AF334842

Order in Variety

Donald E. Stanford

Order in Variety

Essays and Poems in Honor of Donald E. Stanford

Edited by R. W. Crump

Newark: University of Delaware Press
London and Toronto: Associated University Presses

Associated University Presses
440 Forsgate Drive
Cranbury, NJ 08512

Associated University Presses
25 Sicilian Avenue
London WC1A 2QH, England

Associated University Presses
P.O. Box 39, Clarkson Pstl. Stn.
Mississauga, Ontario,
L5J 3X9 Canada

The paper used in this publication meets the requirements of the American National Standard for Permanence of Paper for Printed Library Materials Z39.48-1984.

Library of Congress Cataloging-in-Publication Data

Order in variety : essays and poems in honor of Donald E. Stanford / edited by R. W. Crump.
    p. cm.
   Includes bibliographical references.
   ISBN 0-87413-420-X (alk. paper)
   1. American literature—History and criticism. 2. English literature—History and criticism. 3. American poetry—20th century. 4. English poetry—20th century. I. Stanford, Donald D., 1913– . II. Crump, R. W. (Rebecca W.), 1944– .
PS58.074 1991
820.9—dc20   90-50934
                                       CIP

Contents

Foreword
Jay L. Halio

Readers of Edward Taylor's poetry, like students of Robert Bridges and his circle, are well familiar with the meticulous scholarship of Donald Stanford. Similarly, readers of *The Southern Review* are aware of the many contributions, direct and indirect, that Donald Stanford has made as coeditor of this important quarterly. Revived in 1964 after a distinguished but foreshortened run under the joint editorship of Cleanth Brooks and Robert Penn Warren, *The Southern Review* under Stanford and Lewis P. Simpson continued and extended the traditions earlier established. Thanks to their efforts, we are the richer for the essays, poetry, fiction, and reviews that have appeared for nearly three decades, bringing credit to the editors as well as to the authors, and to the Louisiana State University, which continues to support the enterprise.

Less familiar to the general reader or specialized scholar, but no less important in accomplishment or significance, is Donald Stanford's poetry, about which David Middleton has written eloquently in an essay included in this volume. Middleton also chronicles Stanford's work on *The Southern Review*, placing it in its historical context, and describes his value to him personally as friend and mentor. Had space permitted, Middleton would have included sections as well on Stanford's accomplishments as a scholar and critic and his long association with Yvor Winters. But his poetry, editorship, and teaching are aspects of a career in letters that deserve special notice, particularly in a volume of this kind. For, as Middleton says, his poetry, classic in its beauty, must not be forgotten, and his teaching has influenced countless students of every age and rank or walk in life. As for his editorship, I can speak personally of his generosity and encouragement; as a subscriber, I can also testify to his astute eye and his sense of relevance of what counts.

The other essays and poems collected here are further testimonials to Donald Stanford's stature. They range from studies of

Shakespearean sonnets and Edward Taylor's verse through Mark Twain and D. H. Lawrence to T. S. Eliot and Wallace Stevens. Of course studies of Bridges, Yeats, and Sturge Moore are also included, but so are welcome essays by Cleanth Brooks on the place of the humanities and by Roy Fuller on his experience as Professor of Poetry at Oxford. No dedicatory volume honoring Donald Stanford would be complete without poetry, and heaven's plenty is here provided, with an unusual contribution by Donald Davie: a verse drama in three acts for three voices. All are by friends and colleagues, and had not limitations of space forbidden, still others would appear. The volume concludes with a bibliography of Stanford's published work, but does not mention his many lectures, presentations, poetry readings, and the like, which again would have extended the volume beyond feasible limits.

It is fitting that the University of Delaware Press, publisher of several of his most recent books, should also publish this *Festschrift* honoring Donald Stanford. Because my association with him goes back even longer than our association with the Delaware Press, I join with the other contributors in the pride and pleasure we feel in knowing and working with him. He is a rare individual, as perhaps his devoted wife of many years, Maryanna, knows better than any of us. He has brought poetry and wit and wisdom into all our lives, and above all he has brought warmth and friendship. For everything he is and has done, we express our gratitude and best wishes for a career happily still active.

Order in Variety

Alphabets
Edgar Bowers

I now think nature's way of bringing love
To humans is as strange as any myth
Of us or of our origins. The snail,
Still selfish in its house, has such an ease
As had contented Adam's innocence
Before the Lord divided him in two
And even a pair of legs seen at a distance
Would be enough to bring him, all year long,
The poignant hope, that new wish for a difference
Pygmalion made a copy of in clay
Responsive to his breath. I thought of you
As that first alphabet, bird shape and beast shape,
Which opens to desire the rule beginning
And ending with the 3, the two of us
And love, that spells the two as one; but Proteus
Is truer to himself than we can be
For long to our first word. Bewildering changes!
Water and sunlight! cockroach, parrot, shark
And what is not the same enough to name,
The newborn *nous* itself a mystery
Tormented in some pool beside the Nile,
Now lonelier than Adam or the snail.

Edward Taylor's Love Affair with Sounding Language

Percy G. Adams

Much has been written about Edward Taylor's curious and fascinatingly attractive mind, his similarities to George Herbert, his poetic kinship with Emily Dickinson, his typology, his passionate love of Christ, his Meditations—so many of which were inspired by the sensual Canticles, his homely and even shocking metaphors, his images from nature and music and everyday life and the Bible, his vocabulary in general, his "imperfect" rhymes, and the "dialectical" features of those rhymes, but almost nothing has been said about his great and lasting love of sounding language.[1] This love was not just of individual words but, more particularly, of combinations of words that echo consonants and vowels in stressed syllables. Is it that we defend our neglect by dismissing the sounds in poems as less important than the meaning and imagery? Or is it that we are prone to read only with the eye and mind and not with the ear also? Whatever the reason we can quickly demonstrate that Taylor, at least as much as his poetic descendant Emily Dickinson, employed phonic echoes[2]—that is, consonant and vowel echoes—in profusion, often in great profusion, and, as many readers will agree, often with attractive results. In this respect he is close to his great British contemporaries Dryden, Pope, and Gay and quite different from Herbert, one of the least echo-conscious of great poets. In order to hear these echoes, however, some readers may need to tune down the dials on form, sense, and imagery.

Alliteration is considered the most easily recognized of phonic echoes in poetry and, with varying definitions, has almost universally been a more popular device than rhyme. Today it is best defined as the repetition of an initial consonant or consonant cluster in stressed syllables close enough to each other for the echo to affect the ear. As perhaps every reader of Taylor knows, alliteration was as popular with him as with any fine poet. While the examples are legion, here each line or part of a line has the same initial consonant or consonant cluster in at least three stressed syllables.

> The Bare that breaths the Northern blast. (465)[3]
>
> And Pavements of Rich Pearles, Precious Stone. (130)
>
> Whose sap a sovereign sodder is. . . . (48)
>
> Sins thick and threefold at my threshold lay. (123)
>
> . . . all Stuntedness, or Stately Stintedness. (139)
>
> Astonisht stand, my Soule; why dost not start. (31)[4]
>
> My person with apparel thou prepar'st. (181)
>
> Its Cabbinet wherein it keeps its Case. (368)
>
> What flying Flakes of rapid flames of Love. (174)

Here are two pairs of such consonants in each line.

> Studded with Pretious Stones, Carv'd with rich Curles. (36)
>
> Thou Rod of David's Root, Branch of his Bough. (49)
>
> With Veans of Venom o're my Spirit Sprawle. (108)

Or an initial consonant or cluster can run through consecutive lines, *p,* for example, occurring nine times in one stanza, six times in two of its lines:

> Me pitty, pardon mee and Lord accept
> My Penny Prize, and penny worth of Praise.
>
> (273)

Here is the same initial consonant in four strong syllables:

> Though faith in firy furnace flags, . . . (417)
>
> Earths Golden Fleece, and Flourish, Fruits, and Flower. (241)
>
> Here bud sweet blushing blossoms, sparkling brave. (235)

While none of these examples of polysyllabic or complex alliteration is by any means unique, almost any page of the Stanford edition of Taylor's poems has a number of alliterations of two syllables, some more than two, that seem to come instinctively to the poet. That is, the repetition occurs within a line or, normally,

within any ten consecutive syllables and is thus audible to a
sensitive ear. In fact, a page seldom has fewer than ten such
repetitions, and page 62, not unusual, has twenty-seven, most
rather obviously intended, among them

> appeare-Pass, sentence-suits, Christ-Advocate-Cause-Client, books-
> abounds, pass-pure, Fret-flaw, lost-Laws, Satan's-suit-books-abounds,
> pass-pure, Fret-flaw, lost-Laws, Satan's-suit-same, plead-Pauperis,
> red-Arrest, Loads-Love.

These examples, as with all others given here, do not include
Taylor's abundant word repetitions, of which there are six on this
page, for example, "Respect-Disrespect," "Honour-Dishonour."

As alliteration has to do with the beginning of stressed sylla-
bles, consonance has to do with the end. Although still ambigu-
ous for many students of poems, it is a term not used enough and
should replace altogether the term *slant rhyme*, normally
thought of as a substitute for end rhyme, as in Emily Dickinson's
Locomotive poem, where in each of the four short unrhymed
stanzas the *b* and *d* lines end "up-step," "peer-pare," "while-
hill," "star-door." Because of the word *rhyme* in the term *slant
rhyme*, readers tend to miss the thousands of consonant echoes
at the ends of internal stressed syllables. Dickinson, for example,
in the same short poem has ten other stressed syllables involved
in final consonant echoes. That is, of her some sixty-four ictic
peaks, eighteen consonate. Dickinson, of course, is only one
major poet who knew how to work with this device. Browning,
for example, in "Rebuckled the cheek-strap, chained slacker the
bit" helps to stress the "buck-cheek-slack" peaks in his anapestic
rhythm by repeating the final *k* sound. Taylor's contemporaries
Dryden and Pope were expert with the device, as in Dryden's
onomatopoeic line in which every strong syllable ends with the
sound of *z*, the first such sound coming in the lexically potent
syllable "buzz-": "A buzzing noise of bees his ears alarms"
(*Georgics* 4.801). The term *consonance* permits us to talk of this
kind of internal echo that has become more and more popular
with poets as rhyme has become less popular. It is this term, thus
defined, that will appear in the third edition of the *Princeton
Encyclopedia of Poetry and Poetics:* "consonance is the repeti-
tion of the *sound* of a final consonant or consonant cluster in
stressed syllables near enough to each other for the echo to affect

the ear."[5] And Taylor liked consonance at least as much as Dickinson did later. Here he has the final *z* sound four times in one line, always in a heavy syllable:

> . . . to face
> Mine Eyes, and Nose, and Charm mine Eares with Chimes.
>
> (50)

Here it comes three times:

> Whose Rayes out Shine all pimping Stars that rise. (177)

Here there is an effective three-syllable echo of "-nd":

> Thy hand alone that wound this Clew I finde. (68)

Here final *t* is in five of six stressed syllables:

> . . . into raptures put
> Of right delight of an Extatick cut.
>
> (305)

Here it is in three syllables:

> This doth unbolt the Doore, and light impart. (289)
> I cannot bite a bit of Bread or Roote. (50)

Here *l* is consonated:

> As pure as in the Well: not foule at all. (66)
> Cold Sorrows fall into my Soule as Steel. (58)

Here, in a favorite line, Taylor has final *n* in three stressed syllables and *l* in two:

> And reele the yarn thereon spun of thy Wheele. (467)

Most examples of Taylor's consonance, as with his alliteration, are of course of two syllables and may be lost in a hurried reading, as with "black as inke," "nest-lust," "bran-yawn," "scarce can toss," and "brire-pare." On the other hand, he often employed a kind of internal consonance that is easily heard because it accompanies alliteration in the same words, a phenomenon sometimes called bracket alliteration or bracket consonance, as with "Cast-Curst" (70), "aloft-lift" (126), "Rugged-Ragged" (192). The most difficult echo for a fast reader to hear, however, is the repetition of a consonant that comes at least once at the end of a strong syllable followed in the same word by one or more syllables, as with "Extatick cut" (305), "fine Phansy" (217), "Coale-bellows" (91). Such echoes are heard more easily in "Lord! read the riddle" (254), when the final d in "Lord" and "read" prepares us for the final d in "riddle." The same preparation is made in "My Inke too thick and naught (though liquid Gold)" (181), where the k in "Inke" and "thick" readies the ear for the final k in "Liquid." And, of course, readers with sensitive ears will interject, the vowel in "Inke" and "thick" prepares us for the same vowel in "liquid"—just as in a number of the examples given above, there is a vowel echo; or just as consonance is sometimes combined with alliteration, for example, in "charm mine eares with Chimes," where the initial ch goes with the final z sound.

And that brings me to the third chief phonic echo-assonance, defined as the repetition of the sound of a vowel or diphthong, but not of a following adjacent consonant or consonant cluster, in stressed syllables near enough to each other for the echo to be discernible. That is, if the following adjacent consonant or cluster is the same, we have both assonance and consonance, thus rhyme ordinarily, of the stressed syllables, as in "ballad" and "callous" but not in "callous" and "bastion," where the stressed syllables assonate. Partly because Taylor's poems employ end rhyme, or end-rhyme substitutions, he has even more vowel repetitions than he does alliteration. Nevertheless, he obviously worked—or played—hard at echoing vowels within the line. Considering such repetitions, then—where at least one vowel is not in an end-rhyme word—we find hundreds of striking examples of assonance, especially if we remember that with Taylor, as with Dryden and other British poets of his day, "Devil," "yet," and "get" were often spelled with i and were pronounced to rhyme with "civil" and "fit," that words like "boil" rhymed correctly with "file," that "Mudd" and "good" had the same vowel—not the modern American sound in "rug"—and that "beast" and "feast" actually rhymed with "rest."[6]

Listen then to these rather obviously intended assonances. Here Taylor has the diphthong of "light" in strong syllables three or more times in a line:

Lighten the Eye which Light Divine did spill. (28)
When thy Bright Beams, my Lord, do strike mine Eye. (36)
On Bible Covers, shine in Types out bright. (90)

Here it is the *o* of "so":

That darkness gross his noble Soule doth tip. (156)
That I am clothed in Holy robes for glory. (467)

Here it is the vowel in "sit":

. . . Divells, Wicked ones and sin. (297)
Till when let this unskilful ditty skill. (175)
And tilting stilts do stick within the mudd. (394)

Here is the vowel of "set":

To handle their weapons well and dextrously. (297)
That ever Heaven held or ever kisst. (300)
Oh! that I ever felt what I profess. (56)

Here it is the popular vowel of "late" or "bait":

Oh! let our Praise his Grace assaile. (420)
Grace by the Aide of Justice wins the day. (402)
A mighty Plague rag'd in Arabia. (495)
. . . Assay / To brave the raging Waves of Adria. (429)

Here it is the vowel of "sat":

Up in the Banner Standard of the Camp. (191)

Here is Taylor's vowel in "stuck" and "good":

Stuck in the Bosom of such Stuffe as wee. . . . (45)
A Wooden Wall with Husky Coverlid. (194)

Here, three times, is the diphthong of "view":

That they may view thy Spouses Beauty pure. (349)

Each of a number of these lines, of course, includes alliteration or consonance—as with "Wooden Wall," "rag'd in Arabia," and "unskilful ditty still"—but Taylor also liked a line with a second assonance:

> And that the Righteous, Gracious, Pious, Grave. (447)
>
> Scowl, Glout, and Frown, on honest poverty. (411)
>
> Hath every step with wealthy grace inlaid. (350)
>
> The whiteness, Sope and Nitre can bestow. (143)

And on that same page 62, used above, there are some seventeen assonances without counting echoes in end rhymes. Of these, some of course are probably accidental, as with "Sergeants are," but others—"Bribe-hide," "Client-slide," "State-make-case"—are probably not.

Once we see how much Taylor employed both assonance and consonance we can more easily understand, and explain, his "incorrect" end rhymes. Certainly we can again see why *split rhyme* is not a satisfactory term, for the great majority of his untrue rhymes are either assonance or consonance. First, however, we need to remember this: end rhyme is by no means a favorite sound device in all national poetries, as it has been, but is much less so today in French, German, and English-speaking nations. And with poets of England and the United States, both assonance and consonance have often been used as substitutes for end rhyme. That is true not just with Emily Dickinson but with twentieth-century poets such as Crane and Cummings and dozens of others. Theodore Roethke, for example, gives the first stanza of "The Partner" (in "Four for Sir John Davies") six lines with end rhyme but ends the six lines of stanza 2 with "feet-fond-fate-ground-else-pulse"; that is, every end word is a stressed syllable involved in at least one phonic echo—alliteration of *f* in three words and consonance in all six (*t, nd, s*). Then in "The Gibber" ("The Lost Son") Roethke's third stanza ends its four lines with "whined-cried-briars-die"—that is, with assonance. Why, then, do we speak of improper rhymes of other centuries?

With Taylor we need to remember also that some rhymes imperfect with Americans today were good with him: "one-upon," "prove-love," "come-Womb," "tongues-belongs," "perchance-advance," "unfit-yit" (yet), and, especially, "advice-rejoyce," "Winde-lin'de," "flies-joyes." And he correctly rhymed "Sweate-Heate" (205) and always—at least fifty times—rhymed "would" and "should" with words like "gold" and "hold." Furthermore, as all readers know, certain kinds of "rhymes" imperfect today were imperfect but popularly accepted in Taylor's day, among them these: doe-so, pass-was, crave-have, "Taffity-Deity" (75), "Righteousness-Feebleness" (70). And even "yee-glory" and "play-Fly" were with him very close. Seldom, for an end rhyme, did he repeat a word instead of finding some kind of phonic repetition, as he did with "faile-faile" (423) and "define-fine" (198). It is a fact, then, that Taylor had few really bad rhymes, that he simply gave up, as with "come-defray" (253) and "fruite-hook" (344), for nearly all of his remaining "imperfect" rhymes are either consonance or assonance.

Of these, perhaps one hundred in the Stanford edition repeat the final consonant or cluster but not the vowel of the stressed syllable. Here, however, one must be wary of citing r consonance because in English then and now a following r makes two different vowels sound much alike. Taylor, for example, sounded "are" as he did "air" and like his contemporaries in England constantly rhymed air-ware-appear-far-hear. As a result, what to some of us may seem like an r consonance as we read him is really, at times at least, part of a good rhyme, as when he couples "were-cleare," "are-fair," or "far [pronounced 'fur']-cur." At other times, as with "her-fire," "more-cure," the vowels were probably not sounded the same and so we have an intriguing kind of consonance. Other examples of end consonance are by no means ambiguous or startling today. Of these, some ("streams-Veans," "beams-Stains," "grain-beame") may not be perfect consonances, but the nasal sound of m is so close to that of n that Taylor worked the near-identical sounds hard. Among the other, perhaps clear-cut, end consonances are "those-lose," "fame-Rome," "white-Weight," "them-gum," "disht-feast," "salve-resolve," "breath-Earth," and two fascinating ones—"Antioch-Smoake" (494) and "bred-brudled" (103)—the làst word having three syllables (brud-l-ed) and consonating the d twice with "bred."

Thus we have left the end words in Taylor's poems that echo the vowel or diphthong but not the following consonant in stressed syllables. To be be sure, as with Milton or Dryden or Pope, or any rhyming poet in English, perhaps 12 to 15 percent of all Taylor's rhyme words end with a vowel sound (bee-see, spy-I, you-due, display-pray, joy-glorify) and thus set a kind of precedent for substituting assonance for full rhymes. And Taylor has hundreds of such substitutions. He was often able to find two words that assonated and that also echoed the final of two or more consonants in a following cluster, as with "knocks-drops," "deckt-fret," "fix-eclipse." And with dozens of other rhyme substitutions he employed stressed syllables with the same vowel followed by a nasal but not the same nasal, as with "fling-sin," "presume-tune," "him-sin." In this group belong polysyllabic pairs such as "bespangled-inam'led," where each stressed vowel is followed by a nasal and a weak syllable. As with n, m, and ng, the sounds of s, z and sh are close enough to each other that Taylor used them interchangeably after an assonance, as he did with "His-this," "fresh-dress." One frequent rule-breaker that he favored was an s added to one consonant or cluster but not the other, as with "paint-Saints," "stands-demand," and "worms-turn." And then there is a great mass of unlike consonant sounds to go with assonance, as with "harpe-starte-sparks" in one stanza (491). All of these kinds of assonance substitutions account for the great majority of Taylor's imperfect end rhymes.

Far more important, however, than the phonic echo or echoes that Taylor employed instead of rhyme is the use he made internally of such auditory repetitions, not just for decoration or what Dryden called "music" but to aid the cognitive content and, at times even, to assist the rhetoric.

The first and, with him, favorite structural use was to let such echoes help stress the ictic peaks in a single line or in successive lines of iambic rhythm, whether in the stanza form of the Meditations or in his heroic couplets and other verse forms. Not only does every one of the early examples here help to show that fact, but Taylor's poems provide examples that are countless. In this one line, for example, "That for thyself is fit to set before" (308), the five ictic peaks are strengthened by the alliteration of f and s, the assonance in "-self-set," and the consonance in "fit-set," while "for" and "-fore" were probably pronounced alike. Sometimes we need a sound from the previous line in order to hear every peak echoing, as in ". . . whereby / I may have sight, and Grace in mee may blaze" (29), where the six peaks alliterate b and m and assonate five vowels. But Taylor was no slave to his rhythm, just as Dryden would not "have his sense a slave to syllables,"[7] for in the line "Bleeds royall Wine: and grapes Sweet Raisens make" (106), although the five peaks are marked by the assonance in "royal Wine" and a "grapes-Raisens-make," the words "Bleeds" and "Sweet" have at least a secondary stress as well as the same vowel. And many of Taylor's lines do break the normal iambic rhythm, as with this slow, heavily stressed line, "Christ backt the Curtain, Grace made bright the day" (123), where each of the seven stressed syllables is involved in an echo-alliteration in "Christ-Curtain" and "backt-bright," assonance in "Christ-bright" and "Grace-made-day," and consonance in "Christ-backt-Curt-(ain)-bright."

And over and over, Taylor ran vowels and consonants through the strong syllables of two or more lines to keep the echoes going and the stresses stronger, as here:

> Be Arkd in Christ, or else the Cursed rout
> Of Crimson Sins their Cargoe will them Sinke
> And suffocate . . .

> (135)

Even if "Car-" and "Arkd" may be too far apart for the repeated sound to be heard, we can hear the echoes in "Sins-Sinke-suff-," "Christ-Cursed-Crimson-Cargoe-cate," "Arkd-Christ-rout," "else-Curs(ed)," and "Crimson Sins . . . will . . . Sinke," all in addition to the rhymes with "rout" and "Sinke." Amazingly, such examples are merely representative for this poet.

Especially for Taylor's day in Britain, one important use poets had for phonal echoes was to stress the rhetoric, to aid the idea, for example, to parallel two or more grammatical or structural elements. Not that the twentieth century has not followed the eighteenth in this respect, as one can hear when Eliot alliterates and assonates the verbs that open two successive lines—"Licked its tongue . . . / Lingered upon . . ."—or when Pound begins two of his lines with a kind of anaphoric assonance—"I have played . . . / I have staked. . . ." And while Taylor never worked this sort of parison so hard as the masters Dryden and Pope, he has an astounding number of consonant and vowel echoes that aid the rhetoric. He balanced sounds in parallel verbs, as in examples given above—"Me pitty, pardon mee," "Scowl, Glout, and Frown"—but then this was a favorite use for him:

> I'll walk this Rosy Path: World fawn, or frown. (13)

> Then Wrince, or Wring me. . . . (66)

> That foule . . . and do defile the aire. (219)

> Accept of this, reject the rest. (383)

Perhaps the best sounds in balanced verbs occur in a favorite poem where in one line there are six verbs, two that consonate and four that assonate: "I frown, Chide, strik and fight them,

mourn and Cry" (63). He balanced nouns: "In Bulk, or Bright-
ness" (106), "New Words, new Wayes" (49), "The inward Tacles
and the outward Traces" (357). The nouns could be direct objects:
"I'le give him Grace: he'st give me praise" (406). They could be
predicate nouns or subjects of verbs:

Hence thou a Sinner art, or I a Saint. (413)

Your Faith's a Phansy: Fear a Slavery. (422)

Furthermore, Taylor often paralleled more than one gram-
matical element in a line or a series of lines. And here he left
some evidence that he had read Dryden, for his line "Some
seeming Friends prove secret Foes . . ." (399) repeats the four
phonic echoes in Dryden's line in *Absalom and Achitophel*
". . . from seeming friends, and secret foes" (466). Taylor, in fact,
liked to echo sounds in any kind of parison, adverbs, for exam-
ple, in "To handle their weapon well and dextrously"; or pairs of
like words in a line that has a caesura after the sixth syllable:

Studded with Pretious Stones, Carv'd with rich Curles. (36)

Thou Rod of David's Root, Branch of his Bough. (49)

And these lines, loaded with balance and phonic echoes, would
be amazing in the work of almost any other poet:

My Soile is sandy; brambles o're it grow;
My Stock is stunted; branch no good Fruits breeds.
(87)

Not only does the first part of each line alliterate the same pair of
like words, but noting that "good" as an ictic peak is indeed
stressed more than "Fruits," we realize that Taylor has every
strong syllable echoing at least one sound: "Soile-sandy," "Stock-
stunted," "brambles-branch-breeds," "grow-good," "sandy-bram-
bles-branch," "o're-grow," and "stunted-good." Counting no
rhyme, we have in the ten peak syllables sixteen vowels and
consonants or clusters that echo.

Poets everywhere and always have seemed instinctively to join
adjective to noun with phonal echoes, and Taylor liked this kind
of auditory linkage more than most poets, as any page of his
poems will attest. Beginning, for example, on that same page 62
and going through page 68, one finds that each page has from one
to five such combinations, with page 68 having "admiring style,"

"silver pictures," "Jasper Cask," and this remarkable line—"And Loveliness in Lumps, tunn'd and enrin'de," in which the adjective "tunn'd" assonates with each noun involved and the two adjectives have a distinctive consonance. Among Taylor's adjective-noun echoes, one can include at least twenty-five found in the examples given in paragraphs preceding this one. Wherever we look, however, they can be alliterations:

> Loves liquor, Hells Horrour, Gyants Jaws, Rabble rout, China changes, Sparkling Spangles, fond Affections, empearld pill, Glorifying Glances, flowing flakes, perfumed face, Linsy-Wolsy Loom, stately stature, sinsunk Souls.

They can be assonances even more often:

> Milkwhite Rivers, Silken Skin, Immanuels Land, Holy Soap, Bucking tub, Anger's Anvill, Sparkling Carbuncle, Natures operations, Saphire Battlements, Counsills Tower, Choicest Vine, poison Serpentine, 'Bellisht Definitions, Paradisall joy, tilting stilts, Typick Dispensations, Clayey faces, Spouses Countenance.

They can occasionally be consonances:

> Lapst Estate, Ecstatick cut, a worm eat nut, rotten heart.

They can even echo two phones:

> Graces Lace, Crabtree Cask, Backward Bashfulness, a sovereign Sodder, Dish Delicious (asson. + cons.), Wealthy'st Web, blesst Bellows, Weedy Seed, Lilly Lips, Lumpish Lookes, tripping Slippers, Silver pillow, Glories Palace Doore, bottomless abyss (*b* allit. + *s* cons.).

These combinations can, in fact, frequently be intricate, astounding, with a polysyllabic echo, with more than one adjective, or often with more than one kind of echo:

> My tell tale Tongue, thy footstoole Stepping Stone, The Worlds wild waves, Tabernacles Cap, Christs Antitype Isaac, Rich Quick'ning things, her sattin jacket hot (allit., asson.), her velvet hemlet high (allit., asson., cons.), bare staring bones, Pharao's fatted ware, a rich, fine Phansy ripe, Zions Pasty Plate-Delights (allit., asson. twice, *s* cons.), a little tittle tattles Clatter.

But with Taylor there are so many of these that the extraordinary almost becomes the ordinary:

This Bud of Civill, and of Sacred Faith (154) (Adjs. allit., adj.-noun, asson.)

Upon God's Table Plate Divinely bright (212) (adj.-noun. asson., adv.-adj. asson., *t* cons. of noun-adj.)

Infinities fierce fiery arrow red . . . (287) (3 adjs. allit.)

One needs to remember, however, that these combinations should not be taken out of context. Here in two lines, for example, are three adjective-noun pairs that cross-echo with each other and with a verb:

> My tatter'd Fancy; and my Ragged Rhymes
> Teeme leaden Metaphors . . .
>
> (233)

That is, two of the pairs assonate, one pair alliterates, and "Ragged" echoes the vowel of "tatter'd Fancy" while, without anyone's arguing that it was intentional, "Met-a-phors" consonates with "tatt-er'd" and its second ictic peak alliterates with "Fancy." Likewise, in "Psammitch's Labyrinth, (arts Cramping Task)" (180), not only does each adjective-noun pair assonate but "Lab-" cross-assonates with "Cramping Task." Finally, here is an example of such echoes imbedded in an especially complex ear-appealing passage found in the Hooker Elegy:

> To see thy Freckled Face in Gospell Glass:
> To feele thy Pulse, and finde thy Spleen's not well.
>
> (480)

Note first the vertical balanced assonance in the infinitives "see-feele," the vertical balanced consonance in the noun objects "Face-Pulse," and the alliteration in the parallel verbs "feele-finde." Then note the noun-adjective echoes in "Freckled Face" and "Gospell Glass." And after all that, listen to the total effect of "see-feele-Spleens," "Freckled Face-feele-finde," "Face-Gos(pell)-Glass-Pulse," "Gospell Glass," and "feele-well," all to go with end rhymes that echo other words also—"Alas-Glass," "well-swell," By no means unique these two lines employ heavy echoes in rhetorically balanced words and in noun-adjective pairs but each echo is merely a part of what amounts to a crashing chorus of sounds.

Related in a curious way to Taylor's use of sounding language to affect the cognitive content of his poems is his now well-known love of punning, a love that had ample precedent in poets such as Aeschylus and Shakespeare. Puns of course depend on the repetition of phonic sounds, but with Taylor the echoes in his puns are nearly always related to the echoes around them. Some of his puns are partially hidden. For example, in "The Curse now Cures, though th'Griefe procureth groans" (32), a reader may become so occupied with "Curse-Cures" and "Griefe-Groans" that the pun completed in "procureth" may slip by. And in "Such joy as would an Adamant unjoynt" (35), the assonance in the one word "Adamant" and the attractive consonance of -*nt* perhaps cause the reader to hesitate a second before smiling—or frowning—over the pun on "joy." But in "Full of it's Fulgient Glory of that Hall" (248), the *l* echo in "Hall" strikes us so late that we have already caught the pun and perhaps paused, thereby missing the effect of the three-syllable consonance.

Very often the play on words is not a pun but the repetition of more than one important phone in two or more words, as in, "Then halter up this Cur that is so Curst" (414), or when the Soul orders Satan,

> Begone, therefore; to him I'le send a groane
> Against thee drawn, who makes my heart his throne.
>
> (413)

Taylor's play on the name of the great New England ecclesiastic Hooker is no doubt his most famous pun:

> And no more fish he took
> That thou callst home thy Hooker with his Hook?
> Lord, spare the flock: uphold the fold from falling.
> Send out another Hooker of this Calling.
>
> (482)

Although the pun here, coupled with the abrupt shift in metaphor, may close the reader's ear to the nearby sounds, note that the "Hooker-Hook" pun alliterates with "home" and "uphold," actually has the same vowel as "home," and consonates with "flock," all to go with the end rhymes, the internal rhyme "uphold-fold," and the alliteration of "flock-fold-falling." Perhaps one of Taylor's best puns comes in the last of these three lines,

> Who'le slay a Friend? and save a Foe?
> Who in my War do take delight,

> Fight not for prey, but Pray and Fight,
>
> (305)

where the pun is associated not only with the neat balance of "Friend-Foe," "slay-save," and "Fight-Fight" but with the end rhyme and the vowel echo that begins in "slay-save," runs through "take," and comes to a crescendo in the punning words "prey-Pray."

Taylor, then, employed phonic echoes both for decoration and for rhetorical and cognitive effects, and although he did not create so many opportunities for onomatopoeia as certain other poets have done, he does have some most attractive sound-sense passages, all of which depend heavily on consonant and vowel repetitions accompanied by the proper lexical introduction. Just one year before Taylor's death, Pope in the *Dunciad* (1728) was echoing initial and final *d* and the vowel of *mud* and *dull* and *Dunce* for ugliness,[8] as here:

> How here he sipp'd, how there he plunder'd snug,
> And suck'd all o'er, like an industrious Bug.
>
> (Ll. 129–30)

In two similar and wonderful lines Taylor surely matched Pope's mastery of such "representative meter":

> Lulld in the lap of sinful Nature snugg,
> Like Pearls in Puddles cover'd ore with mudd.
>
> (401)

That is, the "ugly" *u* of "mudd," which starts in "Lulld" and runs through five stressed syllables, is accompanied along the way by the alliteration in "Lulld-lap" and "Pearls-Puddles" and the consonance of *d* in "puddles-mudd." Just as devastating, perhaps, is the line "Like Dunghill Cocks over their Conquourd, Crow" (33), in which the *o* of "Conq-" is pronounced like the *u* of "Dung-" to go with the harsh *k* sound of "Cocks-Conq-Crow." A favorite trio of lines has the vowel of "ugly" in eight ictic peaks:

> This Flood's too stately to be rode upon
> By other boats, which are base swilling tubs.
> It gulps them up as gudgeons. And they're gone.
>
> (Ll. 134–35)

But the dominant vowel is surrounded by an astounding number of other echoes—"stately-base," "rode-boats," "boats-base," and

the harsh g of "gulps-gudgeons-gone." Occasionally Taylor could
fit the sound to the sense in a softer way, as in "Thy Bell may tole
my passing Peale to Hell" (41), which, besides the alliteration of
p, rings the l of "Bell" three more times. And there are a number
of choice passages in Taylor's poems that can be called
onomatopoeic. But, for many readers perhaps, extended analysis
of such lines would go too far. In every such passage one can
choose, however, repetitions play a major role.

Without insisting further on the notion of onomatopoeia, then,
what I have said is that Taylor chose unusual, striking, some-
times idiomatic, often—as with Dickinson—startling words that,
as he put them together, force us very often to call the results
attractive and appropriate. Let us listen again to the sounds in
some of these passages. First, there is this favorite line, "The little
pinking Stars playing boe peep" (360), with its polysyllabic allit-
eration of p and its assonating adjectives. Then there are these
two Donnesque lines,

> The Poles may kiss and Parallels meet I trow
> The Sun the Full moon buss, e'er I do so,
>
> (363)

where the u of "Sun-Full-buss," is not ugly because the lexical
setting is anything but ugly, and then we also have the allitera-
tion of "Poles-Parallels" and "Sun-so," the assonance of "Poles-
trow-so," and the very noticeable consonance in "kiss-buss." The
"Poles-Parallels" contrast is used again in the famous short-line
poem "Christs Reply." This time the two key words echo better
because "Parallels" is pronounced with three syllables and un-
like the use above stresses the third syllable as well as the first,
thereby consonating as well as alliterating with "Poles":

> The Poles shall sooner kiss, and greet
> And Parallels shall sooner meet
> Than thou shalt harmed bee.
>
> (415)

And here in a third passage, one with rough language more
nearly unique in poetry generally than it is with Taylor: "The
mantle I would make," he says,

> will run all Counter buffe,
> To my design, and streakt be like a Snake,
> That's new crept out of 'ts garment, a slunk Slough,

> Or have a smoaky Smell, and Choaky lodge
> Within its Clasp.

(382)

Often slow and grating, these lines are made so by three pairs of successive stressed syllables, one pair—"streakt be"—assonating, another pair—"crept out"—consonating, and the third pair—"Slunk Slough"—alliterating and assonating, and the first word of each pair ending in a consonant that forces slow reading. But there are many other echoes also: "run-buffe," "my design-like," "smoaky-Choaky"; "smoaky Smell"; and "run-Coun(ter)—design," "streakt-crept out," "like-Snake-slunk-smoaky-Choaky." It may be that these echoing phrases are the kind that some of us consider distinctively Taylorsque.

At any rate, in order to make the point conclusively, look at three more of literally a hundred memorable and typical passages. First, in these three lines

> Mudd made with Muscadine int' Mortar Rich,
> Dirt wrought with Aqua-Vitae for a Wall
> Built all of Precious Stones . . .

one will of course note the language that is Taylor's in "Mudd," Muscadine," "Mortar," Aqua-Vitae," and perhaps note that each line begins with two successive strong syllables. Then discounting any end rhymes, we hear the alliteration in "Mudd-made-Muscadine-Mortar," "Rich-wrought," "-dine-dirt," the assonance in "Mudd-Muscadine" and "Mortar-wrought-Wall-all," and then the striking consonance in the parallel constructions "Mudd made" and "Dirt wrought" as well as in "Wall-all" and in these five syllables—"Mort(ar)-Dirt-wrought-Vit(ae)-Built." Second in these six lines, the poet, addressing "My blessed Lord," says,

> I fain would thee advance
> But finde my Pen is work'd to the very Stumps.
> My tongue my Speeches tabber stick can't dance
> Unto thy prais as I would have it jump.
> My Drumb Stick thin of Dogtree Wood is made
> And is unfit to beat thy praises trade.

(361)

Here the first and third lines have fewer auditory repetitions than some, but as a group the six lines have them in abundance: "fain-finde," "Stumps-stick," "tongue-tabber-unto," "Drumb-Dogtree";

"advance-tabber-dance," "Stumps-tongue-jump-Drumb-Wood," "Stick-thin-is-unfit," "made-praises trade"; "fain-pen," "advance-Stumps-dance," "Wood-made-trade," "unfit-beat," and last,

> Words are befould, Thoughts filthy fumes that smoake,
>   From Smutty Huts, like Will-a-Wisps that rise
> From Quaugmires, run ore bogs where frogs do Croake,
>   Lead all astray led by them by the eyes.
>   My muddy words so dark thy Deity,
>   And cloude thy Sun-Shine, and its Shining Sky.
>
> (159)

This stunning stanza would be remarkable with almost any poet but Edward Taylor. While stressing certain extra syllables, it has the poet's usual "unusual" language as well as four adjective-noun groups, each of which echoes at least one phone. And also, not forgetting the two end rhymes good today, it has so many phonic echoes that we can hardly count them: alliteration in "befould-filthy-fumes," "Smoake-Smutty," "Will-a-Wisps," "rise-run," "Lead-led," "dark-Deity"; assonance in "filthy-Will-a-Wisps," "Smutty Huts," "rise-mires-eyes-by-by-eyes-Shine-Shining Sky," "frogs-bogs," "smoake-Croake"; and consonance in "smoake-Croake," "Lead-led-Muddy word(s)-cloude," "bogs-frogs," and the z sound in "fumes" that runs through six other strong syllables to end in "words." All of these echoes surely have much to do with the effect of Taylor's images in "befould," "filthy fumes," "smoake," "Croake," "Smutty Huts," "Quaugmires," "bogs," and "frogs."

In the privacy of his study, without help from an Addison or any other learned critic, usually thinking thoughts for a coming sermon, Edward Taylor for at least forty years wrote poems that, since their real discovery half a century ago, have intrigued and even enraptured us. In truth, some of them are not successful and others are attractive only in parts. Any reader can find certain of the Meditations and a number of passages in *Gods Determinations* that are hurried, unfinished, labored, or heavily doctrinaire. Meditation 32 (Second Series), for example, has some of these shortcomings—unfinished lines, awkward word inversions ("them down pitch"). Nevertheless, even in the dullest of his poems, Taylor at times let his ear collaborate with his mind and his emotions. For example, while the poems in *Gods Determinations* have frequently been called less attractive than the Meditations, they can be brought to life with fine images and sounding lines. "The Effects of Mans Apostasy" is one poem that will probably never be chosen to represent the poet's best work, and yet in it we are suddenly confronted with "Do scale the outworks where there's Scarce a Scout" (389), a line that may not save the poem but a line that reminds us of Taylor's penchant for auditory adornment. "Mans Perplexity when called to an account" is undoubtedly much more successful, perhaps because of the long "tenant-landlord" metaphor at the end, perhaps also because half of the thirty-two lines appeal to the ear, as in

> He on his skirts with Guilt, and Filth out peeps,
> With Pallid Pannick Fear upon his Cheeks,
> With Trembling joynts, and Quiverring Lips, doth quake.
>
> (398)

Surely, even out of context, such images cloathed in such ear appealing phrases should cause any reader to react with pleasure. And while one can select half a dozen lines that need to be revised in "An Extasy of Joy let in by this Reply returned in Admiration," this poem from *Gods Determinations* may be as beautiful as any of the Meditations, this stanza being typical, both in imagery and sound:

> If all the Earthy Mass were rambd in Sacks
> And saddled on an Emmet small,
> Its Load were light unto those packs
> Which Sins do bring on all.
>
> (419)

It is this kind of sense-appealing and ear-appealing language that the maker Taylor received as inspiration when he prayed God's angels to pluck from their "Wings a Quill. / Make me a pen thereof" in order, he begged, with phonal echoes sounding,

> To treat this Theme, more rich than Rubies bright.
> My muddy Inke, and Cloudy fancy dark,
> Will dull its glory, lacking highest Art.
>
> (189)

Notes

1. For years I have wanted to do this essay on Taylor. Occupied with other demands on my time, however, I have been forced to postpone the confession of

my love affair with his poems. Now, at last, comes the inspiration offered by this *Festschrift* for my great friend Donald Stanford, who has done so much for the poems of Taylor.

Note that I am avoiding the term *musical* for poetic language because it has so often been attacked, best perhaps by Calvin Brown. Nevertheless, many poets have not only used the term but loved to read their sounding poems aloud— from Milton and Tennyson and Hopkins to the dozens of our contemporaries who read publicly or have their readings taped. For only three in our century who have found "music" in poems, Empson called Virgil "most melodious," Pound talked of the "musical property" that directs a poet's meaning, and Aiken wanted "musical effects." For these and many related examples, see my *Graces of Harmony: Alliteration, Assonance, and Consonance in Eighteenth-Century Poetry* (Athens: University of Georgia Press, 1977).

2. I am using the word *phone* and not *phoneme*, *phonic* or *phonal* and not *phonemic* because, as Roger Brown is only one to explain, "what we think of as vowels and consonants are not single invariant sounds but rather categories of sounds (phones)" while "the phoneme is often called the smallest unit of speech that 'makes a difference' to a listener or speaker. . . . Phonetic transcription is a culture-free system for recording any speech. It does not take account of all the physical differences that are significant in any language" (*Words and Things* [Glencoe, Ill.: Free Press, 1925], 22ff). Phonemic symbols are placed between slashes and phonetic symbols are placed within brackets. In this essay I have been able to avoid the symbols.

3. Each quotation in this essay is located by page number in the Stanford edition of Taylor's poems (*The Poems of Edward Taylor* [New Haven: Yale University Press, 1960]).

4. Although some poets seem to have been unaware of the practice, an initial cluster beginning with *s* is normally said to alliterate only with a like cluster. In this line, then, the *s* of *Soule* is not heard as alliterating with "-stonisht-stand-start."

5. The question of where a stressed symbol starts or ends is sometimes difficult to answer. See *Graces of Harmony*, 211–12. Here the reader's or speaker's ear is, at times, the criterion, for othopoesits do not always agree. For example, most of us have no trouble hearing the final *l* in "valley lill-ies" but purists may argue over the *d* in "moody madness" or the *k* in "vocal oak." I have tried to avoid examples of Taylor's consonant repetitions that may not be the best "consonance," even though most ears may very well hear the end sounds repeated.

6. For a long essay on late-seventeenth-century British pronunciations of vowels and diphthongs, see *Graces of Harmony*, 199–211, which is heavily dependent on H. C. Wyld (*Studies in English Rhymes from Surrey to Pope* [London: J. Murray, 1923]), E. J. Dobson (*English Pronunciation: 1500–1700*, 2 vols. [Oxford: Clarendon Press, 1957]), and Helge Kokeritz (*Shakespeare's Pronunciation* [New Haven: Yale University Press, 1953]). See also the essay by Gene Russell in the introduction to his *Concordance to the Poems of Edward Taylor* (Washington, D.C.: Microcard Editions, 1973). Fortunately one can make the point about Taylor's assonance without becoming overly involved in a discussion of how he pronounced his vowels, partly because he is often obviously echoing a vowel no matter how he pronounced it.

7. Preface to *Tyrranic Love* (1670), l. 141.

8. See *Graces of Harmony*, 109–11.

Mark Twain's Quarrel with God
Everett Emerson

I cannot see how a man of any large degree of humorous perception can ever be religious—except he purposely shut the eyes of his mind & keep them shut by force.

Mark Twain, *Notebooks and Journals*

It is a paradox that America's greatest humorist—the warm, vulnerable family man Mark Twain—was throughout much of his adult life angry with the Christian church, angry with religion, and at the end of his life even angry with God. How he reached such a destination is a story often misunderstood, especially because of the undue attention given to Clemens' grief over the loss of first his eldest daughter, then his beloved wife.

Samuel Clemens, Son of Missouri, was brought up in a community that was strongly church-oriented, a Protestant community that gave particular emphasis to the Bible. In Hannibal Sam Clemens inevitably went to Sunday School but without the results his mother and the church might have hoped for. In his autobiography he tells how he collected blue tickets every Sunday in order to get to own a religious book. Each Sunday to win his tickets he recited five verses of the Bible. The teacher was, he reports, "always satisfied with his performance. He never seemed to notice that these were the same five foolish virgins that he had been hearing about every Sunday for months."[1] This memory seems to have inspired the amusing account of Tom Sawyer's experience at Sunday School.

Clemens's mother, to whom he was very close, was a churchgoer and strongly religious. In his sketch of her Clemens tells how she was so compasssionate that she even prayed for the devil.[2] She was a Presbyterian. On the other hand, Clemens's father—well described by Dixon Wecter—was an agnostic or freethinker. Possibly the father's influence on his son was to suggest that religion is a woman's concern, an attitude that was and still is a familiar one. The religious atmosphere of Hannibal was fundamentalist, and the notion that all Christians are fundamentalists stayed with Clemens. At the end of his life when he was writing "Letters from the Earth" he supposed that "the Christian thinks every word of it [the Bible] was dictated by God."[3]

Because of—or in spite of—the religious atmosphere of his youth, Clemens was fascinated by the Bible, which he came to know well. In his later years he complained that "the unfaithful guardian of my young life . . . compelled me to read an unexpurgated Bible through before I was 15 years old."[4] A good many of his writings have the Bible as their basis, such as "Adam's Diary" and "Shem's Diary." An investigation shows that he alluded in his writings to twenty-three of the thirty-nine books of the Old Testament and to fourteen of the twenty-seven New Testament books. He cited the Gospel of Matthew a total of fifty-eight times. Thirty-two different copies of the Bible or the New Testament that Clemens owned or used have been identified, several of which are heavily annotated.[5]

Along with biblical fundamentalism, religious life in Hannibal included a strong focus on revivals. The adult Samuel Clemens recalled from his boyhood, "Campbellite revival. All converted but me." Then he added, "All sinners again in a week."[6] Clemens was never to forget the fear he was made to feel of hellfire and damnation. He associated them so closely with Christianity that at the end of his life he was to attack Jesus Christ as the inventor of Hell. Growing up in Hannibal was not a very good beginning for life as a Christian in more sophisticated circles. Moreover, for young Clemens religion was at the heart of the painful socializing process and thus was identified with discipline and rigid adult ways. Hannibal's religious atmosphere also may have encouraged hypocrisy of the sort that our humorist-to-be could readily detect.[7]

Old Clemens recalled in an autobiographical dictation of 1906 that Young Clemens was particularly distressed by the discovery that his first schoolteacher had misled him. She had said that "whosoever prayed for a thing with earnestness and strong desire need not doubt that his prayer would be answered."[8] His prayer was not answered. "I remember the shock yet. I was as astonished as if I had caught my own mother breaking a promise to me. Was the doubt planted then, which in 50 years grew to a certainty: that the X [Christian?] and all other religions are lies and swindles?"[9] This experience appears to have been the first of a series of traumas.

According to what Clemens told his biographer, the great shock of his early religious life came when he was a cub pilot on the Mississippi River. At that time he read Thomas Paine's *The Age of Reason,* still a classic critique of the Bible by a deist and still a work that can shake the faith of young people. There Clemens would have read:

> The Bible represents God to be a changeable, passionate, vindictive Being, making a world and then drowning it, afterwards repenting of what he had done and promising not to do so again. Setting one nation to cut the throats of another, and stopping the course of the sun till the butchery should be done.[10]

What was Clemens's reaction to Tom Paine's *Age of Reason?* He reports that he read it "with fear and hesitation"; he marveled "at its fearlessness and wonderful power."[11] A recent commentator goes so far as to say that "the book converted him" to deism and that in unpublished writings on religion Clemens repeatedly echoed Paine.[12]

But a more subtle factor in the development of Clemens's adult religious attitude also should be identified. Though later he could create in *Roughing It* an entertaining account, Clemens's experiences in Nevada and later in California were for him, as Forrest Robinson has observed, "an innocence-shattering practical joke from which he never recovered."[13] One way he coped with his bitterness was by becoming a humorist critical of the dominant culture, especially when he found it pretentious or hypocritical. It is from his California years that we have Mark Twain's wonderful imaginary "Important Correspondence" with Bishop Hawks, the Reverend Phillip Brooks, and the Reverend Dr. Cummings, all of whom he imagines are yearning for a choice, high-paying job at the Episcopal cathedral in San Francisco.[14]

Perhaps his change of locale from the West to the East might have permitted Clemens to leave behind his old attitudes as he became more sensitive to what eastern audiences wanted from him. But after he left California, he was to have, in 1867, an experience that was to change his life: his trip to Europe, the Mediterranean, and the Holy Land. The passengers that Clemens accompanied on the cruise of the *Quaker City* were nearly all moderately well-to-do Protestants who felt they could justify such a pleasure jaunt because it was a trip to the land of the Bible. This voyage changed Samuel Clemens's life in that it provided him with the subject of his first successful book, *The*

Innocents Abroad. After this publication he had a career as an author, not as a journalist. But the voyage had another effect not sufficiently recognized. It profoundly affected his attitude towards the Bible. In the Holy Land he wanted to see with his own eyes what he had read about ever since childhood. Sadly, Clemens did not see what he had been led to expect, nor did he like what saw: squalor and repulsive people. He declared that the good Samaritan was "probably the only good Samaritan the province ever produced"[15] and confided that "I cannot be imposed upon any more by that picture of the Queen of Sheba visiting Solomon. I shall say to myself, You look fine, madam, but your feet are not clean, and you smell like a camel."[16] Again and again what the Bible had led him to expect was not what he found. Moreover, he was deeply offended by the behavior of the orthodox Christians in the group, those people he called the Pilgrims. They did not acknowledge what was there before their eyes. Presbyterians, he noted, "found a Presbyterian Palestine, and they had already made up their minds to find no other."[17]

With his belief from childhood that all Christians were expected to believe that both the Old Testament and the New were literally true, he had no notion of progressive revelation and referred to the God of the Old and New Testaments as "the Jekyll and Hyde of sacred romance."[18] Since he had a very strong sense of the force of natural law, he rejected the miracles of the Bible. As he later put it, "A miracle is by far the most wonderful and impressive and awe-inspiring thing we can conceive of, except the credulity that can take it at par."[19]

Clemens was alert to the scientific findings of his day. His recognition that the universe is incomprehensibly large made it difficult for him to suppose that its creator could care very much about the insignificant planet Earth. In a letter he wrote to Olivia Langdon before they were married, he asserted, "The world we are so proud of is to the universe of careening globes as one mosquito is to the winged & hoofed flocks & herds that darken the air & populate plains & forest of all the earth."[20]

Because of Olivia Langdon, the woman he was courting, it appeared that Clemens would adopt the ways of the dominant culture that earlier he had ridiculed. In her hometown of Elmira, New York, he saw a better life than the one he had known. John T. Frederick puts it this way:

> After years of poverty, of uncertainty—the printing offices—and
> the cheap boarding houses, the gaudy drama of the river and the

diggings, the hecticness and hazards of journalism as he had known it—Mark had at last tasted in the Langdon and Fairbanks homes [in Elmira and Cleveland] the flavors of security and respectability. They tasted good. He wanted Livy, and he wanted Livy's world too. Professed Christian faith was a part of it, or seemed to be, and on such grounds as the Reverend Thomas Beecher (The Langdons' liberal pastor) represented, that didn't seem too great a requirement. Mark Twain wanted to meet it sincerely—or thought he wanted to, which amounted to the same thing.[21]

Thus we find him declaring in a letter in late 1868, "I shall seek the society of the good—I shall be a *Christian*. I shall climb—climb—towards this bright sun that is shining in the heaven of my happiness until all that is gross & unworthy is hidden. . . ."[22] A letter of January 1869 indicates his struggle to accept the Langdons' religion and achieve a religious faith that Clemens went through while he was courting Olivia. At this time he was on the lecture circuit. "I am 'dark' yet," he wrote. "I see I am still depending on my own strength to lift myself up, and upon my own sense of what is right to guide me in the Way—but not always, Livy, not always. I see the Savior DIMLY at times, and at intervals very near. . . . Sometimes it is a pleasure to me to pray, night and morning in [railroad] cars and everywhere, twenty times a day, and then again the whole spirit of religion is motionless (not dead) within me from the rising, clear to the setting of the sun . . ."[23] Why did Clemens struggle so? The reason is because he thought he needed to become a Christian in order to marry Olivia Langdon. He found he could admire both the Reverend Thomas Beecher of Elmira and the Reverend Henry Ward Beecher of Brooklyn, whose teachings emphasize the fatherhood of God and the brotherhood of man. In a letter to his future mother-in-law he emphasized his dedication to reform. He admits that he had been "a profane swearer," "a man of convivial ways and not averse to social drinking," "a man without religion." "But now I never swear; I never taste wine or spirits upon any occasion whatsoever; I am orderly, and my conduct is above reproach in a worldly sense; and finally I now claim to be a Christian. I claim it, and it only remains to be seen if my bearing shall show that I am justly entitled to so name myself."[24] He was to make such a claim only very briefly.

The religious experience that Clemens had in Elmira was not wholly favorable to the development of his appreciation of Christianity. Thomas Beecher was so popular here that the other Elmira ministers asked him, jealously, to withdraw from their regular Monday morning meetings. Mark Twain wrote for a newspaper an amusing but highly critical report of the ministers in which he noted that Beecher's "great mistake was in supposing that when he had the Savior's endorsement of his conduct, he had all that was necessary. He overlooked the fact that there might possibly be a conflict of opinion between the Savior and the Ministerial Union of Elmira. And there was. Wherefore, blind and foolish, Mr. BEECHER went to his destruction."[25] Lack of charity on the part of professed Christians was already a phenomenon familiar to Clemens.

If there were forces struggling over the immortal soul of Samuel Clemens, the forces opposed to those of the Langdons and Thomas Beecher were those of contemporary science, forces more potent than that of the Elmira Council of Ministers. A month before their wedding, Clemens wrote to Olivia Langdon:

> I have been reading some new arguments to prove that the world is very old and that the six days of creation were six immensely long days. For instance, according to Genesis, the STARS were made when the world was, yet this writer mentions the significant fact that there are stars within reach of our telescopes whose light requires 50,000 years to traverse the wastes of space and come to our earth. How insignificant we are, with our little pigmy world! an atom glinting with uncounted myriads of other atom worlds in a broad shaft of light streaming from God's countenance—and yet prating complacently of our speck as the Great World, and regarding the other specks as petty trifles made to steer our schooners by and to inspire the reveries of "puppy" lovers. Did Christ live 33 years in each of the millions & millions of worlds that hold their majestic courses above our heads? Or was our globe the favored one of all?[26]

Ironically, when Clemens chose Oliver Wendell Holmes's *Autocrat of the Breakfast Table* as a courting book (a book that he would read and mark up, then Olivia would have her turn), Clemens's deistic tendencies were strongly reinforced, for Holmes explained persuasively "the automatic mechanisms of mind and body."[27] Later, much later, he would set forth these ideas in "What is Man?" where he argues that man is a machine.[28]

There was a time after their marriage when the Clemenses read the Bible together and went to church. But it did not last. What Clemens found objectionable was the notion of reading the Bible for the sake of his soul. He found it too full of mythology to be suitable for this purpose. He judged himself a hypocrite and gave up trying to become a Christian. Apparently Olivia gave up her

Christianity too. While the Clemenses were living in Hartford, two years after their wedding, with her mother visiting from Elmira, Olivia went to church. She tells how the minister, Joseph Twichell, prayed for those who had fallen away, but, she explained, she had fallen away too many times to go back again.[29] Later Clemens was to admit that he was responsible for taking his wife's Christian faith away from her.

A simple treatment of what Clemens felt in the late 1870s, specifically in 1878, is contained in a letter he wrote to his brother; it shows how Clemens's views were changing and were to continue to change. He declares that he did not believe in hell or in the divinity of Jesus Christ, but he then adds, "the savior is nonetheless a sacred Personage, and a man should have no desire or disposition to refer to him lightly, profanely, or otherwise than with the profoundest reverence."[30] This reverence towards Jesus Christ was not to last for long.

It was not God that Clemens quarreled with in the 1860s, 1870s, or even the 1880s but the attitude of Christians towards God—*and* the God that Christians believed in. Thus Clemens after giving up the devotional reading of the Bible, wrote a statement in which he distinguished between the God of the Bible and what he called the "true God," whose "beneficent, exact, and changeless ordering of the machinery of his colossal universe is proof that he is at least steadfast to his purposes; whose unwritten laws, so far as they affect man, being equal and impartial, show that he is just and fair."[31] What Clemens condemned was what he understood to be a false attitude towards God, in particular the view that God would intervene in the normal courses of nature to answer prayers. In the late 1870s he wrote an amusing but bitter sketch, "The Holy Children." First published in 1972 in *Fables of Man,* it concerns three little girls, Hope, Mary, and Cecelia, who are deeply devoted to God. Their motto is that faith like to a mustard seed will enable its possessor to remove mountains. They are determined to achieve a faith that would be so powerful and their wish is fulfilled. First, Hope finds that when there is a drought, her prayers for rain are answered. Unfortunately, they are answered with a vengeance and soon there is a flood. The rains stop only when Hope offers up a petition that they do so. Her sisters soon acquire similar powers:

They were asked to pray for cold weather, for the benefit of a poor widow who was perishing of a wasting fever. Although it was midsummer, ice formed, and there was a heavy fall of snow. The woman immediately recovered. The destruction of crops by the cold and snow was complete. This made the children many enemies among the farmers. The children changed the weather many times, every day, to benefit various persons, and these changes were very trying to the general public, and caused much sickness and death, since alternate drenchings and freezings and scorchings were common, and none could escape colds, in consequence, neither could any ever know, upon going out, whether to wear muslin or furs.[32]

Problems continued to occur until the community gathered together and passed a resolution: "That the promise, Ask and ye shall receive, shall henceforth be accepted as sound in theory, and true; but that it shall stop there; whosoever ventures to actually follow the admonition shall suffer death."[33] The sketch illustrates effectively Mark Twain's attitude towards "special providences."

It used to be thought that Mark Twain was an inspired genius who wrote his books from memory and inspiration. As Alan Gribben has shown, he was a profoundly bookish man. Clemens was widely read in science at a time when scientific thought was having a profound influence on many religious people and intellectuals. His was also a time of increasing biblical criticism. He bought a three-volume work entitled *The Bible for Learners* in 1878 and through it learned a great deal about the so-called higher criticism of the Bible that was being undertaken in Germany. Later he was to say, "When religion and science elect to live together, it is a plain case of adultery."[34] He also wrote that mixing geology and theology was mixing fact and fiction. In a more generous moment he wrote, "is there any word of God except geology, paleontology, and astronomy?"[35]

In the late 1870s and early 1880s Samuel Clemens might be said to be a deist. But since he knew that his readership included a great many devout Christians, Clemens was greatly concerned not to alienate any of them. He therefore went to great lengths to hide his heterodox opinions. Perhaps for that reason he undertook regularly to set forth his opinions in writings that he left unpublished. A collection of them, including many works previously unpublished, entitled *What is Man? and Other Philosophical Writings,* includes three statements of belief composed in the 1880s. They are remarkably modest and cautious; in them Mark Twain can be seen trying to make peace with his Hartford friends and neighbors. One of them observes:

Latter-day Protestantism, by seeking the humaner passages of the Bible, and teaching them to the world, whilst allowing those of a different sort to lie dormant, has produced the highest and purest and best individuals which modern society has known. Thus used, the Bible is the most valuable of books. But the strongly-worded authority for all the religious atrocities of the Middle Ages is still in it, and some day it may become as heavy a curse to the world as it formerly was.[36]

Here we have, in Frederick Crews's words, Mark Twain's "religious feelings warring against his devotion to fact for its own sake."[37] Repeatedly Mark Twain wrote down a statement of his religious belief. Why? Perhaps, as John Q. Hays observes, it was because he wanted "to write it down to understand it himself."[38]

In 1884–85 Clemens went on a lecture tour with the Louisiana novelist George Washington Cable. According to Clemens's account, Cable was a pious ass, "A Christ-besprinkled, Psalm-singing Presbyterian," who was so cheap that he practically starved himself when he had to pay for his meals, and then stuffed himself when his meals came from the expense account. Cable would not go to hear the popular preacher Henry Ward Beecher because he refused to travel on the Sabbath. Clemens complained that Cable saved a whole trunkload of dirty clothes from his vacation in order to have the washing done at Clemens's expense when they were on tour.[39] In a letter to William Dean Howells, Clemens groaned: "You will never know, never divine, guess, imagine how loathsome a thing the Christian religion can be made until you come to know & study Cable daily & hourly. . . . He has taught me to abhor & detest the Sabbath-day & hunt up new & troublesome ways to dishonor it."[40]

In his essay "The Pessimism of Mark Twain," Howard Mumford Jones suggests that it is possible

> to say that in condemning the Christian God, the Bible, Christian history, the churches, and the Christian world, irascible, passionate, short-tempered, and egotistical as he frequently was, Mark Twain was the foremost Christian of them all. He judged Christianity not by its performance but by its principles. He appealed from Christian fact to Christian-idealism. . . . Mark Twain's indictment of cruelty, past, present, and to come, is an indictment possible only of a man who truly believes he should love his neighbor, fear God, and keep his commandments. What Mark Twain asked the world was that it permit Christianity to sit in judgment on Christianity."[41]

This attractive interpretation of Samuel Clemens's quarrel with Christianity fails to recognize the later stages of the quarrel, which become a quarrel not with Christianity but with God.

How did Samuel Clemens feel about his lack of a religious faith? No doubt he had a variety of feelings about religion, for he was a profoundly changeable person. When his old friend Charles Warren Stoddard wrote to Clemens that he had at last found peace of mind in becoming a Catholic, Clemens wrote in response: "Peace of mind is a most valuable thing." Then he added, bitterly, "The Bible has robbed the majority of the world of it [peace of mind] during many centuries: it is but fair that in return it should give some to an individual here and there. But you must not make the mistake of supposing that absolute peace of mind is obtainable only through some form of religious belief. No, on the contrary, I have found that a perfect peace is to be found in absolute unbelief. I look back with the same shuddering horror upon the days when I believed as you do upon the days when you did not believe."[42]

Much has been made of the devastating effects on Mark Twain of the death of people close to him. No doubt death was as hard for him to accept as it is for most people. But his first experience with it in his mature years did not come with the death of his daughter Susy. In the summer of 1889, Theodore Crane died. He was Olivia Clemens's brother-in-law, the host of the Clemenses during their summer stays at Elmira's Quarry Farm, and a close friend of Clemens; both he and his wife often talked about religion with Clemens. The death of Theodore Crane shook Clemens. About this time he received a letter from his friend William Dean Howells, whose religious opinions were quite similar to his. Howells had recently lost his daughter Winifred and reported that he had found a little consolation in a book. Howells wrote: "I read something in a strange book (*The Physical Theory of Another Life*) that consoles a little; namely, we saw and felt the power of Deity in such fullness that we ought to infer the infinite Justice and Goodness which we do not see or feel."[43] Olivia saw Howells's letter too, and in a letter that Clemens wrote to his wife he observed, "We do see and feel the *power* of what we call God. We do see it and feel it in . . . measureless fullness."[44] Clemens seems to be trying to find his way back to some kind of faith, but the effort was not to last long.

Even in the 1890s there was a side of Mark Twain that was a believer, as readers of his most underrated book, *Personal Recollections of Joan of Arc*, know. He was attracted to the Maid Joan because she was strong, good, and godly, and because she resembled his daughter Susy his admiration for the young woman who was to be canonized as Saint Joan is obvious to any reader of the book. The man who wrote *Joan of Arc* had a side of him that needed to believe in innocence and purity, in goodness and godliness. He admired Joan of Arc as much as the man who had followed her, Louis de Conte, who is Mark Twain's supposed author of the book. As Frederick Crews has written, Mark Twain was "both sentimental and cynical," the result being "that we can never be quite sure we have got Mark Twain right."[45]

All of Clemens's other writings indicate that his attitudes towards Christianity and God were growing more and more negative and hostile. When he experienced personal misfortune such as his bankruptcy, the death of his daughter Susy, the death of his wife, Livy, and finally the death of his youngest daughter, Jean, he did not decide that he now had a grievance with the God he judged responsible for his misfortunes. Rather his skeptical and pessimistic attitude had been developing even while he was prosperous and expecting to become a multimillionaire. It is too easy to dismiss Clemens's negative view of God by saying that the poor man had suffered.

Whereas for a time Mark Twain was attacking man's notions of God, by the late 1890s he was developing his final beliefs about God. That year he wrote two pieces. One is a credo that Paine published in his 1935 edition of selections from Mark Twain's notebooks; here he contrasts his deistic belief in God "the perfect artisan, the perfect artist," a god revealed by the "bible of nature," the "Book of Nature," with the God of "man-made Bibles."[46] Very different is the first clear account that I can locate of Mark Twain's later, one might say final, beliefs about God occurring in a dialogue he wrote the same year; originally it was planned as a continuation of his philosophical dialogue *What is Man?* But later, perhaps in 1905, the author marked it "NOT TO BE USED." Like *What is Man?*, which Mark Twain did publish, this work is a conversation between an old man, a version of Samuel Clemens, and a young man. The publication finally occurred in 1973 but since it is in a supplement to the volume *What is Man? and Other Philosophical Writings*, it is very little known. It is entitled "GOD."

First the old man declares that he believes that God exists: "I do not claim to know, but I believe it and with all my might. I think He is not a bunch of Laws but a personality." This personality, according to the old man, has revealed himself to man by his deeds and works, by his works and his deeds. Man's experience of God begins with his birth. "The day we are born he begins to persecute us. Even our littleness, our innocence, our helplessness cannot move him to any pity, any gentleness. Day after day, week after week, month after month, the wanton tortures go on. Pain, pain, pain—in the teeth, in the stomach, in the bowels. . . . [Then follows a long catalogue.] Would you treat a little child so, that had done you no harm?"[47] So Mark Twain's first grievance against God is that he is responsible for human suffering. He asks, "Is there some way to explain or justify this more than tigerish spirit, this age-long unappeasable appetite for the blood and misery of the innocent?" The young man's answer is that God's actions must be right since they proceed "from the Source of all justice."[48]

His second grievance is that the God who made the laws of nature, man, and man's nature is responsible for man's sinful nature and his eagerness to break God's laws. Man murders and tortures. He is avaricious, indecent, vulgar, and obscene. Man is what he is, according to Mark Twain's spokesman, because God made him so.

Two other later works set forth Clemens's attitude towards God in his last years. The first of these is the series of autobiographical dictations that he made in the summer of 1906, published in book form in 1987 as *The Outrageous Mark Twain*—the title that Charles Neider, who published them, gave the five dictations of 1906 which Twain called "Reflections on Religion." Clemens wrote to Howells after the dictations were behind him, "I have been dictating some fearful things . . . for no eyes but yours to see until I have been dead a century—if then. But I got them out of my system, where they have been festering for years—& that was the main thing. I feel better, now."[49] Later he wrote on the title pages of two of the chapters, "Not be exposed to an eye until the edition of A.D. 2406." He wanted the world to know what he thought, but he did not want to damage the sale of his books till five hundred years had passed.

Clemens appears to have enjoyed dictating such remarks because of the discrepancy between how the public viewed him, as a genial humorist, and his own sense of himself as one who had penetrated to a profound understanding of the nature of things. Moreover, like Tom Sawyer he liked to show off and shock those close to him. Here is the strongest passage of all. Note that it is not intended as a comment about man's conception of the deity; it is a comment on the deity.

> In His destitution of one and all of the qualities which could grace a God and invite respect for Him and reverence and worship, the real God, the genuine God, the maker of the mighty universe, is just like all the other gods in the list. He proves every day that He takes no

interest in man, nor in the other animals, further than to torture them, slay them, and get out of this pastime such entertainment as it may afford—and do what he can not to get weary of the eternal and changeless monotony of it.[50]

Did Samuel Clemens really believe *that?* There is no evidence that he did not. No doubt his attitude originated very early when he adopted an unsympathetic view of Christianity, a view that wrongheaded Christians themselves had adopted, though they somehow found such ideas comforting rather than disturbing. But the sentiments expressed in this dictation can only be said to represent what Mark Twain felt and thought on one occasion.[51] As Louis Budd has written, he was "less consistent than ever during his last years" and though he had "his nihilistic moods," he "kept adding to the confusion with occasional statements of faith."[52] As late as 1907 he told Albert Bigelow Paine, "I have never seen what seemed an atom of proof that there is a future life." Then he added, "And yet—I am strongly inclined to expect one."[53]

The last work to be taken up here, rather better known than "Reflections on Religion," is *Letters from the Earth*, which is still available in paperback. Back in the 1960s it was on the best-seller list for a long time. Most of what Clemens has to say in this work he had said already; what is different now is that he is in a better humor, much more genial. Even the contrast between the Old and the New Testaments that Clemens likes to emphasize is presented amusingly. The quarrel that Clemens had been having with God is now also a quarrel with Jesus Christ, the Christ that Clemens had referred to so reverently in the late 1870s when he wrote to his brother. In "Letters from the Earth," he says,

> Now here is a curious thing. It is believed by everybody that while he [the Deity] was in Heaven he was stern, hard, resentful, jealous and cruel, but that when he came down to earth and assumed the name Jesus Christ, he became the opposite of what he was before: that is to say, he became sweet, and gentle, merciful, forgiving, and all harshness disappeared from his nature and a deep yearning love for his poor human children took its place. Whereas it was as Jesus Christ that he devised hell and proclaimed it! Which is to say, that as the meek and gentle saviour he was a thousand billion times crueler than he was in the Old Testament—incomparably more atrocious than ever he was when he was at his very worst in the old days.[54]

One cannot determine whether Clemens is discussing the historical Jesus or the Jesus of the hellfire and damnation variety of

Christianity. A charitable view is that once again Clemens was a victim of his own ignorance.

The simple-minded fundamentalism that he believed Christianity to be was one major source of Sam Clemens's later religious position. He was convinced that Christianity was strongly associated with hellfire and damnation. His experience in the Holy Land made him think that the Bible was hardly accurate. Though he questioned for a time the presentation of God in the Bible and preferred a different set of notions concerning God, later he seems to have found that the picture of God found in the Bible, especially the Old Testament, was accurate, and such a God he heartily despised. Clemens profoundly misunderstood Christianity, though he understood very well that some people who prided themselves on being Christians were pious hypocrites.

One must also recognize that Clemens was a humorist, as I have tried to suggest in my epigraph. He liked to satirize and make fun of things and to be irreverent.[55] This attitude was partly responsible for his severe criticism of religion and of God. But he also liked to think of himself, especially in his last years, as a philosopher who had thought about the most profound questions. He told an interviewer in 1907, "Everything I have ever written has had a serious philosophy or truth as its basis."[56]

Clemens's mature religious thought evolved, as we have seen, over a period of many years. If one were to consider the final phase of his religious thinking in the context of the ideas set forth in "What is Man?" it could surely be described as the result of training and temperament. The simplistic teachings on the nature of the Bible he was provided in Hannibal and the heavy emphasis there on hellfire and damnation, plus the barrage of attacks on his adolescent beliefs—Thomas Paine, his experiences in the West and the Holy Land, his reading in the scientific literature of his age, his fear of public recognition of his unorthodox opinions combined with the pleasure he took in showing off—all make it easy to understand Clemens's attacks on God in his last years. If his best works are for all time, his religious thinking was, not surprisingly, that of his age.

Notes

1. Samuel L. Clemens, *Mark Twain's Autobiography*, 2 vols. (New York: Harper, 1924), 2:214.

2. Samuel L. Clemens, "Jane Lampton Clemens," in *Mark Twain's Hannibal*,

Buck and Tom, ed. Walter L. Blair, The Mark Twain Papers (Berkeley and Los Angeles: University of California Press, 1969), 44–45.

3. Indeed it is Satan whose words are quoted, but in this work Satan speaks for Clemens.

4. Albert Bigelow Paine, *Mark Twain: A Biography*, 3 vols. (New York: Harper, 1912), 1281.

5. Alan Gribben, *Mark Twain's Library: A Reconstruction*, 2 vols. (Boston: G. K. Hall, 1980), 1:63–64.

6. Quoted in Samuel L. Clemens, *Mark Twain to Mrs. Fairbanks*, ed. Dixon Wecter (San Marino, Calif.: Huntington Library, 1949), 88, from DV #243, Mark Twain Papers.

7. Forrest G. Robinson's *In Bad Faith: The Dynamics of Deception in Mark Twain's America* (Cambridge: Harvard University Press, 1986), sees the adult Mark Twain's fictional version of Hannibal, *The Adventures of Tom Sawyer*, as an exploration of small-town hypocrisy (or "bad faith").

8. Samuel L. Clemens, *Mark Twain in Eruption: Hitherto Unpublished Pages about Men and Events*, ed. Bernard DeVoto (New York: Harper, 1940), 108.

9. Paine, *Biography*, 277; quoted in Sherwood Cummings, *Mark Twain and Science: Adventures of a Mind* (Baton Rouge: Louisiana State University Press, 1988), 19.

10. *The Age of Reason*, ed. Moncure Daniel Conway (New York: Putnam, 1924), 197.

11. Paine, *Biography*, 1445.

12. Cummings, *Mark Twain and Science*, 21–23.

13. "'Seeing the Elephant': Some Perspectives on Mark Twain's *Roughing It*," *American Studies* 21 (1980): 53.

14. Samuel L. Clemens, *Early Tales & Sketches. Volume 2, 1864–1865*, ed. E. M. Branch and R. H. Hirst, The Works of Mark Twain (Berkeley and Los Angeles: University of California Press, 1981), 2:149–62.

15. Samuel L. Clemens, *Travelling with the Innocents Abroad: Mark Twain's Original Reports from Europe and the Holy Land*, ed. Daniel M. McKeithan (Norman: University of Oklahoma Press, 1958), 258.

16. Samuel L. Clemens, *The Innocents Abroad*, 2 vols., Author's National Edition (New York: Harper, 1911), vol. 2, chap. 24.

17. Ibid., vol. 2, chap. 21.

18. Quoted from 1904 notebook in Gribben, *Mark Twain's Library* 2:664.

19. *Mark Twain's Notebook*, ed. Albert Bigelow Paine (New York: Harper, 1935), 393.

20. *The Love Letters of Mark Twain*, ed. Dixon Wecter (New York: Harper, 1949), 33–34.

21. *The Darkened Sky: Nineteenth-Century Novelists and Religion* (Notre Dame and London: University of Notre Dame Press, 1969), 139.

22. *Mark Twain to Mrs. Fairbanks*, 50.

23. *Love Letters*, 133.

24. Ibid., 65.

25. Robert D. Jerome and Herbert A. Wisbey, *Mark Twain in Elmira* (Elmira, N.Y.: Mark Twain Society, 1977), 120.

26. *Love Letters*, 133.

27. Cummings, *Mark Twain and Science*, 141.

28. Cummings points to Charles Darwin's *The Descent of Man* (1871) and W.

E. H. Lecky's *History of European Morals* (1874) as having a profound influence on the development of his determinism. Cummings's treatment of Mark Twain's religious thought is far better than that of any of the three book-length studies dealing with Clemens's religious thought.

29. *Love Letters*, 167.

30. *Mark Twain's Letters*, ed. Albert Bigelow Paine, 2 vols. (New York: Harper, 1917), 1:323.

31. Paine, *Biography*, 412.

32. John S. Tuckey, ed., *Mark Twain's "Fables of Man"* (Berkeley and Los Angeles: University of California Press, 1972), 73.

33. Ibid., 32.

34. Caroline Harnsberger, *Mark Twain's Views of Religion* (Evanston, Ill.: Schori Press, 1961), 13.

35. Ibid., 27, 43.

36. Samuel L. Clemens, *What Is Man? And Other Philosophical Writings*, ed. Paul Baender, The Works of Mark Twain (Berkeley and Los Angeles: University of California Press, 1973), 57–58.

37. "The Parting of the Twains," *New York Review of Books*, 20 July 1989, 39–44.

38. *Mark Twain and Religion: A Mirror of American Eclecticism*, ed. Fred A. Rodewald (New York: Peter Lang, 1989), 107.

39. Guy A. Cardwell, *Twins of Genius* (East Lansing: Michigan State College Press, 1953), 108.

40. Samuel L. Clemens, *Mark Twain-Howells Letters: The Correspondence of Samuel L. Clemens and William Dean Howells, 1872–1910*, ed. William M. Gibson and Henry Nash Smith, 2 vols. (Cambridge: Harvard University Press, 1960).

41. Howard Mumford Jones, *Belief and Disbelief in American Literature* (Chicago: Chicago University Press, 1967), 110–11.

42. Quoted in Frederick, *The Darkened Sky*, 152.

43. Clemens, *Mark Twain-Howells Letters* 2:606.

44. *Love Letters*, 253.

45. "Parting of the Twains," 44.

46. *Mark Twain's Notebook*, 361–62.

47. *What Is Man?*, 477–78.

48. Ibid., 479–80.

49. *Mark Twain-Howells Letters* 2:85.

50. *The Outrageous Mark Twain*, ed. Charles Neider (New York: Doubleday, 1987), 47.

51. The day before the dictation quoted was undertaken Mark Twain described the God of the Bible as "by long odds the worst God that the ingenuity of man has begotten from his insane imagination" (*Outrageous Mark Twain*, 41). Clemens thus attacked both "the real God, the genuine God," and the God he thought of as having been invented by man's imagination—an apparent inconsistency.

52. Louis J. Budd, *Mark Twain: Social Philosopher* (Bloomington: Indiana University Press, 1962), 188, 207–8.

53. Paine, *Biography*, 1431. John S. Tuckey, "Mark Twain's Later Dialogue: The 'Me' and the Machine" (in *On Mark Twain*, ed. Louis J. Budd and Edwin H. Cady [Durham: Duke University Press, 1987]) is a helpful account of Mark Twain's changing outlook in his later years.

54. *What Is Man?*, 443.

55. In *The Authentic Mark Twain: A Literary Biography of Samuel L. Clemens* (Philadelphia: University of Pennsylvania Press, 1984), I argue that the literary personality that Clemens created in the West, the one he called "Mark Twain," was regularly characterized by irreverence.

56. Quoted in Louis J. Budd, *Our Mark Twain: The Making of His Public Personality* (Philadelphia: University of Pennsylvania Press, 1983), 22.

The Early Readers of Wallace Stevens
George S. Lensing

For Wallace Stevens, the act of reading is metaphorical, the eye's participation in the capacious world. Reading the world makes it into a text. Poems like "Large Red Man Reading" and "The Reader" recall to their own readers that very process: "All night I sat reading a book, / Sat reading as if in a book. . . ."[1] Like the variety of the world beyond the eye, the views in response to the text of a poem could also be varied, as Stevens himself acknowledged: "Some one said not long ago that a poem consists of all the constructions that can be placed upon it. Its measure is the variety of constructions that can be placed upon it: the variety of meanings that can be found in it.[2] Throughout his life, Stevens' readers were his editors (like Harriet Monroe, Ronald Lane Latimer, and Alfred Knopf), his critics, and even himself as he glossed his poems for the benefit of various interlocutors like Hi Simons and Renato Poggioli. After initial publication of the poems, however, his first readers were his reviewers, those who posted in the various journals and newspapers short commentaries on the volumes as they appeared from *Harmonium* (1923) through the *Collected Poems* (1954). There is evidence that Stevens read his reviews, and, in some instances, reacted strongly, though privately, to them. A few of them had a discernible effect upon future poems.

A review is itself a form of criticism *sui generis*. Usually brief and composed shortly after the appearance of a given collection, it possesses inevitable restrictions. By nature it is a preface or brief introduction, given more to final summation and pronouncement than to rigorous analysis. Whether read hastily or not, the volume being scrutinized elicits a preliminary response. The reviewer must be bold: he evaluates peremptorily, often in general rather than specific terms. His aim is to recommend or to dismiss, and, in so doing, he adopts the authority of certitude. Few reviews are long remembered, but they are not without influence. The prestige of the reviewer can add exceptional force to the power of the evaluation, whatever its conclusion or however fairly arrived at. The reputation and circulation of the organ in which the review appears impose yet other factors of influence. In some cases, and this was especially true of Stevens in the 1930s, the political bias of the journal can be crucial in its attitude toward the subject of review. Reviews are perhaps our best introduction to the general milieu in which the poems were written and first published; they often reflect the climate of ideas, the social, political and aesthetic assumptions of the day; the standards of comparison and judgment; and the reviewer's biases and expectations that may be typical. Their historical proximity to the poems can be uniquely valuable to readers of later generations.

Most of the reviews that followed the publication of Stevens' collections were, for the most part, sympathetic. Some were not, however, and as he wrote to Henry Church on the day of the publication of *Parts of a World*, "I shall go through the next month or two in fear of assassination by some aggressive critic" (*L*, 418). To José Rodriguez-Feo he added some time later that "adverse criticism . . . does one more good than the highly favorable kind of thing" (*L*, 529), and it was just such criticism that most touched the direction of his own subsequent writing.

Stevens' long delay in publishing his first volume is testimony to the seriousness with which he undertook the enterprise. Even as he was piecing it together late in 1922, he wrote Harriet Monroe that he was "exercising the most fastidious choice," indeed, discarding many poems from his "witherlings" (*L*, 232). Though *Harmonium* was not a commercial success, it was noticed by reviewers. Not only did Monroe respond enthusiastically in *Poetry: A Magazine of Verse*,[3] but other notable poets and critics also reacted: John Gould Fletcher, Marianne Moore, Louis Untermeyer, Mark Van Doren, Edmund Wilson, and others. *Harmonium* invariably impressed its reviewers principally for its style. Two words that recur over and over in the reviews are "luxuriance" and "virtuosity." To Moore it was the "riot of gorgeousness"[4] created with a precise diction that she admired. Stevens wielded "the finest and most distinguished weapon of style"[5] in modern poetry, according to Fletcher. "Colors are richer, sounds are sharper in him than in other minds or in the real existence which the mass mind accepts,"[6] said Matthew Josephson, and Wilson began his review in *The New Republic* by declaring that "Mr. Wallace Stevens is the master of a style: that is the most remarkable thing about him."[7] In his *Men Seen, Twenty-Four Modern Authors* (1925), Paul Rosenfeld described Stevens in some detail as the "American poet of distinct Laforguian cut."[8]

The spectacle of rhetoric astonished Stevens' early readers, and, even when they went on to criticize him for other reasons, they acknowledged the wit, the showy language, the musical modulations, and the novel images. Though some of the readers found the rhetoric ostentatious and empty, most ranked Stevens as stylist generously. Van Doren, for example, found that *Harmonium* placed its author "high among those wits of today who are also poets"—including Eliot, Pound, and Williams.[9] Fletcher found certain poems by Stevens "head and shoulders above them all"—namely Eliot's *The Waste Land* and Valéry's "Jeune Parque."[10] Even before the publication of *Harmonium*, Yvor Winters, in a review of the collected poems of E. A. Robinson, called Stevens "the greatest of living and of American poets."[11]

The most skillful discussion of Stevens the stylist was conducted by Gorham B. Munson in an essay that appeared in *The Dial* two years after the publication of *Harmonium*.[12] "The Dandyism of Wallace Stevens," carefully defined by Munson, christened Stevens with a name that would attach itself for many years. By dandy, Munson did not mean a cynical poseur or shallow harlequin. Rather, Stevens' dandyism evolved from the cosmos created by his imagination, one based not upon humanism or religion, but "the discipline of one who is a connoisseur of the senses and emotions." Munson insisted that Stevens' dandyism lifted him above the " 'torments of confusion.' " "Tranquillity enfolds Mr. Stevens," he generalized. The poet feasts upon life without distraction: "None else, monocled and gloved, can cut so faultless a figure standing in his box at the circus of life." Munson cleverly redefined and summarized the verbal panache in Stevens' work that had earlier captured the attention of Moore, Fletcher, Josephson, Wilson, and others. The difficulty of this early, extended view of Stevens was that, without quite stating it, Munson hinted at decadence, a succumbing to the empty gestures of language for their own sake. He suggested, moreover, that such posturing was peculiarly American:

> The American nation drives passionately toward comfort. The aim of the frenzied practical life in which it engages is to attain material ease, and the symbols of its paradise are significant. . . . Naturally, in paradise one would not wish to be annoyed by a suspicion that all was a brilliant fake, a magnificent evanescent dream, but rather, to

refine upon one's luxurious means of existence. This is where in America the artistic intelligence may enter and play, elaborating, colouring, bedecking, adding splendour to the circumstances of one's comfort. Is there not fundamentally a kinship between the sensory discriminations and comfortable tranquillity of Wallace Stevens' poetry and the America that owns baronial estates?

Untermeyer's remarks in the *Yale Review*, preceding Munson's by a year, were more explicit: "There are, in fact, many pages in 'Harmonium' which lead one to doubt whether its author even cares to communicate in a tongue familiar to the reader; he is preoccupied with language as color or contrasting sound values, scarcely as a medium for registering degrees of emotion." An "amusing preciosity," he concluded, was Stevens' only achievement. "He luxuriates in an ingeniously distorted world."[13] Wilson agreed that, upon reading the whole volume through, "you are struck by a sort of aridity" instead of discovering "a poet of rich personality."[14] On these grounds, some of the formalist critics of the 1930s and 1940s would balk at the achievement of Stevens. The comments prefigure the charge of "hedonism" that Yvor Winters was to declare in 1943. In *The World's Body* (1938), John Crowe Ransom identified "Sea Surface Full of Clouds" as one form of modernity, decrying the subject matter as "trifling" and declaring the poem itself devoid of "moral, political, religious, or sociological values."[15] Cast as dandy, hedonist, and nominalist, the maker of aridly impersonal poems, Stevens was never in his lifetime able to escape altogether these designations. It became, in fact, a justification for dismissing him, and many did just that.

One can only speculate on the effect of these early summations on the poet himself. His predilection for *la poésie pure*, poems of musical self-sufficiency, was unmistakable in selected poems.[16] Yet he surely saw that many of the reviews involved a fundamental misreading, especially when *Harmonium* was taken as a whole. Munson's argument that Stevens' "literary cosmos" was one "moving according to calculations, subject to his own laws and hierarchies" necessarily disregarded from consideration other poems that demanded the expunging of the imagination's self-indulgences. *The Comedian as the Letter C*, for example, in spite of all the overwrought and even turgid rhetoric of much of the poem, insisted upon Crispin's forswearing dandyism. He would "stem verboseness" in favor of "the essential prose," "the veritable ding an sich":

> Crispin beheld and Crispin was made new.
> The imagination, here, could not evade,
> In poems of plums, the strict austerity
> Of one vast, subjugating, final tone
>
> (*CP*, 30)

"The Emperor of Ice-Cream" decreed, "Let be be finale of seem," where the lamp would affix its beam upon the horny feet of unromanticized and unexalted death. "The Snow Man," Stevens later told Simons, was "an example of the necessity of identifying oneself with reality in order to understand and enjoy it" (*L*, 462). In short, the earliest readers of Stevens failed to recognize the "interdependence" of imagination and reality, of seeming and being, the coexistence of his romantic constructions of the mind followed by their classical decreations. The austere and autumnal poems of *Harmonium* ("Invective against Swans," "Domination of Black," "Nuances of a Theme by Williams," "Another Weeping Woman," "From the Misery of Don Joost," "Valley Candle," "Depression before Spring," and so on) were overlooked in the fascination with the gaudiness and eccentricity of the early work. A favorite quotation from many of the reviews of *Harmonium* was the third tercet of "Another Weeping Woman": "The magnificent cause of being, / The imagination, the one reality / In this imagined world." In not a single instance, however, did the reviewer note the next and final tercet, which concludes that the same magnificent cause of being "Leaves you / With him for whom no phantasy moves, / And you are pierced by a death" (*CP*, 25). A few readers, like Marjorie Allen Seiffert, acknowledged a "rocky substratum of reality" beneath the "scenery of luxuriant and intricate design,"[17] but this was the exception. Absorbed by the stunning diction, the strange images, and the ruses of wit, most readers failed to probe beyond the glint of surface.

The decade of silence that separates *Harmonium* from the writing of the first poems that would make up *Ideas of Order* may best be explained by the distorted and unbalanced readings that greeted the publication of *Harmonium*.[18] There is no evidence from letters or other sources that this is the case, and Stevens' official accounts point to the demands of business and family. Yet even Harriet Monroe, in her eager praise of the poet, hoped that he would not turn out to be as "baffled" as the hero of *The Comedian as the Letter C:* "We must hope that the poem is not strictly autobiographical, that Mr. Stevens, unlike his baffled hero, will get his story uttered."[19] Fletcher was more direct in his instruction: "But for the future he must face a clear choice of evils: he must either expand his range to take in more of human experience, or give up writing altogether."[20] Josephson saw the poet moving from the strange to the scandalous: "The fallacy of this manner . . . is that it must go on being more and more strange. The cultured sensuousness of Mr. Stevens in his book would have to be more and more intimate and scandalous, *ad absurdum*."[21] Such dire warnings and directives, coupled with incomplete readings of what was already there, perhaps cooled the poet's resolve to go on.

With the publication of the second edition of *Harmonium* eight years after the first, Percy Hutchinson in the *New York Times Book Review* reattacked the book as a "tour de force" that "cannot endure": "From one end of the book to the other there is not an idea that can vitally affect the mind, there is not a word that can arouse emotion. The volume is a glittering edifice of icicles."[22] But with the benefit of the interim separating the two editions, other critics examined the poetry more closely. Morton Dauwen Zabel, for example, challenged Munson's designation of Stevens as dandy, adding that "this style was not a conjuror's garment but an expression for ideas of no given date, and of which he [Stevens] remains in many cases our only exact recorder."[23] Most important of all was the first major extended defense of Stevens, and, still today, a valuable appraisal of his work. R. P. Blackmur's "Examples of Wallace Stevens," appearing in *Hound & Horn* early in 1932, was carefully researched by Blackmur, including correspondence with the poet himself.[24] His essay is a rejoinder to those readers who had dismissed Stevens as a finicky stylist. Blackmur examined the diction of *Harmonium* in detail, noting the precision with which Stevens selected his unusual words in order to enhance ambiguity and to arrive at resolution between "ornamental sound and representative statement." Stevens' rhetoric, Blackmur argued, separated him from the more visual images of Pound or dramatic images of Eliot. Neither allusive nor transcendental, the more meditative poetry of Stevens imitated the impersonal movement of the mind's own dispersals. Instead of condensation, Blackmur found expansion: "His visual images never condense the matter of his poems; they either accent or elaborate it. His dramatic statements, likewise, tend rather to give another, perhaps more final, form to what has already been put in different language."[25]

If Blackmur found precision of diction the key to Stevens' meditative rhetoric, Eda Lou Walton saw the opposite—providing what must be the first deconstructionist reading of the poet. Striking out also against the charge of dandyism, she took the style of Stevens as an act of "creative imagination": "Stevens' highly mannered, technically superb verse is so written because it best expresses his particular creative imagination: to this mind no simple statement is possible, every word has innumerable associations. The poet is sincere in being insincere, since to be sincere would for him be ridiculous."[26] Where every word yields to its associations *ad infinitum*, no sincere or unequivocal reference is possible. Only the insincerity of language itself is the poet's sincerity.

When the second edition of *Ideas of Order* appeared in 1936, thirteen years after the first edition of *Harmonium*, the volume gave evidence of an attempt on Stevens' part to reorient his poetry. To the "high ship" on which he sailed in the book's first poem, "Farewell to Florida," he declared his severance from the past and the "sepulchral South." Though he "loved her once," he now repudiated Florida: "I hated the weathery yawl. . . . I hated the vivid blooms." Instead, his course was northward: "My North is leafless and lies in a wintry slime / Both of men and clouds, a slime of men in crowds" (*CP*, 117–18). These men in crowds, with the suggestion of social unrest and universal disorientation, recurred through the volume in both the 1935 and 1936 editions, but vaguely and certainly without direct political attribution. The fecund South, though joyously reclaimed in "The Idea of Order in Key West," dissolved into a world where "forms have vanished" in "Sad Strains of a Gay Waltz":

> There is order in neither sea nor sun.
> The shapes have lost their glistening.
> There are these sudden mobs of men,
>
> These sudden clouds of faces and arms,
> An immense suppression, freed,
> These voices crying without knowing for what,
>
> Except to be happy, without knowing how.
>
> (*CP*, 121–22)

Stevens' temporary repudiation of Florida in favor of a vaguely defined setting of social upheaval was surely an attempt on his part to convey the impression of social consciousness. Such images, he hoped, would disarm those critics who had deplored his work for its innocence of the world beyond immediate personal perceptions. The strategy failed. Theodore Roethke (his own first volume still five years away), reissued the old complaint: "It is a pity that such a rich and special sensibility should be content with the order of words and music, and not project itself more vigorously upon the present-day world."[27] Geoffrey Grigson, in a review for *New Verse* entitled "The Stuffed Goldfinch," excoriated the volume for "too much Wallace Stevens, too little everything else." In his view, the poet was "still the finicking privateer, prosy Herrick, Klee without rhythm, observing nothing, single artificer of his own world of mannerism."[28] Stevens saw the review and, when Ronald Lane Latimer, editor of the 1935 edition, suggested the possibility of a Pulitzer Prize for *Ideas of Order*, the poet reminded his editor, "After all, there are people who think that IDEAS OF ORDER is not only bad but rotten." Grigson, he noted, was interested in "social revolution," while he, on the other hand, believed in "social reform and not in social revolution" (*L*, 309). Ben Belitt reviewed both *Ideas of Order* and *Owl's Clover* (the volume that followed a year later) for the *Nation*, and he sent a note to Stevens, apparently enclosing a copy or summary of the review. The poet's response is one of his few answers to a reviewer. Belitt's review began with a general observation about the poems, but he went on to lament the poet's failure to fix firmly on "order and certitude," preferring a playful relativism. Stevens rather surprisingly accepted the criticism of the second sentence (italicized below) as "a difficulty that I have long been conscious of and with which I am constantly struggling. Your review helps" (*L*, 314). Belitt had written:

> Though the poetry of Wallace Stevens has not lacked themes of commanding contemporary stature, these have not, until recently, constituted his major concern. *His problem has been a curious one: moved to formal discourse in the quest for order and certitude, his art has not up to the present permitted him to pursue such discourse or his temperament to accept it.* Instead, in an essentially evocative medium, he has continued to qualify definitions to their fractional parts, reducing ideas into images and images into sounds—and then neglected the full circle which returns both sound and image to experience and unites the fractional with the definitive insight.[29]

His poetry, however, would continue to favor "fractional parts," as Stevens set out his anecdotes, thirteen ways, variations, asides, extracts, repetitions, notes, and prologues.

Ideas of Order had its defenders. Marianne Moore saw Stevens as "America's chief conjuror,"[30] while F. O. Matthiessen saw an advance over the *"dandyisme"* of *Harmonium:* "One is tempted to say that this is the nearest approach to major poetry being made in this country today."[31] Blackmur extended the defense laid out in his earlier essay to include *Ideas of Order* and *Owl's Clover*,[32] while Monroe, at a total remove from Roethke and Grigson, detected "tremors of trepidation" that Stevens' "delight in all the beauty and oddity may be shaken by the clamor and confusion of the modern scene."[33]

One other review of *Ideas of Order*, however, struck out at the poet for irrelevancy in time of social crisis. This review disturbed the poet and evoked an elaborate response: "Turmoil in the Middle Ground" by Stanley Burnshaw appeared in *New Masses*, a journal of marked leftist leanings. Burnshaw's impatience with Stevens' aestheticism was undisguised. The poet's sensuousness, he said, was a hardened kernel, a "crystallography," totally divided from the fire of personal emotion. Moreover, the poetry itself was "screeching with confusion"; the poet had simply "lost his footing" and now "scrambles to stand up and keep his balance." The reason for such dizzy imbalance was not, in the final analysis, what the poet said or even how he said it. Rather, it was what was left unsaid: "It is the kind of verse that people concerned with the murderous world collapse can hardly swallow today except in tiny doses."[34]

Burnshaw's review appeared on 1 October 1935. On the last day of the same month, Stevens wrote to Latimer announcing the completing of "Mr. Burnshaw and the Statue." He also acknowledged a question from Latimer that must have been preying upon him: "whether I accept the common opinion that my verse is essentially decorative, and whether my landscapes are real or imagined." His first reaction, he said, was to deny the charge of decorative verse, but then he remembered the writing of certain poems for *Harmonium* where he preferred "the idea of images and images alone, or images and the music of verse together." His next paragraph revealed the process whereby now, in the wake of the review by Burnshaw and his own poetic response to it, he was reexamining the issue of poetry and society: "I still have a distinct liking for that sort of thing [pure poetry]. But we live in a different time, and life means a good deal more to us now-a-days than literature does. In the period of which I have just spoken, I thought literature meant most. Moreover, I am not so sure that I don't think exactly the same thing now, but unquestionably, I think at the same time that life is the essential part of literature" (*L*, 288).

In his commonplace book, *Sur Plusieurs Beaux Sujects*, Stevens made it clear that Burnshaw's accusations had refocused his attention upon the relation between the disorders of society and the orders of art. He copied out a review of the poetry of Charles M. Doughty by Anne Treneer from the *Times Literary Supplement* late in 1935: "He [Doughty] belonged to the 'egotistical sublime' because he insisted on creating a world for himself in his poetry . . . with most of the troublesome humanity left out. . . . That poetic diction of his is not adequate to human behaviour as we know it" (*SPBS*, 46–47). Treneer on Doughty was uncannily close to Burnshaw on Stevens and at exactly the same time. The parallel was not lost on Stevens. Treneer had lamented Doughty's omission of the "passionate disorder in the hearts of men" in his poetry. Six weeks after completing "Mr. Burnshaw and the Statue," Stevens wrote to Latimer: "You know, the truth is that I had hardly interested myself in this [forms of order in Dutch and Italian painting] . . . when I came across some such phrase as this: 'man's passionate disorder', and I have since been very much interested in disorder" (*L*, 300). In fact, he had already resolved the issue in "Mr. Burnshaw and the Statue": "even disorder may, / So seen, have an order of its own" (*OP*, 80). It was a conclusion he would develop further three years later in "Connoisseur of Chaos" ("a great disorder is an order").

At the time of Burnshaw's review of *Owl's Clover* the worlds of American poetry and politics were intertwined to a degree hardly seen before or since. In the very numbers of magazines and journals in which Stevens' poems and the reviews of his volumes were appearing, essays and editorials lashed out against Western capitalism and flirted boldly with Marxist alternatives. Ben Belitt's review of *Ideas of Order*, for example, appeared in the same issue of *The Nation* in which Louis Fischer described the Nationalist assault upon Madrid, then held by the Republicans in the Spanish civil war. Fischer, sympathetic to the Russian-backed Loyalists, deplored the worldwide indifference to their plight in Madrid: "Where is the world which answered the call of Belgium? Where is the humanitarian heart of the millions who go to church and pray to God, or of the millions who call themselves idealists yet go about their business signing letters, having manicures, seeing cinemas, while a city of culture and beauty is being ground into dust?"[35] Theodore Roethke's short review of *Ideas of Order* in *The New Republic* was accompanied in the same issue by an essay entitled "A Brief Manual of Beggary." H. F. Kane's instructions for successful begging were intended for the benefit of "large numbers of newcomers" to unemployment and penury.[36] Beside such reportings, apocalyptic both internationally and nationally, the poems of Stevens were ready quarry for consciences of the left.

In 1961, Burnshaw himself, reflecting back upon the mid-1930s, saw both his review and "Mr. Burnshaw and the Statue" as "nothing more nor less than actions of their time. Judge them out of their context and they become grotesques." The overriding test by which every work of art was measured, Burnshaw added, was "social amelioration."[37] Stevens deliberately refused to abide by that measure, however, and he made *Owl's Clover*, of which "Mr. Burnshaw and the Statue" was one part, into a defense of poetry divorced from the programmatic and political.

The poem itself, as no previous poem by Stevens had done, adopts a vision of the world in highly social and pessimistic terms. Both "rich" and "poor" succumb, not to political revolution, but to death:

> There buzzards pile their sticks among the bones
> Of buzzards and eat the bellies of the rich,
> Fat with a thousand butters, and the crows
> Sip the wild honey of the poor man's life,
> The blood of his bitter brain.

(OP, 81)

If such bitterness on the part of the poor is born of the "thousand butters" enjoyed by the rich, both poor and rich are leveled by death without regard to social class. The world is one of waste, as universally dire as the one depicted by Eliot:

> Parts of the immense detritus of a world
> That is completely waste, that moves from waste
> To waste, out of the hopeless waste of the past
> Into a hopeful waste to come.

(OP, 81)

On what base could a "hopeful waste to come" be posited? To Latimer in the same October letter Stevens explained his strategy: "You will remember that Mr. Burnshaw applied the point of view of the practical Communist to IDEAS OF ORDER; in MR. BURNSHAW AND THE STATUE I have tried to reverse the process: that is to say, apply the point of view of the poet to Communism" (*L*, 289). In the poem he declared that "poets' politics" could never rule because poets "are never of the world in which they live" (*OP*,

80). Or rather, they are never of that world as shapers of political destiny. In telling Latimer that he once regarded literature as superior to life ("Moreover, I am not so sure that I don't think exactly the same thing now.") he meant that even among the "wreckage" of life, the poet could discern "faint, portentous lustres." In a world where misery and waste were universal, one also recognized that same world as constantly changing and yielding inevitably to life and to death. In such a setting the poet could make his own orders:

> But change composes, too, and chaos comes
> To momentary calm, spectacular flocks
> Of crimson and hoods of Venezuelan green
> And the sound of z in the grass all day, though these
> Are chaos and of archaic change. Shall you,
> Then, fear a drastic community evolved
> From the whirling, slowly and by trial; or fear
> Men gathering for a mighty flight of men,
> An abysmal migration into a possible blue?
>
> (*OP*, 82)

Stevens' relevance to the turmoil of the 1930s would have to be as a poet and not a politician or reformer. He could recognize and call attention to social disruption, though in *Owl's Clover* Stevens showed that even this was a forced exercise. The poet could propose no social panacea, no program for remaking society. Even if he acknowledged such a mission, he told Latimer, the task was ill-suited to his temperament: "Unfortunately, I don't have ideas that are permanently fixed. My conception of what I think a poet should be and do changes, and I hope, constantly grows" (*L*, 289). The poet, however, does make his own order; he can find his own "lustres" in the thick "wreckage" that surrounds him ("even disorder may, / So seen, have an order of its own" [*OP*, 80]). Stevens must have known that such a view would never placate the Burnshaws, and he would not be drawn again into such a polemic. Latimer sent him a copy of a review of *Owl's Clover* in the *New York Herald Tribune* that declared him "open to attack from the left." Stevens' response to Latimer was bemusement: "I expect the house to be burned down almost any moment" (*L*, 313). When *Owl's Clover* was reproduced in *The Man with the Blue Guitar* a year later the title of this section of the longer poem was changed from "Mr. Burnshaw and the Statue" to "The Statue at the World's End."

In the writing of a later and major poem, *Esthétique du Mal*,

Stevens also responded to the charge of social irrelevancy. The context now was not the economic upheavals of the 1930s, but world war. In 1944 John Crowe Ransom wrote to request a poem for the *Kenyon Review* and, as a courtesy, enclosed a copy of the spring issue. Within its pages Stevens' attention was fixed upon an essay by Ransom himself, "Artists, Soldiers, Positivists." In the essay Ransom had cited a letter from an unidentified soldier who, in fact, attacked Stevens and Eliot as too removed in their work from the international crisis:

> What are we after in poetry? Or, more exactly, what are we attempting to rout? The commandos of contemporary literature are having little to do with Eliot and even poets of charming distemper like Wallace Stevens (for whom we all developed considerable passion). . . . Men like Karl Shapiro (his "Anxiety," in *Chimera* recently, is notable), John Berryman, Delmore Schwartz transcend the aesthetic of poetry, thank God! I find the poetry in *Kenyon Review* lamentable in many ways because it is cut off from pain. It is intellectual and it is fine, but it never reveals muscle and nerve.[38]

If the soldier found in Shapiro, Berryman and Schwartz a poetry that transcended an "aesthetic of poetry," Stevens resolved to rescue that aesthetic and to remake it as his own "esthétique," but one of "mal," obviously showing he was not "cut off from pain."

Although *Esthétique du Mal* confronts the experience of pain in a context wider than war, section 7 introduces war's casualty. The soldier's fatal wound ("How red the rose that is the soldier's wound . . .") is presented more through pathos than horror, death's apotheosis ("deathless in great size") rather than personal calamity (*CP*, 318–19). What comforts the soldier's survivors is "gaiety of language" (*CP*, 327), the pleasures of the "physical world" of "green corn gleaming" (*CP*, 325) and the "miraculous thrift" (*CP*, 320) of sight and sound. His esthétique, in fact, harks back to "Sunday Morning" (1915) wherein "Death is the mother of beauty" (*CP*, 68), a guarantor of the earth's largesse. Perhaps more humanly and personally, he also proposes an esthétique of human sympathy, a summons to all "true sympathizers" to enter the ring of "the actual, the warm, the near" and to join in "So great a unity" with every brother. In so doing, he concludes, "we forego / Lament, willingly forfeit the ai-ai" (*CP*, 317).

One senses in *Esthétique du Mal*, as nowhere else in Stevens, the raw personality of the poet, the "rotund emotions" of a man facing forthrightly war, evil, conflict with father, the "bitter aspic" of life. It was his reduction to poet of "charming distemper" by Ransom's soldier that had stung him, more sharply even than Burnshaw's reprimand, and provoked the poem.

The remaining volumes by Stevens continued to provoke among the reviewers new formulations of the issues that had separated them in the earlier ones: stylistic adroitness and mastery vs. preciosity and decadent ornamentation; a humanist's affirmation of the powers of the constructive mind vs. an esthete's equivocation, emotional barrenness and dissociation from the world of "hunger of love."[39]

As late as 1954, John Ciardi, reviewing *Collected Poems*, found Stevens to be "American poetry's Great Unread,"[40] though it became increasingly clear with each volume that the poet was difficult to dismiss peremptorily. With the publication of *Parts of a World* in 1942, for example, reviews began to appear for the first time in publications of a wider readership: *The New Yorker, Time, Atlantic Monthly*, for example. Louise Bogan, though her enthusiasm for Stevens would slacken with subsequent volumes, found in 1942 the need for "an enlightened scholar" to take Stevens "in hand."[41] She must have sensed the inadequacies of brief reviews in coming to terms with the poet. William York Tindall, reviewing the same *Parts of a World*, found Stevens "the most interesting and perhaps the best poet now writing in America. Certainly he is the best craftsman."[42] F. Cudworth Flint agreed, declaring him "to share with Robert Frost the first place among living American poets."[43] While his readers were never large in number, a few, including influential poets and critics, made up a loyal and substantive platform of admirers. Rolfe Humphries in 1950 found him, along with Williams, "one of the most be-culted American poets."[44]

The reviews of the second half of Stevens' career give us some indication of how the reputation was secured. The dialectic in his work between imagination and reality, clothed in the images and tropes of his redoubtable rhetoric, was more bold after *The Man with the Blue Guitar* (1937), the poem that spelled out the dialectic most explicitly. *Notes toward a Supreme Fiction* (1942) established the meditative character of the later work and initiated the debate over the superiority of the earlier poetry (usually *Harmonium*) or the later.

The epistemological dynamics of the poetry had been hardly noticed in *Harmonium, Ideas of Order* and *Owl's Clover.* Lloyd Frankenberg, reacting to *The Auroras of Autumn* (1950) in the

New York Times Book Review, saw the theme as all-pervasive: "the history of their [imagination and reality] liaisons, divorcements, reconciliations and final fluctuations comprises the poetry of Stevens."[45] If Frankenberg saw the duality in terms of a sexual metaphor, Harvey Breit adopted Stevens' notion of the " 'war between the mind and sky' ": "Then is Stevens' perspective an absolute of war? I do not know how Stevens would reply. But, though this war is the unrequited theme of the poems, it subsides inside the poems and, at last, *is requited by them.*"[46] Few of the reviewers, however, managed to develop the complexities of the mind's interaction with the world except to name them. An exception was Hi Simons. His review in *Poetry* of *Parts of a World,* "The Humanism of Wallace Stevens," gave evidence of the recent care he had poured upon the poet's work, including his correspondence with Stevens. The "law of inherent opposites," defined in "Connoisseur of Chaos," became his touchstone:

> "Law" is a a metaphor for "feeling," a feeling of supreme pleasure in the recognition of the interrelationships of such contraries as the actual and the imagined, the real and the ideal, order and disorder, man and woman, life and death. Total reality comprises both opposites in each pair; it is not complete, hence not real, without them both.[47]

Victor Tejera, a philosopher reviewing *Transport to Summer* for the *Journal of Philosophy,* found a kinship between metaphysics and Stevens' verse. Here, he insisted, was a poet who could be taken seriously by philosophers. His "realistic epistemological position" was founded upon his recognition of metaphor as "a way of things." While his poetry proceeds from a different origin, it shared with metaphysics a complementary relation: "Thus, if it can be said that metaphysics consists in the analysis of the differentiae of being, then it may also be said that poetry is the quest for similarities in the same domain. Seen in this light poetry becomes a complement, a transliteration of metaphysics." Tejera went on to find three stages leading up to the exercise of metaphorical likenesses, stages that anticipate the later critical development of Stevens' phenomenology. "The first stage is Pyrrhonic: *skepticism* shears away the rubble of old and dead forms. The second is empirical and devoted to *observation* of the now naked and consequently stark reality. The third stage is the strictly poetic one and represents a reconstruing of experience through the *invention* of new and adequate forms; forms which are to one reader at least, a guide to the feelings and a stimulus to the imagination."[48]

A few reviewers were impatient with the direction of the later work. Some eleven years after "Examples of Wallace Stevens," Blackmur began revising his view of the poet. The method had become one of fragmented variations on a major idea, "a piety of the imagination with the effrontery of repetition." Instead of the precise diction he had admired in *Harmonium* and *Ideas of Order*, Blackmur now discovered "special knowledge of fashion and gibberish in vocabulary and idiom."[49] Later, in *Transport to Summer*, he found too many poems about poetry and poets, obliterating "what the poet ought to see."[50] Louise Bogan found the Stevens of the 1940s "obsessed by his defense of the imagination against 'the world of fact.' In his earlier work, when that argument was implicit, his point was made more convincingly."[51] Louis Untermeyer, adamant in his pre-*Harmonium* objections, found no advance in the later volumes: "Stevens seems to be less anxious to establish a relation between imagination and 'the' world than making 'a' world—another world of the intellect; a forced creation, an incongruity of serious wit and irresponsible whimsy."[52] Vivienne Koch, writing after the publication of *The Auroras of Autumn*, saw the danger of a "jejeune solipsism,"[53] while G. S. Fraser labeled Stevens a "pragmatic solipsist" in 1955.[54] Stevens himself told Simons in 1940 that "people say that I live in a world of my own: that sort of thing. Instead of seeking therefore for a 'relentless contact,' I have been interested in what might be described as an attempt to achieve the normal, the central." By the "central," Stevens seems to have referred to the experiences of ordinary lives and circumstances, and he told Simons that a knowledge of his commitment to it "may be useful to you in understanding some of the later things" (*L*, 352). Whatever recent poems he had in mind, they did not succeed in persuading later reviewers like Untermeyer that his work had found such a "center." The reviewers here demonstrate a problem in reading Stevens that has carried over into longer and more sophisticated critical studies as well: the tendency to judge the poet generally on the basis of isolated poems. It is indeed possible to single out poems as solipsistic or eccentrically private, poems where the imagination either remakes the real or ignores it altogether. Any final assessment of Stevens has to include the shifts in poetic emphasis from poem to poem, however. Other poems contest with equal demand the hegemony of the imagination: "Sometimes I believe most in the imagination for a long time," Stevens told Heringman, "then, without reasoning about it, turn to reality and believe in that and that alone. But both of these things project themselves endlessly and I want them to do just that" (L, 710). Only in rare cases did the contemporary reviews of Stevens' volumes, even those of the *Collected Poems*, recognize fully these shifting "beliefs."

Melita Schaum has shown how Stevens' later poetry displeased those formalist critics who had found in *Harmonium* a workshop for their own ideals:

> Stevens' early poetry was easily received into formalist readings, for it so readily satisfied the aesthetic interest in semantic and imagistic complexities in both verbal and tonal play. But Stevens' later work, "devolving" as it were into theory, provided greater problems for both formalist critics and those critics of transformation, such as the later Blackmur, who, though respecting formal craftsmanship, still demonstrated a desire for . . . an aesthetic which could move beyond "coherence and significance" into a type of "significant coherence."[55]

Poems of union and separation between mind and world, especially after *The Man with the Blue Guitar*, evoked a consideration of Stevens as a poet of ratiocination or meditation. After reading *Notes toward a Supreme Fiction* and *Esthétique du Mal*, Louis Martz was convinced that Stevens had "mastered a conversational, meditative style."[56] His important essay "Wallace Stevens: The World as Meditation," would appear more than a decade after this review, but already he was calling attention to this aspect of Stevens' style. F. Cudworth Flint came to the same conclusion after reading *Parts of a World*. Stevens, he asserted, was "trying to discover through his poetry what we can know and how we can know it." Such knowledge as the object of poetic quest was attained "not by denying objects or explaining them away, but by dwelling on them, by clinging to them intently with our minds."[57]

Of all Stevens' reviewers, it was the poet Delmore Schwartz who consistently recognized the patterns of thought that underlay the "sense of play and jocular attitudinizing" that so often seemed to preempt the attention of the reviewers. In his review of *The Man with the Blue Guitar*, for example, Schwartz cited the lines, "To strike his living hi and ho, / To tick it, tock it, turn it true," adding, "If we dig into just such usages and then come back to the poem as whole, we understand the justice of such verbalism, its necessity, and we are confronted with a mind of the utmost seriousness."[58] The point was reiterated after the publication of *Transport to Summer*,[59] and, following the appearance of the *Collected Poems*, Schwartz spoke of the conversion of aestheticism into contemplation "in the full philosophical and virtually religious sense of the word."[60] After reading *Parts of a World*, William York Tindall found Stevens "nonchalant, precise, precious, and, it must be admitted, not a little decadent." With a backhanded sweep, he singled out a motive behind other attributes of the poetry: "But, as in a dream . . . it is never altogether clear what the thinking is about. Concealing his thoughts, if any, in indirection, nonsense, and exquisite goofiness, Stevens conveys the sensation of thinking, which for most of us is all that thinking comes to anyway."[61] To locate Stevens as a meditative poet, one needed to see behind the flashy surfaces of his poems; such views emerged only in the 1940s, especially after the publication of *Notes toward a Supreme Fiction*.

Some, however, preferred the "goofiness" for its own sake. Finding the later poems too cerebral, repetitious, and undramatic, these reviewers maintained a preference for the poems of *Harmonium*. Toward the end of Stevens' life there began to emerge, in fact, a division between those who found the poet never to have surpassed the success of the earliest poems and those who championed the triumph of meditative poems like *Notes toward a Supreme Fiction* and *Esthétique du Mal*. Robert Lowell, writing a year after the publication of his own *Lord Weary's Castle*, distrusted the "structural differences" of a poem like *Notes toward a Supreme Fiction*: "It rambles and rambles without gathering volume, and many of the sections are padded to fill out their twenty-one lines." He preferred "the concrete, gaudy wit of 'Harmonium.'"[62] Other poets agreed. Louise Bogan decried the more recent "explicit, logical, and rather word-spinning defense of the role of the imagination," a mode that "weakened or destroyed a good deal of his original 'magic.'"[63] Louis Simpson[64] and John Ciardi[65] each came to the same conclusion.

In their disapproval of his later poetry, the defenders of the early Stevens often followed the argument put forth by Yvor Winters in his essay "Wallace Stevens or the Hedonist's Progress." Appearing in *The Anatomy of Nonsense* in 1943, it became one of the most influential in Stevens' lifetime. While finding much to admire in "Sunday Morning" and a few other early poems, Winters categorized the early work of Stevens as "the most perfect laboratory of hedonism to be found in literature." The hedonism consisted in "the cultivation of the emotions as an end in itself,"[66] and that cultivation fed upon a radical nominalism that portended a breakdown for Stevens as a poet. Hedonism and nominalism, argued Winters, left the poet incapable of moving beyond mere descriptive verse, incapable of positing judgments and thoughts apart from description. There could be, he concluded, no growth for such a poet. Winters cannot be said to have preferred *Harmonium* over the later work, finding the hedonism present from the beginning. But the reviewers who did justify the first poems often did so on the basis of Winters' prediction that the subsequent poetry would necessarily be stillborn. Donald Davie, for example, after reading the *Collected Poems*, harked back to Winters' judgment: "The more one reviews Stevens's later career, the more one sees the point of Yvor Winters's verdict that from 'Harmonium,' despite its technical variety, there could be no way forward. There was, in fact, one development that Winters did not foresee: the poetry could thereafter live on its own fat, gnaw its own vitals, conduct a running commentary on itself."[67]

Other critics found the rewards of the later poetry greater. Jean Garrigue, for example, reviewing *The Auroras of Autumn*, found a happy respite from the "caracole-cutting and figured somersault-turning . . . delicate quiddities, and secretive, half-concealed antics" of the earlier work.[68] Hayden Carruth admired both early and late Stevens, though the former was "not as good" as the latter,[69] and Joseph Bennett admired the "quieter manipulation of effects, and an economy of means that gave it [the later work] an increasingly dexterous emotional range and an intellectuality that is markedly more luminous."[70]

Because of the impact of Stevens' first volume and the continuing popularity of many of its contents as anthology pieces, *Harmonium* was an inevitable yardstick against which the succeeding volumes were measured. Reviewers, expecially toward the end of Stevens' career and as the longer meditative works became absorbed, judged the later work in the shadow of the poet's initial impression. Stevens' readers still manifest their preference between various poems early and late, but the criticism of the poet has long outgrown the simplistic distinctions that were never completely valid. The meditative penchant was already present in poems from *Harmonium* like "Sunday Morning," "Le Monocle de Mon Oncle," while the rhetorical array of wit, nonsense sounds, and unfamiliar diction persisted in each volume after *Harmonium*. Donald E. Stanford has correctly noted that Stevens "had the gift of language to a superb degree, and he enjoyed playing with it as much as he enjoyed playing with ideas."[71]

Stevens's letters are remarkably free of recrimination against his harsher critics, as his remarks to Latimer on Grigson and his review of *Ideas of Order* ("A Stuffed Goldfinch") indicate. A few months following that review he recommended Grigson's *New Verse* to Van Geyzel as a poetry magazine "the most vigorous of its kind" (*L*, 332). Blackmur he admired though he found his criticism circumlocutory (*L*, 484). Winters' famous essay "The Hedonist's Progress" he claimed never to have read, but he was familiar enough with it to offer a mild defense against the charge of hedonism to Theodore Weiss (*L*, 463). He later endorsed Allen Tate's nomination of Winters for membership in the National Institute of Arts and Letters (*L*, 633).

Stevens was himself a reviewer only once, responding to a request to assay Marianne Moore's *Selected Poems* in 1935. The review begins by commending the formal prosody of Moore and her preference for commonplace objects. The second half defends her as a romantic. His aim is to convey a general feeling of her poetry in the aggregate. The quality of the romantic as "the living and at the same time the imaginative, the youthful, the delicate and a variety of things which it is not necessary to try to particularize at the moment" constituted "the vital element in poetry" (*OP*, 220). The one fault Stevens found in the reviewers of his own work was their reticence to speak of the feelings of pleasure wherever they found it. For the reviews of *Parts of a World*, he told Church, he had not found "so much as a suggestion that the book gave the man who read it any pleasure" (*L*, 430). That failure preoccupied him, and he reiterated the point to Simons a few weeks later: "All this is proved by the fact that I have yet to see any review in which the reviewer let himself go and said that he really enjoyed the book. . . . Possibly one never has more than a very few readers who pick up the feelings that one puts into one's poems" (*L*, 436). Marianne Moore's romanticism was charged, not only with an "uncommon intelligence," but with the very feelings he found the reviewers so often ignoring: "It means in a time like our own of violent feelings, equally violent feelings and the most skilful expression of the genuine" (*OP*, 220).

In other shorter commentaries, not formally reviews, Stevens wrote tactfully of the early poems of Martha Champion and

Samuel French Morse, an introduction to the poems of Williams and another short tribute to him, and a commentary on the regionalism in the poetry of John Crowe Ransom. The method of loosely organized impressions and the informal style of his other essays suggest that Stevens might have made an excellent reviewer, but the pencil for that task remained in the drawer. One reason for his silence on the work of his contemporaries was the fact that he seldom read them.

Stevens defended the role of the reviewer as promoter. Standing between poet and common reader, the critic gave heart to the latter, who, according to Stevens, needed rousing: "About the reviews: It is hard to speak of the value of reviews. Looking at them wholly from my point of view, their value is in bringing about a certain amount of acceptance. People never read poetry well until they have accepted it; they read it timidly or they are on edge about it, afraid that something is going to go wrong with the sentence after next" (L, 436). Such a plea comes from a poet who had experienced, both privately and in print, complaints about the abstruseness of his own work. The reviewer was the poet's ally, reassuring him that the poet was, after all, worth the trouble.

Though he obviously read many of the reviews of his poems, Stevens claimed that he usually avoided them. The essay by Winters was one of the latter: "I . . . have not read a line of his essay on my own poetry. This is out of pure virtue, because I think it disturbs one to read either praise or blame" (L, 484). Another part of that potential disturbance was self-consciousness, a vice, he told Simons, that was fatal to a poet (L, 493). He returned to the same point five years later when Rodriguez-Feo asked him if he had read William Van O'Connor's new book on his poetry (L, 676).

In the later years, when reviewers and critics (Hi Simons, Bernard Heringman, Charles Tomlinson, Samuel French Morse, Sr. Bernetta Quinn, Robert Pack) sent copies of their published remarks, Stevens invariably responded gratefully. An early essay by Howard Baker he characterized as "an extremely intelligent analysis of my work" (L, 292). He identified Simons as one of the "two or three" readers who "pick up the feelings that one puts into one's poems" (L, 436). A later essay by Heringman he acknowledged to its author as "one of the most understanding things about my poetry that I have ever read" (L, 695).

Stevens was obviously moved by some of the early criticism—not merely because it promised to steer his work to "acceptance," but also because it showed to the poet himself the scope and complexity of his achievement. Even the unfriendly reviews recalled him to a certain sense of his identity as a poet. The unsympathetic critics who found his work unrooted in the world of anguish and other basic human emotions account as much as anything else for the relentless reorientation in poem after poem toward the real, the normal, the center. Such returns were always temporary, but they were corrective and renewing—and not merely so in the aesthetic or epistemological senses, but in the social and personal as well.

Frank Doggett is correct when he notes that Stevens' response to all his criticism "neither improved nor reduced the quality of his poetry."[72] The reviewers, in fact, never succeeded in arousing the self-consciousness that might have harmed the confidence and firmness of his own voice. "Mr. Burnshaw and the Statue" is only the most explicit evidence of this resistance. Yet, perhaps more than that of most poets, Stevens' poetry benefited from the kind of "acceptance" that his first readers made possible.

In their own right, most of the reviews are deservedly forgotten today except as historical markers on the route to later and more ambitious assessments. All of them help define a climate of standards and expectations contemporaneous with the poet, a period when critics were finding modernism sometimes confusing, sometimes vital, but unquestionably new. A few of the reviewers, like Monroe, Blackmur, Schwartz, and Simons, made important forays in defining the complex value of the poetry. Robert Lowell was correct when he wrote in 1947 that Stevens lacked the popularity of Frost and the international reputation of Eliot and Pound,[73] but that "he has, nevertheless, been fortunate in the criticism he has received." He went on to mention the names of Blackmur and Winters, adding, "But Winters' evaluation is corrective to Blackmur's appreciation; and by combining the two essays one can come to a calmer and more objective understanding of Stevens than is, perhaps, possible with any other contemporary American writer.[74] Because Stevens' popularity as a poet was not widespread, it was, in fact, his reviewers who secured his reputation and guaranteed, even in dissent, his seriousness.

Notes

1. *The Collected Poems of Wallace Stevens* (New York: Alfred A. Knopf, 1961), 146; hereafter cited in text as *CP*. In a similar way, *Opus Posthumous* (New York: Alfred A. Knopf, 1989); *Letters of Wallace Stevens*, selected and edited by Holly Stevens (New York: Alfred A. Knopf, 1966); and *Sur Plusieurs*

Beaux Sujects (Stanford: Stanford University Press, 1989) are cited in text as *OP, L,* and *SPBS* respectively.

2. From George S. Lensing, "Wallace Stevens and Stevens T. Mason: An Epistolary Exchange," *Wallace Stevens Journal* 4 (Fall 1980): 36. In his *Implied Reader: Patterns of Communication in Prose Fiction from Bunyan to Beckett* (Baltimore: Johns Hopkins University Press, 1974), Wolfgang Iser speaks of the "inevitable omissions" in the flow of prose narratives, "gaps" left for the creative act of reading to fill. His conclusion is not unlike Stevens' defense of the "variety of constructions" placed upon a poetic text: "These gaps have a different effect on the process of anticipation and retrospection, and thus on the 'gestalt' of the virtual dimension, for they may be filled in different ways. For this reason, one text is potentially capable of several different realizations, and no reading can ever exhaust the full potential, for each reader will fill in the gaps in his own way, thereby excluding the various other possibilities; as he reads, he will make his own decision as to how the gap is to be filled. In this very act the dynamics of reading are revealed" (280).

3. For a thorough treatment of the Wallace Stevens–Harriet Monroe relationship, see George S. Lensing, "Harriet Monroe and *Poetry: A Magazine of Verse*," in *Wallace Stevens: A Poet's Growth* (Baton Rouge: Louisiana State University Press, 1986), 245–67.

4. "Well Moused, Lion," *The Dial* 76 (January 1924): 84.

5. "The Revival of Aestheticism," *The Freeman* 8 (19 December 1923): 355.

6. Untitled, *Broom* 5 (November 1923): 236.

7. "Wallace Stevens and E. E. Cummings," *New Republic* 38 (19 March 1924): 102.

8. (New York: Dial Press, 1925), 158.

9. "Poets and Wits," *The Nation* 117 (10 October 1923): 400.

10. "The Revival of Aestheticism," 355.

11. "A Cool Master," *Poetry* 19 (February 1922): 287.

12. "The Dandyism of Wallace Stevens," *The Dial* 79 (November 1925): 413–17.

13. "Among the New Books," *Yale Review* 14 (October 1924): 159–60. Untermeyer's disapproval of Stevens had begun several years earlier. In his *The New Era in American Poetry* (New York: Henry Holt and Co., 1919) he had spoken of the "attenuated preciosity" of Stevens, citing "The Florist Wears Knee-Breeches" (317). Conrad Aiken, reviewing Untermeyer's book in *New Republic* 19 (10 May 1919): 58–60, defended Stevens, Eliot, Pound, Bodenheim, and others as poets who worked more "through a play of implication than through matter-of-fact statement." In his rejoinder in the same issue (60–61), Untermeyer referred to the "mere verbal legerdemain of the Pound-Stevens-Arsenberg-Others."

14. "Wallace Stevens and E. E. Cummings," 102.

15. *The World's Body* (New York: Charles Scribner's Sons, 1938), 59.

16. See George S. Lensing, "Stevens on Stevens," in *Wallace Stevens: A Poet's Growth* (Baton Rouge: Louisiana State University Press, 1986), 294–99.

17. "The Intellectual Tropics," *Poetry* 23 (December 1923): 160.

18. Frank Doggett has noted the "speculation that this kind of [critical] condescension toward *Harmonium* was to some degree responsible for his long silence after 1923" (*Wallace Stevens: The Making of the Poem* [Baltimore: Johns Hopkins University Press, 1980], 120).

19. "A Cavalier of Beauty," *Poetry* 23 (March 1924): 327.

20. "The Revival of Aestheticism," 356.

21. Josephson, untitled, 236.

22. "Pure Poetry and Mr. Wallace Stevens," *New York Times Book Review*, 9 August 1931, sect. 1, p. 37.

23. "The Harmonium of Wallace Stevens," *Poetry* 39 (December 1931): 149.

24. Stevens' letter to R. P. Blackmur, dated 16 November 1931, with his comments on "The Emperor of Ice-Cream," was published by Holly Stevens in an essay, "Flux," *Southern Review* 15 (October 1979): 771–74.

25. "Examples of Wallace Stevens," *Hound & Horn* 5 (January–March 1932): 223–55.

26. "Beyond the Wasteland," *The Nation* 133 (9 September 1931): 264.

27. Untitled, *New Republic* 87 (15 July 1936): 305.

28. 19 (February–March 1936): 18.

29. "The Violent Mind," *The Nation* 143 (12 December 1936): 708.

30. "Unanimity and Fortitude," *Poetry* 49 (February 1937): 268.

31. "Society and Solitude in Poetry," *Yale Review* 25 (March 1936): 606.

32. "The Composition in Nine Poets," *Southern Review* 2 (Winter 1937): 558–76.

33. "He Plays the Present," *Poetry* 47 (December 1935): 156.

34. 17 (1 October 1935): 41–42. A second review, by Isidor Schneider, continued the attack against *Ideas of Order* one year later. He decried the limitation of Stevens' imagination to the mere "processes of art." He called for a much wider range of play: "But imagination is a process of all creative minds, and the imagination of a Lenin, a Freud, an Einstein, a Stalin, a Wright, an Amundsen is of a Dantesque range" ("Order Limited," *New Masses* 21 [27 October 1936]: 24).

35. "Under Fire in Madrid," *The Nation* 143 (12 December 1936): 694.

36. "A Brief Manual of Beggary," *New Republic* 87 (15 July 1936): 288–89.

37. "Wallace Stevens and the Statue," *Sewanee Review* 69 (July–September 1961): 356, 358.

38. "Artists, Soldiers, Positivists," *Kenyon Review* 6 (Spring 1944): 276.

39. The charge of G. S. Fraser, "The Aesthete and the Sensationalist," *Partisan Review* 22 (Spring 1955): 271.

40. "Wallace Stevens' 'Absolute Music,'" *The Nation* 179 (16 October 1954): 346.

41. "Verse," *New Yorker* 18 (10 October 1942): 62.

42. "Literary Signposts," *American Mercury* 56 (January 1943): 119.

43. "Images of Secret Life," *Virginia Quarterly Review* 19 (Winter 1943): 133.

44. "Verse Chronicle," *The Nation* 171 (30 September 1950): 293.

45. "'Secretions of Insight,'" *New York Times Book Review*, 10 September 1950, sec. 7, p. 20

46. "Sanity That is Magic," *Poetry* 62 (April 1943): 50.

47. "The Humanism of Wallace Stevens," *Poetry* 61 (November 1942): 449.

48. Untitled, *Journal of Philosophy* 45 (26 February 1948): 138, 139.

49. "An Abstraction Blooded," *Partisan Review* 10 (May–June 1943): 300, 299.

50. "Poetry and Sensibility: Some Rules of Thumb," *Poetry* 71 (February 1948): 274.

51. "Verse," 62.

52. "Departure from Dandyism," *Saturday Review of Literature* 25 (19 December 1942): 11.

53. "The Necessary Angels of Earth," *Sewanee Review* 59 (Autumn 1951): 665.

54. "The Aesthete and the Sensationalist," 271.

55. *Wallace Stevens and the Critical Schools* (Tuscaloosa: University of Alabama Press, 1988), 0.76.

56. "Recent Poetry," *The Yale Review* 37 (December 1947): 340.

57. "Images of Secret Life," 133, 134.

58. "New Verse," *Partisan Review* 4 (February 1938): 50.

59. "Auden and Stevens," *Partisan Review* 14 (September–October 1947): 528–32.

60. "In the Orchards of the Imagination," *New Republic* 131 (1 November 1954): 17.

61. "Literary signposts," *American Mercury* 56 (January 1943): 119.

62. "Imagination and Reality," *The Nation* 164 (5 April 1947): 401. According to Steven Axelrod, Lowell copied into his notebook the following poems from *Harmonium*: passages from "Sunday Morning" (thrice), "Le Monocle de Mon Oncle" (third stanza), "On the Manner of Addressing Clouds," "Of Heaven Considered as a Tomb," "The Death of a Soldier." *Robert Lowell, Life and Art* (Princeton: Princeton University Press, 1978), 246.

63. "Verse," *New Yorker* 26 (28 October 1950): 130.

64. Untitled, *American Scholar* 24 (Spring 1955): 240.

65. "Wallace Stevens' 'Absolute Music,'" 347.

66. "Wallace Stevens or the Hedonist's Progress," *The Anatomy of Nonsense* (Norfolk, Conn.: New Directions, 1943), 88–110.

67. Untitled, *Shenandoah* 6 (Spring 1955): 64.

68. "Search for Reality in New Haven," *Saturday Review of Literature* 34 (10 February 1951): 17.

69. "'Without the Inventions of Sorrow,'" *Poetry* 85 (February 1955): 291.

70. "Some Notes on American Poetry," *Nine* 3 (April 1952): 262.

71. *Revolution and Convention in Modern Poetry* (Newark: University of Delaware Press, 1983), 83.

72. *Wallace Stevens: The Making of the Poem*, 129.

73. For an examination of Stevens' difficulties in publishing a volume in England, see George S. Lensing, "Wallace Stevens in England," in *Wallace Stevens, A Celebration*, ed. Frank Doggett and Robert Buttel (Princeton: Princeton University Press, 1980), 130–148.

74. "Imagination and Reality," 400.

To Jonathan Edwards
David Levin

. . . there came into my mind, a sweet sense of the glorious majesty and grace of god, that I know not how to express. I seemed to see them both in a sweet conjunction: majesty and meekness joined together: it was a sweet and gentle, and holy majesty; and also a majestic meekness; an awful sweetness; a high, and great, and holy gentleness.

—Spiritual autobiography

Unconverted men walk over the pit of hell on a rotten covering. . . .

—"Sinners in the Hands of an Angry God"

In sweet conjunction holy gentleness,
An awful majesty of sovereign meekness,
Shadows your insistent eagerness
To crown your highest thought with proofs of weakness.

Not only in consigning us to Hell,
But in your definition of true virtue,
You bend your Sovereign's doctrines to a will
As deep as any sin for which we search you.

Consent to Being sounds a harmony,
An *Exsultate* just as glorious
As any Mozart wrote in any key.
Even when you are most censorious,
Standing us on the rotten covering,
You make us hear the angels, hovering.

On Gari Melchers' "Writing" (1905) in the Los Angeles County Museum

> The house was quiet and the world was calm
> —Wallace Stevens

Helen Pinkerton

How often did she make such quiet, one wonders,
This woman writing at a covered table—
Full summer light warming the roseate hues,
Mauve, red, and pink of dress and cloth and room.
A Wedgewood pier-glass shows three Roman figures
In ritual dance—cool neoclassic Graces—
Beside a clay pot of geraniums.
Her taste eclectic—like our modern lives—
Loving the past but settle in the living,

She seems meticulous—even, perhaps,
Like Edith Wharton, passionate for order,
Feeling, as she did, that in house and novel,
"Order, the beauty even of Beauty is."
Stevens, though you sought order in the sea
And grander heavens, the threat of nothingness
Unmanned you. Most women have no time for such,
For fate constrains them to immediate means,
The quiet art of keeping calm the house.

Forsan et Haec
Janet Lewis

For Don Stanford

"Forsan et haec olim—" How does it go, that line?
Perhaps this, even this . . . one day—
My father wrote it in the copy of the Aeneid
Which he gave you that summer, that summer
When you read Latin together. That summer
When you gave of your young strength
To lengthen his, in the hewing of wood,
And the drawing of water, all the work
About dock or cabin that the years made
Too heavy for him. That summer
When we were all together on St. Joseph's Island,
Three generations, and friends, at Everens Point.
"Perhaps even this, one day
It will rejoice us to remember."
Even this.

Aeneas and his companions
Had grief enough to remember,
The streets of Troy in flame, the ships
Storm-tossed.
I remember no disaster,
No storm, such as harassed Aeneas.
I wish only to draw that summer nearer.

In that quiet place there was always
The sound of the wind in leaves, the lapping
Of water, and the voices of the freighters
Coming upstream, as they signaled for the Lookout
At the turn where the river narrows.
The blast echoed within the wooden walls
Of the sunlit cabin, familiar, reassuring.

From that upland meadow
Where cedars overhung the granite rock
Where the sheep took shelter,
We could look down
On the open stretches of the river and watch
The long freighters riding high in the water,
Going unloaded toward Superior.
We saw the puff of steam,
The white flash by the funnel, and waited
Moments for the sound to reach us,
A soft thunder rolling wide in the moving air.

Look back on this with me now. To no one else,
After these fifty-seven years, can I say:
Forsan et haec olim meminisse iuvabit.

Janet Lewis in Her Eightieth Year Arriving at Dusk with a Basket of Persimmons

Stanford, California, 8 November 1979

Maclin Bocock

Dear Friend, you have come so many times,
(All those years gone now)
With gift from garden or mind,
And you have never let me leave your shaded yard
Without a poem or blossom
Or words that mend.
Now you're here once more,
A quiet Demeter at the end of day.

Oh, Janet, your are that fruit
Dazzling to sight, to inner eye!
Through all your spinning seasons
You have used the earth
Wisely, gently,
And grown to perfect ripeness.

Your radiance, a benediction.

Whose Worth's Unknown, although His Height Be Taken

Wesley Trimpi

For Donald Stanford

I have taken the eighth line of Sonnet 116 as my title for this essay, whose purpose is to explain Shakespeare's distinction between knowing the "worth" and taking the "height" of a star. Because the star is a metaphor for the subject of the poem itself, understanding the contrast between these activities is essential to our grasping the kind of love the poet wishes to describe. If the antithesis remains obscure, our response to the sonnet must remain incomplete.

Since this line in Sonnet 116 has continued to give difficulty to commentators, I would like to clarify briefly the tradition that provided Shakespeare with his distinction. I shall not be concerned with the biographical implications of the poem nor with the question of whether the author is speaking of love between friends or between lovers, men or women. The interested reader will find amply diverse speculation on such issues in the secondary literature but will not find a satisfactory explanation of the navigational metaphor in the eighth line.

> Let me not to the marriage of true minds
> Admit impediments. Love is not love
> Which alters when it alteration finds,
> Or bends with the remover to remove:
> O, no! it is an ever fixed mark,
> That looks on tempests and is never shaken;
> It is the star to every wandering bark,
> Whose worth's unknown, although his height be taken.
> Love's not Time's fool, though rosy lips and cheeks
> Within his bending sickle's compass come;
> Love alters not with his brief hours and weeks,
> But bears it out even to the edge of doom:

> If this be error and upon me proved,
> I never writ, nor no man ever loved.

The kind of love capable of overcoming the impediments usually imposed by temporal circumstances and human weakness has the power not to change even when faced by changes in the beloved. The possession of this power is compared first to that of a sea-mark such as a beacon, unshaken by tempests, and then to a star whose position is sufficiently constant to permit reliable navigation.[1] As clear as these comparisons are on the surface, two difficulties arise with the clause "whose worth's unknown."[2]

The first is the meaning of the word "worth." If the value of a navigational star for those in a "wandering bark" lies in its being able to be sighted, why would its worth be unknown even though "its height be taken?" Its worth should consist in its being sighted.[3] But clearly Shakespeare is making a distinction here between "worth" and the art of navigation, and various meanings have been offered for the first term. Since the nineteenth century some form of astrological influence has been the most recurrent misinterpretation.[4] And even when the star's value has been correctly seen as its (relative) invariability, either no reason is given for its "worth's" being unknown or its "constancy" is regarded as correlative with (or necessary for)—rather than as distinct from—sighting its height.[5]

The second difficulty is the meaning of "unknown." Unknown to everyone, hence perhaps unknowable? Or, if not unknowable in general, unknown to whom? The meaning of "worth" as the power not to alter, to remain constant, will be clarified by the context of Shakespeare's distinction to be established below, but I want to comment on the second difficulty here.

> It is the star to every wandering bark,
> Whose worth's unknown, although his height be taken.

The worth clearly cannot be unknowable to all, since in the course of the sonnet the speaker explicitly states what it is.[6] It must be unknown then to those in the wandering ship, the "dull sublunary" lovers caught up in the tempests of conflicting desires, since it is clearly these who have just profited from taking the height of the star whose worth remains unknown to them. Such lovers are in motion, from the speaker's point of view, and do not know this worth—this power not to alter—for if they did know it, they would not be wandering but rather trying to participate in its stability. Yet, as wanderers they may, indeed must, take the height of the star to find their temporary locations; and, in fact, the more times they must sight the star, the greater and more erratic their motion is revealed to be and the less likely they are to "know" (recognize, share in) its constancy.[7]

Shakespeare's distinction between knowing the worth and taking the height of the star has Stoic, Peripatetic, and Platonic roots. I shall begin with its most simplified, polemic, and (probably) available form in Seneca's observations to Lucilius on the relation of the liberal arts to philosophy and then summarize briefly the Aristotelian and Platonic anticipations of the Stoic argument. In order to criticize the current state of the liberal arts, Seneca contrasts their specialized subject matter and expedient objectives to those of philosophy, particularly ethics, which alone has retained the end, long abandoned by the arts themselves, of literally "setting men free." Among the individual arts contrasted with philosophy, Seneca discusses the objectives of the mathematical disciplines at greatest length, and I turn to the two extended analyses of these objectives in *Epistle* 88.

In the first of these (88.10–17), he says the mathematician (*geometres*) teaches him "to lay out the dimensions" of his estate, but should have taught him "what is enough for a man to own (10);" he teaches him to calculate his wealth but does not show him how useless property is to one who does not know how to share it with his brother (11). Addressing such a teacher directly, he says

You know how to measure the circle; you find the square of any shape which is set before you; you compute the distances between the stars *(intervalla siderum dicis)*; there is nothing which does not come within the scope of your calculations. But if you are a real master of your profession, measure me the mind of man! Tell me how great it is, or how puny! You know what a straight line is; but how does it benefit you if you do not know what is straight in this life of ours? (13)

Seneca then questions the value of astrological knowledge. Should he, as a philosopher, be disturbed

Because Saturn and Mars are in opposition, or when Mercury sets at eventide in plain view of Saturn, rather than learn that those stars, wherever they are, are propitious, and that they are not subject to change? They are driven along by an unending round of destiny, on a course from which they cannot swerve. They return at stated seasons;

they either set in motion, or mark the intervals of the whole world's work. But if they are responsible for whatever happens, how will it help you know the secrets of the immutable? Or if they merely give indications, what good is there in foreseeing what you cannot escape? Whether you know these things or not, they will take place. (14–15)

(Cum Saturnus et Mars ex contrario stabunt aut cum Mercurius vespertinum faciet occasum vidente Saturno, potius quam hoc discam, ubicumque sunt ista, propitia esse, non posse mutari? Agit illa continuus ordo fatorum et inevitabilis cursus. Per statas vices remeant et effectus rerum omnium aut movent aut notant. Sed sive quicquid evenit faciunt, quid inmutabilis ret notitia profeciet? Sive significant, quid refert providere quod effugere no possis? Scias ista, nescias fient.)

The more valuable knowledge of the philosopher, as we shall see, concerns the permanent reliability of the stars, "their unending round of destiny," whereby they "mark the intervals of the whole world's work" rather than the accidental coincidences (from the human point of view) upon which astrologers base their predictions. So Shakespeare says that the kind of love, whose constancy he compares to the worth of the star, is "not Time's fool," altering with its 'brief hours and weeks, / But bears it out even to the edge of doom."[8]

Seneca's second passage (88.24–30) brings us even closer to Shakespeare's distinction. Here he responds to a defender of the mathematician's claim to be regarded as a philosopher on the grounds that mathematics is very important to that part of philosophy concerned with physical nature (*naturales quaestiones*). Though we philosophers, Seneca answers, get some help from mathematics in the same way that the carpenter may be said to aid the mathematician, "carpentering is not a part of mathematics, nor is mathematics a part of philosophy" (25).

Moreover, each has its own limits; for the wise man investigates and learns the causes of natural phenomena, while the mathematician follows up and computes their numbers and their measurements. The wise man knows the laws by which the heavenly bodies persist, what powers belong to them, and what attributes; the astronomer merely notes their settings and their risings, and the occasional periods during which they seem to stand still, although as a matter of fact no heavenly body can stand still. (26)

(Praeterea utraque fines suos habet. Sapiens enim causas naturalium et quaerit et novit, quorum numeros mensurasque geometres persequitur et subputal, qua ratione constent caelestia, quae illis sit vis quaeve natura, sapiens scit; cursus et recursus et quasdam observationes, per quas descendunt et adlevantur ac speciem interdum stantium praebent, cum caeslestibus stare non liceat, colligit mathematicus.)

The wise man, he continues, will know what causes that reflection in the mirror; the mathematician can merely tell you how far the body should be from the reflection. "The philosopher will demonstrate that the sun is a large body, while the astronomer will compute just how large, progressing in knowledge by his method of trial and experiment; but in order to progress, he must summon to his aid certain principles" (27). These principles must be borrowed from philosophy, since no individual art like mathematics "is sufficient unto itself"; only philosophy builds totally upon its own ground. In fact, only philosophy "brings the soul to perfection" through its "unalterable knowledge of good and evil," which it alone can investigate (*una re consummatur animus, scientia bonorum ac malorum inmutabili; nihil autem ulla ars alia de bonis ac malis quaerit*, 28). To illustrate the nature of this "unalterable knowledge," Seneca then describes in some detail a number of specific virtues, among which are *fortitudo, fides, temperantia, humanitas*, and *clementia* (29–30). As this comprehension of ethical conditions is the objective and the possession of the wise man (*sapiens*), so it is the possession of the speaker in the sonnet from his very first words: "Let *me* not . . ." (my italics). As the possessor of philosophical insight into the virtue of love, he compares that type of love which he is defining to the star whose essential quality will be unknown to those lovers on "the wandering bark"—lovers who can, like the mathematician, only navigate by taking its height, an art arrived at by their "method of trial and experiment" (*usu quodam et exercitatione*).[9]

Mathematics and philosophy each have their individual *fines*: that is, their particular "ends" or "objectives," as Lodge translates the word in the previous note. The "wise man investigates and learns the causes (*causas*) of natural phenomena" and, therefore, he "knows the laws by which (*qua ratione*) the heavenly bodies persist, what powers belong to them, and what attributes"—*quae illis sit vis quaeve natura*. He knows their "worth," that is, a word that might, in this context, be rendered *causa, ratio, vis*, or *natura*. *Vis*, in addition to meaning "power" or "force," connotes "virtue" in the sense of the Italian *virtu*, the essential potency, activity, or efficacy of a thing. It is just this sense that permits Caesar to see in the "true fix'd resting quality" of the northern star, as cited in note 1, an essential "property" of his own nature—of his own "worth." Such properties are primarily "inner" qualities and would be, according to Aristotle, better known with respect to their own nature—"absolutely" *(haplos)*—than with respect to our own perceptions—"to us" *(hemin)*.

Absolute knowledge, as distinct from the accidental knowledge of the sophist, is achieved from Aristotle when an event cannot be otherwise than as it is known and when its cause is certain. It is obtained by demonstration from premises that are true, primary (indemonstrable), causative (and hence prior), and better known than their conclusions. But we must remember, he says, that

> There are two senses in which things are prior and more knowable. That which is prior in nature is not the same as that which is prior in relation to us *(pros hemas)*, and that which is <naturally> more knowable is not the same as that which is more knowable by us. By "prior" or "more knowable" in relation to us I mean that which is nearer to our perception, and by "prior" or "more knowable" in the absolute sense *(haplos)* I mean that which is further from it. The most universal concepts are furthest from our perception, and particulars are nearest to it; and these are opposite to one another. (*Post an.* 1.2; 71b16–72a6)

Aristotle applies this broad, logical discrimination between kinds of intelligibility to his treatment of the more specialized mathematical, physical, and ethical subject matters. But in considering types of knowledge, he repeatedly warns us that

> We must not look for equal exactness in all departments of study, but only such a degree as is appropriate to the particular line of enquiry. A carpenter and a geometrician both seek after a right angle, but in different ways; the former is content with that approximation to it which satisfies the purpose of his work; the latter, being a student of truth, looks for its essence or essential attributes. (*EN* 1.7.18–19)

For the Stoic Seneca, to whom Ethics appears the most important branch of philosophy, the philosopher will hold the same superior position to the mathematician with respect to knowledge as both he and Aristotle say the geometer holds to the carpenter.[10]

The Platonic anticipations of Seneca most relevant to Shakespeare's distinction occur in the *Republic* (521d–33d) and the

Philebus (55d–59c). In the first Plato is describing the educational curriculum proper for the guardians of the State. In this curriculum the mathematical disciplines of arithmetic, geometry, and astronomy play an important role for their contribution to economic and civic affairs. Astronomy, for instance, cultivating a quick "perception about the seasons and the courses of the months and the years is serviceable, not only to agriculture and navigation (nautiiai), but still more to the military art" (527d). But as currently practiced, these arts fall short of their potential realization. In limiting itself primarily to phenomenal objects, geometry, which should pursue "the knowledge of the eternally existent," fails to "draw the soul to truth" and to produce "a philosophical attitude of mind, directing upward the faculties that now wrongly are turned earthward" (527b). Likewise astronomy, whatever its practical applications, has the power to make the soul look upwards (525d, 526e–27b, 529a): the stars should be studied, not as moving objects, but as forms of motion, as patterns of reality, which can be apprehended only "by reason and thought, but not by sight" (529ce). Yet even at their best, while these arts contribute to a philosophical receptivity of mind, they are not themselves philosophy. In not being able to give any account of their assumptions, they are but "dreaming about being," while dialectic remains "the only process of inquiry that advances . . . doing away with hypotheses, up to the first principle itself in order to find confirmation there" (533bc). Dialectic alone, then, in being able to account for its first principles, best represents for Plato that spirit of philosophical inquiry that reveals to Seneca's "wise man" the nature of the universe *(totius mundi naturam).*[11]

In the *Philebus* Plato categorizes the arts and sciences according to their degree of exactness or "purity." The less exact arts are those based, like music, on practice, experience, and educated conjecture and include medicine, agriculture, piloting *(kubernetiken),* and generalship (55e–56b). The more exact arts, like shipbuilding and architecture, are those more dependent on arithmetical reckoning, but even in a numerical art there will be degrees of accuracy according to whether—to borrow Aristotle's example cited above—a carpenter or geometer employs it (57bd). Be they arithmetical or not, it should be remembered that for the most part the arts are based on opinion and, developed to create perishable productions from transient models, can acquire little certainty (59ab). True and exact knowledge can be derived only from the study of "things which are eternally the same without change or mixture" (59c), and such knowledge is only achieved, again, through dialectic, which is an art "which has to do with being, reality, and eternal immutability" (58a).[12]

These, then, are some of the texts that establish the tradition from which Shakespeare has borrowed his distinction between knowing the "worth" and taking "the height" of the star. The speaker in the sonnet takes the persona of the "wise man" (*sapiens*) and addresses his metaphorical discrimination between different kinds of love to us as well as to his friend—to us as readers who may well be too caught up in our own perceptions to understand how love might be considered "in itself."

Notes

1. *Shakespeare's Songs and Poems*, ed. E. Hubler (New York: McGraw-Hill, 1964). The star is usually taken to be the Polestar, whose variation is minimal, yet any star whose location might be predicted could do. Commentators since Kinnear (*Cruces*, 1883, 501) have observed the parallel with Julius Caesar's claim: "But I am constant as the northern star, / Of whose true fix'd and resting quality / There is no fellow in the firmament" (3.1.60–62). "Resting quality" means the "essential property"—as opposed to "accidental attribute"—of remaining in the same position, and as a "quality" in the categorical sense, supports the meaning of "worth" described below.

2. It has frequently been observed that Sonnet 116 is linked to Sonnets 115 and 117. This is particularly clear in "But reckoning Time, whose million'd accidents . . . Divert strong minds to th' course of alt'ring things" (115.5–8) and "That I have hoisted sail to all the winds / Which should transport me farthest from your sight" (117.7–8). I see nothing in the following explanation of Shakespeare's distinction in 116.7–8, which either tightens or loosens such connections.

3. Compare the analogous figure in *As You Like It*. Rosalind says to Celia: "My pretty little coz, that thou didst know how many fathom deep I am in love! but it cannot be sounded: my affection hath an unknown bottom, like the bay of Portugal" (4.1.200–203). Rosalind is saying that Celia cannot know the extent, quality, or essential nature of her affection precisely because its depth *cannot* be sounded; its bottom (metaphorically, its "ground" or first principle, potential force or vitality), like the star's "worth," remains "unknown."

4. Some recent commentators, such as W. G. Ingram and Theodore Redpath, recognize that "there is no need to tie the sense of 'worth' down, as a number of commentators have, to occult or astrological influence" (*Shakespeare's Sonnets* [New York: Barnes & Noble, 1965], 268) and others, such as Stephen Booth, have not mentioned it at all (*Shakespeare's Sonnets* [New Haven: Yale University Press, 1977], 384–92).

5. In his *The Sonnets of Shakespeare* (New York: Houghton-Mifflin, 1916), 274–75, R. M. Alden cites Ingleby: "Surely, then, the 'worth' spoken of must be *constancy*. . . . The sailor must know that the star has this worth, or his latitude would not depend upon its altitude" (*The Soule Arayed*, 5)—this in the face of Shakespeare's explicit statement that the star's worth is "unknown"!

6. Yvor Winters makes this point forcefully, but he argues that the comparison is unrealized on the grounds that "there is simply no such separation between the two functions of true love as there is between the two functions of the star [i.e., navigational and astrological], yet the comparison is made in such a way as to indicate a separation." There are, of course, not two functions of "true love," but one of true (or permanent) love and one of "altering" love (or desire) subject to time, which Shakespeare's distinction aims to bring out. Granted that Winters has not grasped the distinction, which separates the two categories of love, any better than other commentators have, he nevertheless forthrightly comments that, given the current state of interpretation, a separation that is expected is regrettably left obscure (*Forms of Discovery* [Chicago: Swallow Press, 1967], 54–55). Stephen Booth, on the other hand, who takes "unknown" to mean "unknowable," also finds that "worth is imprecisely used," its "general sense dictated by context," but proceeds to justify the imprecision because its evocative power somehow acknowledges the fact "that the actual topic remains a distant impalpable essence, sensorily apprehensible by imperfect proxy" (*Shakespeare's Sonnets*, 385, 388).

7. Many commentators simply regard "unknown" as some form of adverbial intensifier: inexpressible, incalculable, beyond estimation, immense—such as Pooler's "incalculable or incalculably great" (Arden, 1918) or Booth's "the North Star and ideal love—which is the highest rung on the Platonic ladder and the highest kind of love—are both beyond human estimation, too high to be measured" (*Shakespeare's Sonnets*, 385). Why, then, the concessive "although?" Is taking the height to be thought to diminish this greatness? Or does "incalculably" great mean "inexhaustibly" great, making "although" mean "even after"—thus, the star's worth is so inexhaustible that although its height has been taken (once or many times), it can be still profitably taken an indefinite number of times in the future? But this becomes very arbitrary, and gradually the cognitive force of "unknown," implied by the antithesis disappears.

8. *Seneca ad Lucilium Epistulae Morales*, trans. R. M. Gummere, 3 vols., Loeb Classical Library (Cambridge: Harvard University Press, 1962). In the nearly contemporaneous translation of Thomas Lodge, Seneca questions the use of astrology in these words: "What shall it profit to know this? That I may be carefull when *Saturne* and *Mars* shall be in opposition, or when Mercury shall make his evening fall *Saturne* looking? Rather I will learne this, that wheresoever these things be, that they be prosperous, that they cannot be changed. A continuall order and an inevitable course of destinies moveth these: by set courses do they retire. They either move or note the effect of all things" (*The Workes both Morrall and Natural of Lucius Annaeus Seneca Translated by T. Lodge* [London, 1614], 365). The fact that in this passage Seneca makes clear that astrological influences are not the proper objects of philosophical knowledge argues against associating astrology with "worth."

9. Some of Lodge's phrasing is useful here: "Furthermore, both have their ends: for a wiseman both seeketh and knoweth the causes of naturall things, the numbers and measure of which, a Geometrician followeth after and counteth. A wise man knoweth after what manner heavenly things consist, what force, or what nature is unto them: A Mathematician collecteth the courses, and returnings backe, and the observations, by which they descend and be lifted up. . . . A Philosopher will prove the Sunne to be great: the Mathematician will shew how great it is, who proceedeth by a certain exercise and use; but that he may proceede, certaine principles are to be obtained by him. . . . Philosophy [on the

other hand] desireth nothing from another thing, it raiseth up the whole worke
from the ground. The Mathematicks . . . is a superfical Art, it receiveth princi-
ples from others, by the benefit of which it may come to farther things. . . . The
minde is made perfect by one thing, namely, the unchangeable knowledge of
good and bad things; which agreeth unto Philosophy onely. But none other Art
enquireth about good and bad things: let us consider the Vertues in particular"
(*The Workes of Seneca*, 366–67).

10. *Aristotle: Posterior Analytics*, trans. H. Tredennick, Loeb Classical Li-
brary (Cambridge: Harvard University Press, 1966) and *Aristotle: The Nic-
omachean Ethics*, trans. H. Rackham, Loeb Classical Library (Cambridge:
Harvard University Press, 1956). For a discussion of the other principal pas-
sages on the two types of intelligibility and appropriate expectations of their
exactness, see my *Muses of One Mind* (Princeton: Princeton University Press,
1983), 119–29.

11. *Plato: The Republic*, trans. P. Shorey, Loeb Classical Library (Cambridge:
Harvard University Press, 1970).

12. *Plato: Philebus*, trans. H. Fowler, Loeb Classical Library (Cambridge:
Harvard University Press, 1962).

Robert Bridges and the English Musical Renaissance
Catherine Phillips

One of the anecdotes that Robert Bridges told of his childhood was of being taken to hear open-air concerts given by the local military band in Walmer and, escaping from the control of his kindly nurse, stealing "between the legs of the performers into the magic circle" where he could stand "close under the instruments and drink in their peculiar sonorities" to his "heart's content".[1] At Eton he would slip away during afternoon breaks to listen to the organ in the Royal chapel at Windsor, and Hubert Parry noted in his diary that Bridges had made an enthusiastic audience when he displayed what the new organ at Eton could do. Bridges does not seem to have played an instrument to a level at which he was happy to perform but he sang and wrote music. The letters of Gerard Manley Hopkins to Bridges mention an air harmonized that Bridges evidently wrote to a poem, "O earlier shall the rosebuds blow" by William Johnson Cory, a Master at Eton. Hopkins considered that the air was "an inspiration of melody", original-sounding and sweet, indeed at times he considered it too sweet.[2] He also mentions in 1880 a hymn that Bridges had written and that his sister, Grace, had said was not very original but sweet.[3]

Bridges seems later to have destroyed these and other of his musical compositions. However, he continued to sing in musical groups and later he collaborated with musicians, providing words for them to set. Plain chant remained his favorite type of music but he knew Handel's oratories well and at various times mentioned enjoying Purcell, Beethoven, Mozart, Chopin, and others, as well as the modern music of those with whom he collaborated. Such collaboration occurred easily and naturally since his interest in music and art led him to include a number of the important musicians and artists of the day among his friends. While at Oxford he maintained his friendship with Hubert Parry, who was a couple of years his junior, and came to know John

Stainer, four years his senior and university organist. For part of the time that he was studying and practicing medicine in London (1869–77) Bridges shared a house with Harry Ellis Wooldridge, whose extensive knowledge of early music led to his being invited to write the first volume of the *Oxford History of Music*. Wooldridge introduced Bridges to W. O. Rockstro, a church organist in London, who wrote most of the articles on plain chant for Grove's *Dictionary of Music* and produced an edition of Mozart's operas. Rockstro spent extended periods staying with the Bridges.

In 1881 Bridges became seriously ill. This close escape from death and his gradual realization that his gifts were not ideally those of a doctor led him to give up medicine. He moved to the village of Yattendon near Newbury, where among the local responsibilities he took on was the training of the village choir. He remained their precentor for nine years. From this grew the *Yattendon Hymnal*. Bridges explained that he had tried to "provide better settings of the hymns than those in use" and "when I gave up my office, I printed the first twenty-five hymns for the convenience of the choir, and also for the sake of the tunes by Jeremy Clark [whom he considered the originator of English hymnody], which I had been at some pains to restore, and for the preservation of the tunes composed on our behalf by Professor Wooldridge."

The essay, "Some Principles of Hymn-singing," sets out Bridges' reasons for choosing particular composers. He starts from the premise that

> Music being the universal expression of the mysterious and supernatural, the best that man has ever attain'd to, is capable of uniting in common devotion minds that are only separated by creeds, and it comforts our hope with a brighter promise of unity than any logic offers. And if we consider and ask ourselves what sort of music we should wish to hear on entering a church, we should surely, in describing our ideal, say first of all that it must be something different from what is heard elsewhere; that it should be a sacred music, devoted to its purpose, a music whose peace should still passion, whose dignity should strengthen our faith, whose unquestion'd beauty should find a home in our hearts, to cheer us in life and death. . . .[4]

"Good melody," says Bridges, "is never out of fashion" and the plain song melodies whose unbarred rhythms "dance at liberty with the voice and sense" instead of "plumping down . . . on the first note of every bar whether it will or no" have clear advantages.[5] He found that many of the tunes he liked had no suitable words, and of the final collection of one hundred hymns he provided over forty with new words, generally translations. The bulk of the melodies were composed by nine writers: four from Heinrich Isaac (1490); thirteen from Louis Bourgeois (1550); four from Christopher Tye (1550); eight from Thomas Tallis (1560); eight from Orlando Gibbons (1623); thirteen from Johann Crueger (1640); nine from Jeremy Clark (1700); eight from William Croft (1710) and eight from J. S. Bach. Harry Wooldridge wrote seven tunes and Bridges' schoolmate Lionel Muirhead wrote one. Most of the tunes needed to have settings written for them, and these were provided by Bridges' wife, Monica, and by Wooldridge.

The plain song tunes were given Palestrinal harmonization that was unsuitable for unison singing with an instrumental accompaniment but intended for unaccompanied singing in four parts. Bridges ensured that in addition to the luxury edition produced by the Oxford University Press, a cheap but aesthetically pleasing one was also provided. He believed that far too often those who could not afford expensive things had made available to them only the "cheap and nasty." Like William Morris, he considered that it was only by allowing all the nation to be surrounded by beautiful things that Britain would be a nation with good aesthetic taste.

The importance of family hymnbooks has of course greatly declined, but Bridges had grown up enjoying the custom of spending Sunday evenings with his family gathered round the piano singing hymns and had continued the custom, still common at that time, in his own family. The *Yattendon Hymnal* attracted the attention of members of the committee formed to revise *Hymns Ancient and Modern*. They considered it "too short for congregational use" but "within its limits, of incomparable value" and they hoped that "we may some day see it enlarged and made more easily accessible."[6] Bridges was asked to join the committee but finding that it was likely to spend much of its time on hymns that he thought insipid and sentimental, he declined the invitation.

Bridges also took an interest in the pointing of psalms and did a number of these, some in collaboration with Sir Hugh Allen, an old friend who had frequently visited the Bridges when they lived at Yattendon (1882–1906). Bridges wrote three scholarly articles on the setting of psalms, "Anglican Chanting," published in the *Musical Antiquary* (1912), the article on "Chanting" for the *Prayer-book Dictionary* (1912), and the preface to a *MS Collection of Psalms noted in Speech-Rhythm*, which was published posthumously as Essay 25 of his *Collected Essays*. As with Bridges' article "The Principles of Hymn-singing," his article entitled "Anglican Chanting" was designed to show how current chanting could be improved. Sir Hugh Allen was on the committee for revising the psalter and in 1916 was probably behind the invitation to Bridges to join in the work.

Bridges again turned down the invitation but from 1918 began setting the psalms, eventually writing settings for fifty-nine of them. His system was more complex than that normally used in that he employed two units of time that could be represented as regular time values and the reduced values of notes written in triplets or even four notes in the time of three and five notes in the time of four. As with his later experiments in the writing of poetry, he was aiming at greater flexibility of rhythm. "A friend remembers finding [Bridges and Allen] together once in the Museum Road [Oxford]. Bridges was declaiming against the use of Gregorian chants for the English Psalter on the ground that it was using tunes made for a language with the accent usually on the penultimate syllable for a language with quite different accentuation. When Bridges left, Allen said: 'I always like him best when he's violent, but then he generally is.' "[7]

Around the turn of the century there was in England something of a renaissance in music. Several British composers enriched the store of the national music: Hubert Parry, considered the leader of the revival, was especially gifted at writing beautiful melodies; Charles Stanford made interesting use of Irish folk-tunes, and Edward Elgar, who was to become the most famous of the group, enriched orchestration. More concerts and recitals were given, provincial music festivals became larger and more prestigious, and the standard of performance and ensemble work increased. Knowledge of music became more widespread as more people heard music performed and the subject became a respectable one for advanced study. The first of Bridges' collaborations was on an oratorio with Charles Stanford, performed at the Birmingham Festival in 1890. Stanford later wrote an account of the collaboration. He had, he said, been looking at the manuscript of Milton's initial ideas of *Paradise Lost* as a tragedy and had thought that it would make a good oratorio. "There was happily," he said, "one poet, as interested and knowledgeable in music as in his own craft, who was steeped to the lips in Milton, and whose style was more indebted to that master than any of his contemporaries, Mr. Robert Bridges."[8]

Bridges had to write the three-act work rapidly in order to keep to Stanford's busy schedule, and he was not altogether happy with it. The first act was set in Heaven and Bridges suggested its "characteristics" would best be attained using "early modal methods, to contrast with the modern colouring of the second and third (Hell and Earth)."[9] This necessitated that Stanford, then professor of music at Cambridge, have a series of lessons in modal writing. He took these from W. S. Rockstro, Bridges' friend, who was living in Torquay at the time.[10] In fact the modes were also used for their associations with angels and devils in the second act, where the "mi contra Fa est Diabolus in musica" was interwoven throughout in a witty musical parody. Bridges' handling of the fall of. Adam and Eve is far gentler psychologically than Milton's. Adam's concupiscence is not depicted, and it is Eve who, recovering first, persuades the despairing Adam to turn to God in repentance. The third act contains three masques, visions of war, plague and famine, and the vision of the angels of Music and Poetry as comforters of Sorrow. These visions are included in Milton's sketch and in Book XI of *Paradise Lost* in much the same gruesome detail that Bridges uses. The oratorio ends with Christ's words, "Come unto me Ye weary and heavy-laden," and a chorus describing Adam and Eve falling asleep while comforted by the promise of Christianity.

The oratorio received a mixed reception. George Bernard Shaw said of it, "I caught not a single definite purpose or idea at all commensurate with the huge pretensions of the musical design. That pretension is the ruin of *Eden*."[11] Frank Howes has said that "Stanford accepted the classical forms and sought to fill them by orthodox procedures," a fault of which Howes generally finds him guilty.[12] John Porte has commented that "from the purely constructive point of view," *Eden* is "one of the most remarkable of Stanford's large works," but there are stretches where the music is uninteresting and the listener is best advised then to "dip deeply into the libretto." However, "the conflict for first position in the eyes or ears of the audience hardly produces the finest possible effect."[13]

J. A. Fuller-Maitland has suggested that part of the work's unpopularity arose "because the beauty of the ancient modes had not yet dawned even on the more intelligent part of the public, as it has since done."[14] In 1934 he wrote, "now that the ecclesiastical modes are recognized as an enrichment, rather than an impoverishment, of the composer's resources, *Eden* would probably make a great impression, even though the need for engaging six soloists is rather a serious objection to its revival by provincial societies." He describes part of the music:

> The quotation from the hymn "Sanctorum meritis" serves as a motto-theme for the whole of the first part, and the six-part chorus "God of Might!" is a grand conception grandly carried out. The absence of the bass voice in this number is compensated in the baritone solo for the Angel of the Sun, with its most picturesque accompaniment. The climax of the scene is the "Madrigale spirituale" in five parts a *capella*, a thing of radiant beauty. The final chorus "of all angels" still without basses, makes a most effective ending to the "act." In the second "act," after an introduction which recalls that to the second act of *Parsifal*, a chorus of "all devils" parodies the first scene, and the triple apostrophe to Satan is a counterpart to the angels' triple address to God; at the very end of the act the angelic hymn is heard immediately after its parody, carrying out Satan's reference to
>
> > the song, whose echo
> > Sometimes makes vibrate here our iron vault.
>
> The part of Satan needs a singer of the calibre of Henschel, who sang it with perfect conviction both at Birmingham and in London, and the opportunities it gives to a great artist are as many in the third "act" as in the second, if not more, because of the craft the tempter must indicate. The lovely pastoral introduction and duet, the clever *scherzando* movement where the serpent is seen, and the fruitless interjections of the angelic choir warning Eve of her danger, lead to a declamatory solo describing Adam's remorse; there is a prayer, and Michael and two angels join their voices with his (what becomes of Eve, by the way?). What remains can hardly fail to come as an anticlimax; Adam is shown a pageant . . . followed by words of Christ sung by six baritones of the chorus, a kind of lullaby in which the influence of Berlioz is to be detected, and a fine broad final chorus of all angels, this time complete with bass voices.[15]

A letter written by Bridges to Stanford when they were subsequently preparing the text for publication shows Bridges' detailed awareness of the interrelationship between the words and music:

My dear Stanford,

I congratulate you. The words I wrote for the bad place are (I mark the bars and suggested rests)

Behind them [O happy sight]!] my sons I see / crowned and bright as the / Seraphim / that in God's / presence sing the / threefold hymn.

I should like *God's* a semibreve. If you must move on it I myself prefer p.p to pp[16]

He also mentioned a change that Stanford had made to his wording, turning "to soil the glory of God" into "to soil the might of God." The work was dedicated to Hubert Parry, apparently because Parry had projected a similar subject and had abandoned it when he heard of Stanford's intentions.

Bridges' next collaboration, in 1895 on "Invocation to Music," was with Parry, with whom he would have liked closer consultation than Parry's busy schedule at the Royal College of Music allowed. Bridges wrote the ode so that Parry had a choice of musical opportunities and could emphasize some and omit others. The ode marks a new departure in Parry's musical development, a turning away from the style of oratorio towards forms that have been compared with Bach's cantatas. Critics have been divided over how successful they find these works, which include three set to words by Bridges: the "Invocation to Music," "Songs of Darkness and Light," and "The Chivalry of the Sea." Sir Henry Hadow considered that Parry was successfully conveying his own religious feelings in the music but R. O. Morris concluded that ultimately Parry failed to make his style sufficiently flexible to accommodate the subtleties of his belief. The result was "a noble failure [though] a failure more admirable and more inspiring than many another man's victory."[17]

Bridges' letters show that he tried to give Parry as free a hand as he could but that he often felt that the composer was fussing unnecessarily. This may have been the result of the personal significance of the work to Parry. The ode was dedicated to Purcell and performed first at the Leeds Festival and then at the commemoration for Purcell in London. Bridges was away and missed Parry's letter telling him when it was to be performed. He seems in any case to have been of two minds about whether he wanted to hear it. He wrote to Parry, "I am very sorry to have missed the opportunity, but I doubt whether if I had been home I could have managed to make all the prearrangements necessary to secure reasonable comfort. . . . I had to content myself with buying all the penny papers as I came up in the train yesterday, and reading what the critics said. I gathered two things. 1st. that the Ode had really been a success, and 2ndly that the critics are a poor lot. It is extraordinary that they cannot give one a better notion of what has taken place."[18]

Bridges sent the ode to Richard Watson Dixon and, when it was returned, wrote,

> I was rather disappointed at your having nothing to say about the Dirge, which I fancy is as good a thing as I have written. I guess that its Ecclesiastes vein was unsympathetic to you. But the point of it was to express that view of the matter—and the moral of it is that the poetical expression of it is *the* (or at least *a*) cure for the melancholy. This it seems to me is what art has to do. To satisfy by expression. In the ode Sorrow complains that art having left the country she has no expression for her soul—and she asks for comfort. Music gives her the comfort of this most melancholy dirge.—The next movement is more cheerful, and passes off into a sort of triumph.[19]

In *Eden*, Bridges had asserted the power of music to provide such comfort. The Dirge is prepared for by the movement (No. VI) that Bridges described to Dixon in which Sorrow asks Music to give her a means of expressing her grief. Yet in the Dirge itself the refrain of loss appears at the end of the second verse, where it comes almost abruptly to end the description of one's joy in the beauties of nature. In literature and choral work the pervasiveness and unexpected arrival of death is often presented in a more overtly threatening way. Here it is introduced gently, almost with euphemism. It opens a refrain that is lovely and characteristic of Bridges in its ahistorical mixture of diction:

> Then he hideth his face;—
> Whence he came to pass away
> Where all is forgot,
> Unmade—lost for aye
> With the things that are not[20]

It is Fuller-Maitland's opinion that although "it happens very rarely with Parry that his music fails to enhance the beauty of the words he sets; . . . his treatment of Bridges's fine *Invocation to Music* . . . must be admitted to fall below the poem in emotional value. The pastoral pictures at the end of the tenor solo, and the 'dirge' for bass, are its most remarkable points, and there is an impressive seven-part close."[21]

When the "Ode to Music" was published in 1896 Bridges took

the opportunity of prefacing it with an article stating his objection to the popular trend of giving poems declamatory choral settings. Bridges stated that his objections were not to the setting that Parry had given his ode, which "far beyond his deserts, honour'd and beautyfy'd" it, but to Parry's apparent advocacy of the declamatory method in his book *The Art of Music* (1893). Bridges points out that a declamatory method is close to *recitativo secco* and not the most effective way of marrying words and music. It disregards such important considerations as the difference in the use of repetition in the two media: music-building on repetitions that are necessary to enforce the significance of a phrase whereas reiteration in poetry weakens the force of the second phrase. The formal structure of music and verse are different so that rhythms, cadences of phrases, and distribution of climax all have natures that are different in the two. Bridges expresses his belief that if the two forms are allowed a looser partnership then they can be more effectively united so that "the best musical treatment of passages of great poetic beauty is not to declaim them, but, as it were, to woo them and court them and caress them, and deck them with fresh musical beauties; approaching them tenderly now on one side, now on another, and to keep a delicat reverse which shall leave their proper unity unmolested."[22]

Gustav Holst wrote a second setting of the Dirge in 1931. Called *Choral Fantasia*, it was written for the Three Choirs Festival. Imogen Holst, in a detailed description of the work, notes its development of sounds that Holst had "hinted at years ago" when searching for a way out of personal despair. In her opinion the work contains moments in which Holst "manages to find the warmth he had been searching for ever since listening to that performance of the Schubert Quintet [in 1929 when he felt that he had failed to incorporate this most valuable of human experiences in his music]. He was to lose [the warmth] again, in moments of weariness, during the few remaining years. But having once found it, he could shake off the horror of numbness and isolation. There was to be no more despair."[23] It was therefore a composition of personal importance to the composer, as well as one that in his oeuvre shows him "able to move forward with all the strength of his mature experience."

Parry was evidently not too disturbed by Bridges' preface to their work and began a second collaboration with Bridges in 1898. Of this collaboration Bridges told Lionel Muirhead, "I have a 'Hymn of Nature' publishing on October 26 in the September

number of the *Cornhill*. It is the poem which Parry has set for the
Gloucester Festival ["A Song of Darkness and Light"]. It contains
some queer words to sing in a Cathedral, but I hope it won't be
the last time that such things are allowed. I should have told you
that they sing 'Blessed pair of Sirens' for an anthem at Wells
[Cathedral].[24] There is great variety in mood from section to
section, giving opportunities of very different musical settings
within a relatively small compass. Section 4 of the ode is an
example of the way in which Bridges absorbed imagery of con-
temporary society into his verse:

> Or else, in crowded cities gathering close,
>   He traffics morn and eve
>   In thronging market-halls;
>   Or within echoing walls
>   Of busy arsenals
> Weldth the stubborn iron to engines vast;
>   Or tends the thousand looms
>   Where, with black smoke o'ercast,
>   The land mourns in deep glooms . . .
> —(Bridges, *Poetical Works*, 403)

This contrasts with the more rural imagery of some of the other
sections.

Ten years later Parry and Bridges collaborated on a memorial
ode for members of Eton killed in the Boer War. This time Bridges
was adamant that his wording must not be altered since the
audience included a number of women who had lost their sons
and consequently the meaning of the words was more important
than the beauty of the music. The response he received showed
that he achieved this though his son, who was by this time at
Eton, reported that his school friends had not much liked the
piece. Parry also set Bridges' "Chivalry of the Sea" to music in
1916. This has been described as "an eloquent and characteristic
five-part chorus, much of which may be felt by some hearers as
an incursion into the region long ago staked out by Stanford."[25]

Bridges was one of a number of people who considered that
Parry had been very unwise in accepting the position of director
of the Royal College of Music. The objection was that he gave to
this largely administrative task the energy that should have gone
into his creative work. Parry died in 1918 and when two years
later it was decided to place a memorial tablet to him in
Gloucester Cathedral it was Bridges who wrote the poem for it:

> From boyhood's eager play call'd by the English Muse
> Her fine scholar to be then her Master's compeer
> A spirit elect whom no unworthy thought could wrong
> Nor any fear touch thee joyously on life's waves
> Navigating thy soul into her holy haven:
> Long these familiar walls will re-echo thy song
> And this stone engraved remember thy young face
> Thy honour and thy grave and the love of thy friends.[26]

In addition to Bridges' collaborations with composers, on several occasions musicians set his poems to music. In 1891 or 1892 Stanford set "Six Songs of Robert Bridges," considered "among the best of the composer's smaller vocal works."[26] His setting of "Since thou, O fondest and truest" has been called "exquisite."[27] Parry set the sonnet-paraphrase of the Lord's Prayer from *The Growth of Love* as a motet in six parts and found in Bridges' poem "My delight and thy delight" a "thoroughly congenial" subject.[28] Gerald Finzi, a student of R. O. Morris's wrote part-songs to Bridges' poems and in 1916 Frank Bridges' early troilet, "All women born are so perverse." Gustav Holst made a "Choral Fantasia" from seven of Bridges' poems (1927). He brought the girls from Saint Paul's School, where he was music master, to Bridges' home and they performed "Say who is this?," "O, Love, I complain," "Angel spirits of sleep," "When first we met," "Sorrow and Joy," "Love on my heart from heaven fell," and "Assemble all ye maidens." Holst noted in 1925 that "I did the first of the Bridges' poems the moment I caught sight of the words. . . . Since when I've been wondering what they mean."[29] His daughter, Imogen, thought that he had "managed to draw out their magic" of the contrast between the pleasure of the young and the wisdom of the old in the "deep divining" vision of the cellos and basses and the low murmuring voice of that mysterious being "who knoweth things untold." Not for many years had Holst "managed to convey an apprehensive dread with such naked counterpoint." Holst responded to the mixture of irony and tenderness in "O Love, I complain" and altogether wrote with a spontaneity that sounds "as if he was no longer quite so much afraid of sensuous beauty." Bridges wrote to Holst two days after the performance:

> I hope you were as well satisfied as we with the general success of your venture. It was a blessing that there was no rain, but if only we had had the weather on Saturday which came to us á day late yesterday, all would have been perfect. You asked me once or twice

about the music, whether I liked it: if I did not say much it was because I felt it impertinent in me to pretend to judge of your work, and I thought that the pleasure, which I could tell you the professionals were feeling was a better compliment than mine would be, because they are accustomed to modern writing, whereas I am oldfashioned. I was relieved to find that they were somewhat in my predicament: which was that I did not understand any piece well on the first hearing, but I liked it at second hearing and came in the end to full pleasure. I liked all the "Songs" especially, *When first we met* and *Sorrow and Joy*. The only piece that I did not take to was "Assemble all ye maidens" and that could be accounted for by the great dislike that I have for the *poem*. Its history is queer. I will tell you of it someday.

Our gratitude is enormous. We had a most delightful time: all our guests were enthusiastic. We hope you will do it again some day. . . . Your way of treating the words is so novel, and so unlike anything I could have imagined, that I think I got on astonishingly well in appreciating your inventions so far as I did. For I really liked them very much: and want to hear them again.[31]

Bridges' love of music was publicly acknowledged when the committee formed by Siegfried Sassoon to honor Bridges on his eightieth birthday (1924) decided to give him a clavichord made by Dolmetsch, which Dolmetsch played for Bridges. Bridges, who had avoided a public presentation, sent each of those who had subscribed for the gift a photograph of himself seated beside it taken by Lady Ottoline Morrell and accompanied by a note of thanks.

This love of music, characteristic of Bridges all his life, has several far-reaching effects on his poetry, some of them positive and others negative. For instance, in many of his best descriptive poems the vividness is in no small measure due to the sensitivity with which the sounds of the scene have been captured. For example, in "London Snow" the changes in the noises in the city are caught in such lines as "When men were all asleep the snow came flying, / . . . Hushing the latest traffic of the drowsy town; / Deadening, muffling, stifling its murmurs failing; / . . . The ear hearkened to the stillness of the solemn air; / No sound of wheel rumbling nor of foot falling, / And the busy morning cries came thin and spare." Similarly, in "Elegy: The Summer-house on the Mound" Bridges adds in imagination the sounds suggested by the sights he sees through the telescope—"ships in stately motion pass so near / That what I see is speaking to my ear: / I hear the waves dash and the tackle strain. / The canvas flap, the rattle of the chain / That runs out thro' the hawse, the clank of the winch / Winding the rusty cable inch by inch." The sensitivity to sound is clear in Bridges' handling of rhythm. Only a poet with a well-established sense of the rhythms of poetry could have imposed on the loose structure of the decasyllables of "The Testament of Beauty" a sense of poetry. Wallace B. Nichols, writing about Bridges in 1930, said, "no poet in English ever possessed a more delicate ear than Robert Bridges . . . in most of his poems, except those in iambic pentameter, nearly every cadence is a surprise. Technically considered, that was probably his greatest triumph, the continual surprise to the listening ear in his cadences."[32]

The sensitivity to sound led to Bridges' awareness of two problems, which he solved in ways that have done his poetic reputation less good. The first of these is his consciousness of the large number of homonyms in the language. He made this the topic of one of his first articles in the tracts of the Society for Pure English and tried to avoid them by substituting where possible words that had once been used and had fallen into disuse such as "ken" for "know," a change he made in revising a line in "The Testament of Beauty": "no child would know its parent, no parent his child" (Book 2, l. 128); "know" was revised to "ken." Although in the early decades of the twentieth century a number of poets were keenly interested in old and dialect words, today, with the emphasis on hearing the confessional voice of the poet in his work, readers do think, as Hopkins warned, that the use of words that the poet clearly would not use in everyday life means that they are reading an exercise rather than the sincere expression of the poet's feelings.

The second problem Bridges sought to avoid with adverse consequences was that of sibilance. One of the choirboys Bridges trained at Yattendon once described hearing a choir singing in English as listening to a flock of hissing geese, an awareness of sibilance that Bridges no doubt inculcated. Bridges reduced the number of such ugly sounds in his verse by using the "th" endings for the third-person singular of verbs. He favored this because it was sixteenth-century usage found in Shakespeare and the authorized version of the Bible. Bridges thought of these two sources as forming the cornerstone of English literary culture, texts that would be familiar to all succeeding generations, their diction remaining current because of the stature of their content. They would, he expected, keep such language current in a way that anything written in the language of the day of other centuries would not. There has, however, been a shift away from valuing poetry for its musical qualities and towards almost excessive concentration on meaning. Similar changes can be traced in the way actors have delivered their lines in performances of Shakespeare's plays throughout the century.

The result of both of Bridges' solutions to problems in the music of his verse caused by the nature of English has been to give his poems and plays a "dated" effect sometimes thought to be affectation. While this has undoubtably reduced the number of poems that appeal to readers and reduced the number of readers to whom Bridges appeals, he does have many poems in which these things do not matter and numerous poems in which passages are unaffected by these traits. Many of the descriptions of the English countryside such as "November," "The Garden of September," "The evening darkens over," and passages from "Wintry Delights" and "The Testament of Beauty" belong to this category. They all have beautiful imagery and musical cadences and convey in this the sincerity of Bridges' love of the English landcape. Perhaps, if fashion in poetic taste follows the course that fashion in clothing has taken over the last few years and moves towards a greater eclecticism, there will be more room for and a greater appreciation of one of our most musical poets.

Notes

1. Robert Bridges, "The Necessity of Poetry," Essay 23, *Collected Essays* (Oxford: Oxford University Press, 1936), 230–31.

2. *The Letters of Gerard Manley Hopkins to Robert Bridges*, ed. C. C. Abbott, 2d ed. (Oxford: Oxford University Press, 1955), 85.

2. Ibid., 98.

4. Robert Bridges, "A Practical Discourse on Some Principles of Hymn-singing," Essay 22, *Collected Essays*, p. 65.

5. Ibid., 42.

6. W. H. Hadow, *Hymn Tunes*, Occasional Papers No. 5 (London: Humphry Milford, n.d.), 12.

7. Cyril Bailey, *Hugh Percy Allen* (Oxford: Oxford University Press, 1948), 122.

8. Sir Charles Villiers Stanford, *Pages from an Unwritten Diary* (London: Edward Arnold, 1914), 273–75.

9. Ibid., 273.

10. Stanford was so impressed with Rockstro's abilities and the new possibilities that modal writing opened up that he induced Grove to appoint him to the Royal College of Music (ibid., 275).

11. As cited by Frank Howes in *The English Musical Renaissance* (London: Secker and Warburgs, 1966), 153.

12. Ibid.

13. John F. Porte, *Sir Charles V. Stanford* (London: Kegan Paul, Trench, Trubner and Co., 1921), 44–45.

14. J. A. Fuller-Maitland, *The Music of Parry and Stanford* (Cambridge: W. Heffer and Sons, 1934), 58.

15. Ibid., 59–60.

16. Harry Plunket Greene, *Charles Villiers Stanford* (London: Edward Arnold, 1935), 251.

17. Charles L. Graves, *Hubert Parry: His Life and Works* (London: Macmillan and Co., 1926), 205–7. See too Fuller-Maitland, *Music of Parry and Stanford*, 71.

18. *The Selected Letters of Robert Bridges*, ed. Donald E. Stanford, 2 vols. (Newark: University of Delaware Press, 1983, 1984), 297.

19. 5 October 1895, ibid., 298.

20. Robert Bridges, *Poetical Works of Robert Bridges with* The Testament of Beauty *but Excluding the Eight Dramas*, 2d ed. (London: Oxford University Press, 1953), 398.

21. Fuller-Maitland, *Music of Parry and Stanford*, 65.

22. Robert Bridges, "On the Musical Setting of Poetry," Essay 21, *Collected Essays*, 9.

23. Imogen Holst, *The Music of Gustav Holst* (London: Oxford University Press, 1968), 122–25, 198.

24. 5 August 1898, *Selected Letters of Bridges*, 332.

25. Fuller-Maitland, *Music of Parry and Stanford*, 77.

26. *Selected Letters of Bridges*, 923, 966 n.859.

27. Porte, *Sir Charles V. Stanford*, 46.

28. Fuller-Maitland, *Music of Parry and Stanford*, 99.

29. Ibid., 98, 100.

30. Holst, *Music of Holst*, 93–95.

31. 4 July [1927], *Selected Letters of Bridges*, 880.

32. "Poets Laureate," *Bookman* 78 (June 1930): 168.

T. Sturge Moore and Yeats's Golden Bird
Grosvenor Powell

On 16 April 1930 T. Sturge Moore wrote to W. B. Yeats objecting to the final stanza of "Sailing to Byzantium": "Your *Sailing to Byzantium*, magnificient as the first three stanzas are, lets me down in the fourth, as such a goldsmith's bird is as much nature as a man's body, especially if it only sings like Homer or Shakespeare of what is past or passing or to come to Lords and Ladies."[1] Yeats replied, on 4 October 1930, that Moore had misunderstood the poem and that he had therefore written "Byzantium" by way of clarification and further exposition: "The poem ["Byzantium"] originates from a criticism of yours. You objected to the last stanza of *Sailing to Byzantium* because a bird made by a goldsmith was just as natural as anything else. That showed me that the idea needed exposition." Yeats understood immediately just how Moore had misunderstood what the bird represented, both in reality and within his own Completed Symbol, and he saw the way in which the idea represented by the bird had to be clarified. Moore had taken the bird as an instance of qualified reincarnation: the poet, Moore believed, had asked to be "out of nature," not in the sense of existing in a discarnate state but in that of returning to the world as an art object. The mechanical bird would then sing to incarnate lords and ladies about incarnate experience within time. The possibility that Yeats's trope involves discarnate as well as incarnate experience did not seem to have occurred to Moore.

If we take "Byzantium" as the necessary "exposition" designed to explain to Moore how he had misread "Sailing to Byzantium," we shall discover that Yeats's intention in "Sailing to Byzantium" was slightly different from what most readers have always assumed it to be. We shall also find that "Byzantium" remains essentially the poem it was before. The interest, however, in Moore's relationship to and demonstrable influence on Yeats does not lie in the production of new readings of Yeats's poems. It lies rather in what one can learn from that relationship about what two late romantic poets thought about the nature of poetic meaning, the function of poetic language, and the relationship of the necessarily indeterminate romantic subject to meaning and language.

For both poets, as for poststructuralist critics, poetry is concerned with extensions of human consciousness that are necessarily indeterminate. We cannot know what it means to experience the ground of consciousness, to become or to enter another consciousness, or to merge with transcendent consciousness. These experiences, however, create the problems posed by the main tradition of romantic poetry from William Wordsworth through Wallace Stevens and beyond. Do such extensions of consciousness exist at all? If they do exist, what do they feel like? Can poetry capture the experience? If they do not exist, is there some value in the illusion, the poetic fiction, that they do exist?

Yeats developed strategies for dealing in precise terms with these indeterminate extensions, and Moore, in his own poetry, also tried to reproduce the indeterminate experience of romantic extensions of consciousness within determinate poetic structures. Both poets were motivated by the desire to produce maximumn clarity of thought, experience, and language while taking the greatest possible speculative risks. Yeats and Moore both regarded language as a tool, imperfect but useful, for exploring indeterminacy and particularly the indeterminacy of those experiences that takes one to the margins of human consciousness. They found the indeterminacy in the experience rather than in the language, and they both exhibited a refreshing literal-mindedness in their approach to questions of poetic meaning. Moore read Yeats's "Sailing to Byzantium" very literally and concluded that it is impossible to respond to the golden bird because the bird cannot be imagined as a vehicle of consciousness. Yeats understood Moore's difficulty and wrote "Byzantium" to show that the bird is indeed a vehicle of consciousness, but of a sort that had not occurred to Moore.

The Sealed Bottle: Yeats and Moore in Correspondence

Nowhere in the writings of the two men is this literal-mindedness more apparent than in the intense philosophical discussion that occurs in their correspondence during the years immediately preceding the crucial letters from which I have already quoted. The correspondence conveys the sense of a shared recognition that language is a tool for decreasing the indeterminacy of the necessarily indeterminate question of the relationship between consciousness and reality. As we shall see, this question is the one that divides the two men in their conceptions of human consciousness and in their readings of "Sailing to Byzantium," and it is the question that Yeats attempts to resolve in "Byzantium."

"Byzantium" can be read as Yeats's final contribution to the discussion initiated in the letters. The specific question that occasions the discussion is that of whether or not one can make a distinction between a "real" object and a "phantasmal" or hallucinatory object. Yeats maintains that both constitute the mind's experience and that no distinction can be made between them. Moore maintains the commonsense view that each of us is isolated within our own consciousness and that we perceive a shared world. The argument that develops is intense because both men are poets in a tradition in which the nature of the self and its participation or nonparticipation in the life of the universe is the central question. Interestingly enough, each seemed finally to feel that he had won the debate.

The argument arises from Yeats's casual claim that he had recently made a friend see a vision: "Hitherto I have always taken the idealist view of such visions but now, thanks to your brother's *Refutation of Idealism*, I am permitted to think that they exist outside the human mind" (*Correspondence*, 59). In reply Moore points out that Yeats has misapplied G. E. Moore's argument: "Because some appearances have real external causes does not mean that others may not be entirely subjective. Memory may be as vivid and precise as the experience remembered" (*Correspondence*, 59–60). Yeats responds by saying, in effect, that all perceived objects, all sense-data, whether subjective or objective, possess the same degree of reality (*Correspondence*, 63). There are, Moore writes back, commonsense distinctions that can be made: "we call things real as a matter of fact because of those properties in which they differ from dreams. Everybody supposes that an hallucination in the form of a cat looks to the hallucinating person exactly like a cat. As his experience is entirely private nobody can say anything certain about it except himself" (*Correspondence*, 65).

But Yeats will have none of it. Reality is not somehow bifurcated, existing both out there and then repeated in our perception, and the mind is not the superfluous quicksilver at the back of a mirror that merely reflects the external world internally: "Why should nature create that useless quicksilver? My own belief is that we know nothing but 'spirits and their relations,' but if I could escape from the useless quicksilver [I] would see nothing I care for involved if I had to consider the stream of images ('sense-data,' Ruskins's cat and the house cat), which since Berkeley have seemed a part of the mind, as separate from it" (*Correspondence*, 67). Yeats goes on to establish the crucial difference between his own view of perception and that of Moore and the rest of us: "Russell and his school cannot escape from the belief that each man is a sealed bottle. Every man who has studied psychical science by watching his own life knows that we share emotion, thought and image" (*Correspondence*, 68–69).

The point is an extremely important one, not only for the argument with Moore, but for an understanding of *A Vision* and of Yeats's later poetry. Yeats insists on "the impossibility of drawing any distinct line between objective and subjective images. . . . The distinction between objective and subjective images is to any student of the subject obsolete" (*Correspondence*, 70). In other words, mind interacts directly with mind. Reality exists in consciousness, and consciousness can be shared: "The present realist argument breaks down because we have no longer the right to say that there is any image of the mind peculiar to one person: something of it is peculiar, as something of the images we call physical is peculiar, and that is all we can say. It becomes necessary to consider that all minds may make under certain circumstances a single mind" (*Correspondence*, 81). For Yeats, reality only exists in perception, Berkeley's *esse est percipi*. There is a subject, the perceiving consciousness, but there is no object. External to the mind is only a matrix of possibility, a flux of formless and quite literally unimagined and unformulated energy, that only takes form and temporal-spatial existence within a perceiving mind (*Correspondence*, 82–83).

Implicit in Yeats's position is the idealist view that only mind is real. Yeats had always held this view. One can find it in his exposition of Blake's doctrines in the Ellis-Yeats edition of Blake:

Nature, he tells (or rather he reminds us) is merely a name for one form of mental existence. Art is another and a higher form. But that art may rise to its true place, it must be set free from memory that binds it to Nature.

Nature—or creation,—is a result of the shrinkage of consciousness,—originally clairvoyant,—under the rule of the five senses, and of argument and law. Such consciousness is the result of the divided portions of Universal mind obtaining perception of one another.[2]

It appears also in the three doctrines that Yeats sees as lying behind the practice of magic:

(1) That the borders of our mind are ever shifting, and that many minds can flow into one another, as it were, and create or reveal a single mind, a single energy.
(2) That the borders of our memories are as shifting, and that our memories are a part of one great memory, the memory of Nature herself.
(3) That this great mind and memory can be evoked by symbols.[3]

And it occurs elsewhere in his prose, perhaps most notably in *Rosa Alchemica* and *Per Amica Silentia Lunae.*

I have concentrated on Yeats's belief that reality only exists in perception and that "all minds may make under certain circumstances a single mind" to emphasize that Yeats held these views with great consistency and fervor and was prepared to argue against the commonsense view that the object exists objectively and is repeated in the perception of the isolated human perceiver. To my knowledge, the only significant poet truly and literally to agree with Yeats is William Blake, who, like Yeats, was deeply affected by the Berkelian view of reality.

During the years that followed the publication of the first version of *A Vision* in 1925, the years during which Yeats argued the nature of mind with Moore, Yeats systematically educated himself for the first time in his life in metaphysics and the philosophy of science.

> I could not read philosophy till my big book was written. Those who gave me material forbid me to do so; they feared I think, that if I did so I would split up experience till it ceased to exist. When it was written (though the proofs had yet to come) I started to read. I read for months every day Plato and Plotinus. Then I started on Berkeley and Croce and Gentile. You introduced me to your brother's work and to Russell, and I found Eddington and one or two others for myself. I am still however anything but at my ease in recent philosophy. I find your brother extraordinarily obscure.
>
> (*Correspondence*, 83)

It was also during this period, and as a consequence of the argument with Moore and the effort to come to terms with metaphysics and the philosophy of science, that Yeats came to see that his own fundamental views were even more Berkeleian than he had earlier imagined, and it was during these years that he revised *A Vision* in terms of what he had learned from the study of philosophy and from arguing with Moore.[4] As a result of all of these activities he became more convinced than ever of the validity of his crucial distinction between the individual mind as a sealed bottle on the one hand, and as part of a shared mind on the other. But if the mind is shared, surely it is shared by the dead as well as the living. Although such an insight is present in *Vision A,* it is in *Vision B* that it is presented systematically, with Berkeleian precision and economy.

Life in Death: A Vision

Yeats hypothesizes in both versions of *A Vision* that during life the sealed bottle predominates and we have only intimations of the larger sharing with other minds. Experience is dominated by the temporal-spatial norms of individual perception, personal history, temperament, and our sense of unique identity. In Yeats's system, personal, incarnate identity is the province of the Faculties. Yeats learned from the belated self-education in philosophy to which he submitted himself after 1925 that the Faculties in his system can be equated with the Understanding in Coleridge's reworking of Kant in *The Friend* and *The Statesman's Manual,* and that the Principles, which predominate in discarnate experience between incarnations, can be identified with Coleridge's Reason. Although these Kantian distinctions are implicit in the confusing treatment of the Principles and of discarnate experience in *Vision A,* it is only in *Vision B* that they become an explicit element in Yeats's conscious exposition: "But now in a few minutes they [the communicators] drew that distinction between what their terminology calls the *Faculties* and what it calls the *Principles,* between experience and revelation, between understanding and reason, between the higher and lower mind, which has engaged the thought of saints and philosophers from the time of Buddha."[5] This insight provided Yeats with one of the key distinctions by which he completely reconceived his exposition of the experience of the discarnate spirit, the labor that produced *Vision B.*

It is interesting that Yeats retained unrevised from *Vision A* only those parts that are schematizations of incarnate experience and that do not bear on the complex questions of how to talk

about the discarnate soul and the nature of discarnate experi-
ence. The sections of *A Vision* that underwent the greatest
change between the version of 1925 and that of 1937 are those
that describe the Principles—that is, discarnate life. Those sec-
tions relating to the Faculties remained unchanged: "The first
version of *A Vision*, except the section on the twenty-eight
Phases, and that called 'Dove or Swan' which I repeat without
change, fills me with shame. I had misinterpreted the geometry
and in my ignorance of philosophy failed to understand the
distinction upon which the coherence of the whole de-
pended . . ." (*Vision B*, 19).

Even more important, I believe, than the distinction between
Understanding and Reason is the Berkeleian formula *esse est
percipi*. Now, with great economy, Yeats can place reality in
perception, which is where he had always wanted it to be. Like
Berkeley he extended the notion to include the perception of
spirits and of a supreme spirit. The Four Faculties of incarnate
experience are now defined as perceived experience, not as phil-
osophical abstractions. They exist only in the experience of indi-
vidual human beings; a person's experience of life is subjective in
the sense that it exists only within his or her perception and that
of the *Daimon*, one's soul or permanent self that lives through a
sequence of individual incarnations. Between lives the same
principle applies, and being exists solely in perception. Yeats
found that the *Daimon*, which seems to have had no clear func-
tion or definition in *Vision A*, becomes the means whereby Yeats
can express this new perception:

> The *Four Faculties* are not the abstract categories of philosophy, being
> the result of the four memories of the *Daimon* or ultimate self of that
> man. His Body of Fate, the series of events forced upon him from
> without, is shaped out of the *Daimon's* memory of events of his past
> incarnations; his *Mask* or object of desire or idea of the good, out of
> its memory of the moments of exaltation in his past lives; his *Will* or
> normal ego out of its memory of all the events of his present life,
> whether consciously remembered or not; his *Creative Mind* from its
> memory of ideas—or universals—displayed by actual men in past
> lives, or their spirits between lives. (*Vision B*, 83)

The Faculties exist in the memory of the Daimon. Reality, for
Yeats, exists within the consciousness of Daimons. Their ideas
and the relations between them constitute the totality of being. It
is thus that the matrix or substratum exists within the con-
sciousness of spirits and is "living and active" and thus that

Yeats can say, as he did to Moore, that he believed only in "spirits and their relations" (*Correspondence,* 66). This economical assertion that reality only exists in consciousness is precisely Berkeley's *esse est percipi.*[6]

Yeats schematizes the Berkeleian formula and places it within the vital matrix provided by the geometrical schemes through which are shown the interrelationships between all possible modes of consciousness, incarnate and discarnate. Yeats saw clearly that the Berkeleian view developed here is not solipsistic, for, as he informed Moore, "the belief that all is experience does not mean that there is no truth unknown to us for there are unknown minds, but it does mean that there is no truth where there is no mind to know it" (*Correspondence,* 86). This, of course, is Berkeley's own defense: "For though we hold indeed the objects of sense to be nothing else but ideas which cannot exist unperceived; yet we may not hence conclude they have no existence except only while they are perceived by us, since there may be some other spirit that perceives them, though we do not" (*Principles,* 61).

This Berkeleian concept is crucial to our understanding of "Sailing to Byzantium" and to the further exposition of the idea of "Sailing to Byzantium" in "Byzantium," and it is the one not made explicit until Yeats had completed *Vision B:* the most important development that occurs in the revision of *A Vision* is that after death we escape the sealed bottle in ways that enforce a radical alteration in the relationship between identity and perception. The sharing of minds of which we have intimations during incarnate experience becomes more apparent because they are not masked by the norms of individual perception.

I have already noted that the fortuitous element in the development in Yeats's thought, which I am here tracing, related to the remarkable argument that Yeats had with Moore. For reasons that Yeats himself provides in *Vision B,* he had, during his formative years and while writing *Vision A,* stayed away from rigorous philosophical speculation: "For the same reason they [the communicators] asked me not to read philosophy until their exposition was complete, and this increased my difficulties. Apart from two or three of the principal Platonic Dialogues I knew no philosophy. Arguments with my father . . . had destroyed my confidence and driven me from speculation to the direct experience of the Mystics" (*Vision B,* 12). When the argument with Moore forced Yeats to overcome his resistance to metaphysics and to think through his fundamental assumptions, he discovered the simplifying formulas that made it possible for him to restate his system in philosophically comprehensible terms.

The labor that went into rewriting *A Vision* did not alter the indeterminacy of the content. Yeats is, after all, trying to make sense of revealed material that he cannot truly know. And, in any case, the romantic preoccupation with extensions of consciousness, with Wordsworth's "unknown modes of being," encourages the view that this inherent indeterminacy is a sign of the poetic. Even if we believe that Yeats's special revelation is a fiction, it is not presented as a fiction. It is presented as the effort to treat in increasingly determinate formulations the inescapably indeterminate subject matter of the modes of human transcendence and our relationship with the dead. Only by assuming a revelation could Yeats talk about these matters at all.

Byzantium

Yeats was concerned with expressing quite specific meaning in his poems. When F. R. Leavis said disparagingly that Yeats's poetry was a by-product of his other interests, he was expressing a partial truth. Yeats worked intensely on his synthesis of the occult, history, and philosophy, and he took seriously the quite specific conclusions that he reached and that he wished to be understood. It is unfortunate that Yeats's correspondence, his prose writings, even his rough drafts, should prove so useful as glosses on the poetry and on the intention, often more hidden than apparent, in his poems. But useful they are. Without them, one might not be able in the present instance to understand the precise nature of the exposition that Yeats could see was needed to make his meaning in "Sailing to Byzantium" clear to Moore: the bird for Yeats does not itself possess consciousness, and it does not exist exclusively in the perception of incarnate spirits. Although it has its origins in our world, as does all experience, it exists primarily in the perception of discarnate spirits. Incarnate perception is the source for Yeats of all experience. It is the source of the raw material of consciousness, even for discarnate spirits. This is its value and its function, and this is why the dead need us. Unfortunately Yeats had become so accustomed to his own way of thinking that he may not have realized that the poem which he provided as explanation seems more opaque than the original poem to be explained. Yeats's Byzantium exists exclusively in the perception of spirits, some incarnate and some discarnate. It is not anywhere. Like everything else, it is perceived by the living in their time and by the dead under certain conditions and circumstances that, by their very nature, cannot be known.

In the third and fourth stanzas of the first full draft of "Sailing to Byzantium" [B1], we find support for this reading:

> O saints that stand amid God's sacred fire
> As in the gold mosaic of a wall
> Consume this heart and make it what you were
> Unwavering, indifferent, fanatical
> It faints upon the road sick with desire
> But fastened to this dying animal
> Or send the dolphin's back, and gather me
> Into the artifice of eternity
>
> The sensuous dream being past I shall not take
> A guttering form of nature's fashion
> But rather that the Grecian smithies make
> Of hammered gold and gold enamelling
> At the Emperor's order for his lady' sake
> And set upon a golden bough to sing
> To Lords and Ladies of Byzantium
> Of what is past or passing or to come.[7]

A distinction is made in the third stanza between the speaker as a visitor, perhaps in imagination or vision but still in life, and the souls that are carried on the backs of dolphins. The development of the thought through the drafts led Yeats to drop this initial distinction and to drop the dolphins, which seemed, at least in terms of the rhetoric of the draft, to enforce the distinction. In the third stanza of the finished poem, the poet is in the unstable state of the newly arrived and unpurged spirit, but of a spirit already discarnate and "out of nature." We find support for this reading of "out of nature" in the two earlier versions of the line that was eventually to contain this problematic phrase:

> [B2] The sensuous dream being done I shall not take
> [C6] The dolphin's journey done I shall not take

The poet is in the presence of the Byzantine sages in Yeats's syncretistic version of the Heavenly City. The addition of the gyres suggests the dance of purgation of newly arrived souls. The "sensuous dream" is incarnate existence, expressed figuratively as a dying and flickering, a "guttering" flame. The golden bird is an artifice of eternity in that it is an art object that has the peculiar spiritual potency that Yeats attributed to Byzantine art. Yeats seems to have meant by "the artifice of eternity" the kind of spiritual achievement that can impinge on discarnate consciousness and specifically the entire artistic and spiritual achievement of sixth-century Byzantium as Yeats has created it.

The lords and ladies and the subject of the bird's song, then, are not "out of nature," but the bird itself is both in and out, depending on the status in reality of the spirit that perceives it. Lacking consciousness itself, the bird exists, as Yeats always knew but came to understand in more technical terms from his study of Berkeley, in the perception of spirits. In "Sailing to Byzantium" it exists primarily in the perception of discarnate spirits and specifically that of the speaker of the poem who, in the third stanza, becomes a discarnate spirit. "Byzantium" explains all of this partly through reintroducing details of exposition that had been revised out of Yeats's earlier versions of "Sailing to Byzantium."

Perception requires a principle of unity, and the principle usually adopted is that of normal consciousness, life in the sealed bottle of personality. The most difficult conception in "Sailing to Byzantium" and the one missed by Moore, here and throughout the correspondence, is the Berkeleian point that reality exists in the perception of spirits. "Byzantium" provides, as Yeats had hoped that it would, the needed exposition. Most of us, in reading "Sailing to Byzantium," try, as did Moore, to impose the principle of normal consciousness. "Byzantium" is a poetic experiment in describing another state and one in which the principle of the sealed bottle does not apply. In "Byzantium," the indeterminacy of the poem is just the indeterminacy that might be imagined as the state of a newly arrived discarnate spirit.

The only difference between the two poems is that "Sailing to Byzantium" is a form of petition. "Byzantium" is a poem of vision; it presents a discarnate "scene." Although the point of view is roughly that of a newly arrived spirit, one cannot speak here of point of view in the normal sense. The observer is out of body and out of time. In hailing the mummy, like is hailing like. There is no expository petition as in "Sailing to Byzantium." There is the impossible effort to create a persona that can speak the visionary experience of being discarnate. The indeterminacy that a reader perceives in the poem is a functional representation of the poem's subject expressed in language that is as precise as

Yeats can make it. The poem expresses the indeterminacy that must exist in any human imagining of such experience and that is just the indeterminacy that Yeats insists on maintaining with regard to the revelation provided by his communicators.

The details of the poem exist in the perception of an unstable spirit like the newly arrived spirit of stanzas three and four of "Sailing to Byzantium." But here the spirit speaks in the bardic and apocalyptic tone that Yeats reserves for poetic statement that includes an element of the discarnate. Yeats understands that he, as a mortal man, does not "know" what he is talking about, but he can adopt a literary convention that allows him to speak as a discarnate spirit, or, alternatively, the convention of the apocalyptic voice that can speak in trance or vision. The speaker in "Byzantium" shares characteristics of both conventions. Thus, the "unpurged images" of the first stanza, although unequivocally images of incarnate experience, do not exist in incarnate experience; they exist in the shifting perspective of a discarnate spirit for whom the normal distinction between real and unreal does not exist.

The apparent indeterminacy of the details of the poem has the same function: it is a very realistic rendering of a state of being and perception in which no meaning can be attached to incarnate existence as a principle of unity. Normal reality ceases to be a norm. The alternatives, "image, man or shade, / Shade more than man, more image than a shade" and "Miracle, bird or golden handiwork, / More miracle than bird or handiwork," are not intended to be resolved but are visions from the discarnate perspective that cannot make distinctions based on normal (that is, incarnate) perception. The alternatives are alternatives of reality-status, but in this state of the spirit, one cannot talk about or experience a reality-status.

For Wordsworth and most other romantic poets, including Moore, the transcendent moment in which one becomes another is occasional and bounded by the experience of normal life within the sealed bottle. Although Yeats and Moore shared a common literary background, Yeats always carried the shared outlook or procedure further than Moore was willing to. Both were concerned with the limits of experience and the merging with death. But Yeats actually tried to imagine discarnate experience. Both used poetic personae and poetry itself as techniques for creating desired but impossible states of being and consciousness. Yeats, however, was more daring than Moore in his exploration of these margins of human consciousness. With the help of Berkeley's *esse est percipi*, Yeats extended the romantic trope of merging as far as it will go.[8] He, like Blake, believed that, properly perceived, reality is always transcendent and is exclusively spiritual because only existing in the perception of spirits. To place all of reality in the perception of spirits as Yeats does is, after all, to extend in a very single-minded and literal way this romantic trope so that it encompasses all of human experience.

Notes

1. W. B. Yeats and T. Sturge Moore, *Correspondence, 1901–1937*, edited by Ursula Bridge (London: 1953), 162; hereafter cited in the text as *Correspondence*. Further evidence relating to the genesis of the objection stated in this letter and to Moore's critique of the stanza will appear shortly in David Peters Corbett, "T. Sturge Moore, 'Do We Or Do We Not, Know It?', and the Writing of 'Byzantium,'" *Yeats Annual*.

2. *The Works of William Blake*, edited with lithographs of the illustrated "Prophetic Books," and a Memoir and Interpretation by Edwin John Ellis and WIlliam Butler Yeats, 3 vols. (London: B. Quaritch, 1893): 1:xii.

3. W. B. Yeats, "Magic," *Essays and Introductions* (1961; reprint, New York: Macmillan, 1968), 28.

4. For a detailed discussion of the influence of Berkeley and Moore on the revisions that produced *Vision B*, see my article "Yeats's Second 'Vision': Berkeley, Coleridge, and the Correspondence with Sturge Moore," *Modern Language Review* 76 (1981): 273–90.

5. W. B. Yeats, *A Vision* (1937; reprint, with corrections, London: Macmillan, 1962), 22; hereafter cited as *Vision B*. See also W. B. Yeats, *A Vision: An Explanation of Life Founded upon the Writings of Giraldus and upon Certain Doctrines Attributed to Kusta ben Luka* (London: 1925); hereafter cited as *Vision A*.

6. George Berkeley, *A Treatise Concerning the Principles of Human Knowledge*, in *The Works of George Berkeley, Bishop of Cloyne*, ed. A. A. Luce and T. E. Jessop, 9 vols. (London and New York: Nelson, 1948–57), 2:79–80; hreafter cited as *Principles*.

7. Quoted in Curtis Bradford, "Yeats's Byzantium Poems: A Study of Their Development," in *Yeats: A Collection of Critical Essays*, ed. John Unterecker (Englewood Cliffs, N.J.: Prentice-Hall, 1963), 103.

8. Yeats's Golden Bird is only one instance of this trope. The kind of trope that I have in mind, to point to familiar examples that go beyond the concerns of this essay, is that represented by the numerous instances of subject-object coalescence to be found throughout *The Prelude* and also in Wallace Stevens' hypostatizations of this coalescence in the personae that populate his poems: the Hero, the Glass Man, and the Green Queen, for example. The theory of this kind of trope is explored throughout Stevens' prose, especially in "Effects of Analogy," "A Collect of Philosophy," "Two or Three Ideas," and "The Irrational Element in Poetry."

After a Change of Regime

A Drama in Three Acts
and for Three Voices
Donald Davie

For Don Stanford

I
From the Widow of the Head of State
The Countess Remembers
Soliloquy of the Minister for Culture

II
Frankness of the Minister for Culture
The Countess Gives an Interview
From the Widow of the Head of State

III
The Countess Points a Finger
The Minister Disgraced
The Widow of the Head of State, as Ready Reckoner

From the Widow of the Head of State

He was never above the mêlée
Of four bare legs in bed.
But what did the Countess say,
The groomed black head
Over the military typewriter?
I had gone there by mistake.
I saw her lips go tighter
And her hands pause, then take

A cigarette from her case.
Did she seek manhood
In the assassin's face
Of her own man of blood,
The mutilated colonel with the bomb,
As I did in the bed
Of one whose time would come
To be his figurehead?

I ought to have found it more
Difficult to forgive
The role they cast us for:
Removed, contemplative,
Statesmanlike. We paid
The heavier price, all told.
For Heinrich was afraid.
"Will no one help the old
Gentleman?" they said,
Meaning, to press the trigger
He held against his head.
Did he have to cut their figure?
A statesman has to fail
If the wife of a statesman needs
To judge her man by the scale
Of the crippled man of deeds.

They were planning it even then,
At the machine the Countess,
A network of hard-pushed men
And Heinrich. I counted for less
Than she did, less than I thought.
My contemplative man is dead
By violence, who taught
Civility instead.
Those professorial lips
He sealed against me earned
Honours and fellowships
Years ago. I had learned
From him, I had understood
How manhood is in the mind.
Then came this spilling of blood,
And manhood still to find.

The Countess Remembers

I told him enigmatically: "You need
Ventilation." After a pause (he was
Famously imperturbable) he said:
You mean. after all this, Canada?"
                              His wound
Had sobered him so far as not to attempt
The quizzical. "Why, my dear,
Who'd rule it out? Kicking Horse Canyon for
Ever!"
        My limbless horseman
Had ruled out being amused, and yet amusement
Affectionately flickered in those tawny
Eyes that should have been Prussian. Easily he
Indulged me:
              "Yes, Saskatchewan. Why not?"

And yet he knew that, notable horseman though
He was on the sands of Pomerania, his
End had to be in the claustrophobic
Bunker, his bomb, asphyxiation by cordite.
No prairie airs for him.
                        Nor for me. And indeed I knew it.

Soft cats in public places ogled their cream
In the dish of him limping, laurelled by the *regime*.

Soliloquy of the Minister for Culture

Where, where is justice, when the sacred gift,
When deathless justice comes not to reward
Perfervid love and utter self-denial. . . ?
                        Pushkin, *Mozart and Salieri*

Salieri to his Mozart—poisoner,
The sterile rival. If that Muse of his,
So bare and truthful, took it upon her

To know her peers, why here the parallel is,
Exact and banal. Calling him "immature"
Gives me away; my lost youth makes the claim.
Wasted and Moscow-nipped. His never-worked for,
Free, ambiguous mastery, all the same
I have the edge of—he should have a more
Responsible, a more adult concern.
He manages the thing with too much ease.
Expert in skills he never had to learn.
What can he see in them except caprice
Or self-indulgence? But there's more than this:
What Pushkin couldn't know, what this *flâneur*
Ought to know but doesn't, is
The right our guilt affords us. If I were
Free to tell this faithful party-member
All that the Party knows, were I to confess
The cost I know and choose not to remember,
I'd see his golden and unnatural youth
Age on the instant. And his truthfulness!
How cheap that comes, until one knows the truth . . .

Bored tonight, I took down Pushkin's trifle,
"Dubrovsky." Does he know it? Poet's prose,
Bare narrative *resumé*, beautiful.
It made his much-praised spareness look verbose.
And yet I thought of him. Yes, reading through it,
I saw him cast just that cold classic light
On us, on the Revolution. If he knew it,
If only he knew . . . He can't be told outright.
But he's no fool. He ought to know me better
Than to interpret all my talk of "conflict"
According to the letter.
I've tried to tell him, underneath the strict
Seal of our barbarous jargon, what the truth
Is, that he needs—not that he may tell it
(That he may not), but that its resonance
Tell for him. The elegance of the tacit
Informs the life we lead, and reticence
In art reflects it. Therefore all my planned
Exclusions should be seen as right
By a taste like his. Insufferably bland,
His blindness strips me. How unfair it is

That I, who know the truth, am bored tonight,
And he alert among complacencies!

Frankness of the Minister for Culture

"Know your enemy." I know him,
Can whistle Dixie and
The Battle Hymn of the Republic.
I did not waste my time in Washington.

Because their kids are good kids, what their kids
Are avid for, they have to like as well;
Prompt action (swift compliance) has
Earned commendations. BCM (US):
Battle Communications
Maintenance. Crucial in Combat.

Or if their kids are bad kids by
Calvinist definition, what
Their kids have been inured to has to be
Endured by them for patriotic reasons,
For Uncle Sam's sweet sake. Complying, their
Abnegation gets to like the diet.

Parentage in America—there's a study!

AAA (triple A)
Atrocities Awareness
Agency: a boon to every age-group.
Of course it is their arts that are atrocious.

Americans live my acronymns.
And so I fear do we—a distasteful interim measure.
The measures of verse must be that much more cherished and
honoured.

Since we, not they, are the heirs
Of the Enlightenment, an enlightened
Fatherly concern for artists is
A high priority for the Revolution.

I should not need to spell this out, and would not
Except for the dolts among us. Turnip-heads!

The Countess Gives an Interview

Surviving was his business as a schoolboy
During those years of our sleazy triumphs, before
It came to be every one's business. Huge eyes under
The always thin thatch of his straight straw hair, he
Questioned: "Was it not terrible?" I
Embraced him of course, said No, abstractedly;
Pleased by his sensitivity and yet
Uneasy with it, plagued by even then
In his piping treble the note of options kept
Open, and channels open, though of course
In the case of a mere child thinking so was absurd.

The mereness of him, of his or of any childhood
In those years and for people of our rank
Is hard to imagine. His father and I
Interacted so intensely . . . pah,
Where did I learn such gibberish? Our love,
Mine and the Count's, could find no room for him.
And that's no crime. We found superior nurse-maids,
Then *mademoiselle,* then tutors. It was the pattern
In our world that was passing, not yet past.

He has favored the public with precocious memoirs
In which—I have skimmed them—he accounts for
Father and Mother briefly indeed but with
Tenderness even one might say if one
Could so far trust him.
                     Yes, I am a tigress,
But not as you see in defence of her cub. I speak of
My son the poet who is having a great success;
On whose account you interview this non-person.

His patronage, or theirs who for now protect him,
Permits these indiscretions. You have been
Indulgent, comrades. You know better

Than I can do what character best projects him
Before a public that I have no truck with.

From the Widow of the Head of State

The English it was, he relied on.
A frail reed! Who was I
To tell him not to confide in
Their so amusingly drunken
Cultural attaché, their
Embassy spy?
                              I had little
To go on beyond what I heard
(One could hardly avoid it indeed): their
Journalists uproarious at the bar—
                              "Sister Wragg
                              will carry the flag . . .
                              Sister Barker
                              will be right-hand marker . . ."
(My English is good.) I heard them
Commending someone:
                              ". . . would as soon
                              miss Christmas or the Queen as
                              the glorious First of June"
(The anniversary of a naval action,
Heinrich, I researched it.)

More I half-heard, wafted in and out
Of the Danubia's tea-time strings over cream-cakes,
The bar's increasingly loud and intemperate voices:
                              "The mind of Europe stops . . ."
                              "The ideologies rattle . . ."
                              "Nobody's easy touch,
                              Guy Burgess thought
                              Old England's winding-sheet
                              ought to have been sewn
                              by sailmakers and such . . .

                                        "Lest we forget!"
A ragged roar came. Then:

> "One who sold as much
> small dirt as he could get."

The Danubia's tea-room emptied. There came through
one slurred discontinuous prattle:
> "This is a common market.
> trams continue to rattle.
> This is the way the mind
> of Europe stops, has stopped."

> "With a hey, jolly Jack, with a hey
> and hearts of oak come home,"
the voice said, then went dumb.

Heinrich, they spoke of one
Who had betrayed their secrets.
Leibchen, you should have known
Better. Perfidious English,
They trawled to catch only their own;
Their splotched own trout-farmed fish!

The Countess Points a Finger

Who tipped them off about the bunker? Not
Istvan, not Karl . . . The field is appallingly narrow
Seeing that all who knew, who were in the network
Were rounded up and "dealt with," there and then.
Quite in their style to kill their own informant,
That would be thorough. Istvan? Oskar? Karl?
François? . . . I would have let the question go
If it would let me. Some one said the leak
Could have been nearer home: the Count's *factotum*.
That loyal blockhead? Never! Nearer home
Even than that? That's paranoia speaking,
That must be chained and kenneled. Even so
I sniff our gate-posts
                   and come back with what
I cannot prove nor ever could: that drunken
English charmer whom I know my son
At times fell in with, in the Danubia bar.

Timid old Heinrich's Ganymede
A double agent? It's conceivable.

The Minister Disgraced

Slowly destroying each other in transports
Of joy and rage the Count and Countess
Tolstoy lately stalked the stage.

Sheets were over the circle where children's
Voices would chant oh the song of the golden
Goose the principal boy of Panto,

And Claus or Nicholas all the grosser
Gods of the Christmas hissed the holy
Boyar and approved his Countess.

* *

At blood-warm Christmas booby Joseph
Feels a fool since pap and sleepy
Parturition seem the rule.

But I could wait. Their child the poet
Was mine, no other's. Children of my loins
Are not so dear; their several mothers know it.

Slowly destroying each other in torments
Of rage and appetite male and female
Mankind wrote the pre-war page,

Pre-Revolution. But paternity now
Is a considered, not a carnal matter;
Not once for all, but a perpetual Easter.

The spirit of Revolution easing
Out of that blasphemous egg, a mother's ardent
Good of coincident animal goes beg.

* *

I told his mother: It was not for me

To legislate for poetry, nor for her
Tainted by certain "ill-advised connections."

Some pride I took at the time in that
Civilized manoeuvre. Now the light
Leaks into my cell, accusing me over and over:

"Romanticized conception of the poet,
Hectic or pale *naif!*" He took a leaf
Out of my shrewd book, and impaled me on it.

I was the golden goose. This pantomime
Enacts the goose I was, and golden is
The price he has had for me, who dared to choose.

The time will come . . . It may, but I don't think so.
Thirty years on, he'll star in freedom-loving
Congresses where I'll be a dirty word.

The Widow of the Head of State as Ready Reckoner

As a researcher I'm no longer tireless;
Tenacious, though. It's not
The highest virtue, Heinrich let me know,
But has its usefulness. "My little bloodhound,"
He called me once or twice, those years ago,
Smiling. I have my own techniques: I
Never let go,
And—here's a professional secret—I let chance
Work for me; meek short-lived gusts that blow
Crumples of information down the gutter
Bring what I could have slaved for years to know
And nowhere found. My swan's nest of grey hairs,
My reticule and sandwich, are not known
In the Academy of Sciences. I am not
Often saluted there, am seldom noticed,
A corpulent old biddy, but
I know my trade, and I am not afraid.

This time it was the merest air, not in

Metaphor but quite literally, blew
The crimped clue to me. It was the Tannoy
System one learns how not to listen to:
A bad mistake, a failing. Blaring from
Each tenement's or public building's corner
Came to us, day by day, what the *regime*
Thought proper for us. And this summer morning
It was, I perceived belatedly, a poem
Excited, high-flown, urgent. This was not
Anything new. For poetry too was the workers',
The ideology said, if they would only
Reach out and take it. And perhaps they did
For all I know; perhaps in the lonely *puszta*
Some herder of long-horned cattle half-remembered
What the Tannoy had blared as he scuffed his feet
Stumbling at dawn in his mired village. My
Allegedly muddier origins
In the small *bourgeoisie* had muddied me.
In our circles poetry was permitted,
Was even at times extolled: it fabricated
Idylls one might day-dream in. But this
Poetry made an idyll of our present
And thereby lied, it lied. I have been made
Indignant on this account—which will not do
For a researcher who should always be
Dispassionate, who very nearly this time,
Pulled by her passions, missed the straw in the wind.

The exalted diction, once and then again,
Swooped on to "turnip-heads": not a locution
Altogether current yet, it seemed
(The poetry was ambiguous, as usual),
A slogan of class-division and resistance
In some one or other's mouth.
                              For the researcher,
States like ours present a special problem:
Much that is said is said in code. Decoded.
This drop from aureate diction signalled, if
I may be excused the vulgarism, some one,
And some one of some eminence, "for the chop."

My cattle-herder on the *puszta*, what
Could he have made of it? It was not meant

For his decoding. The researcher knew
And knew right: fall of some one eminent.

Scholarship? No, hardly scholarship;
A matter of life and death. But it's on this—
What some one said, what someone else let slip,
The coral-insect's inching edifice—
That erudition grounds its hierarchies.

The obtuse researcher gets there after all
Or rather, first of all. The annalist
Sees in the tyrant's circle this one rise
And that one, who was more deserving, fall.

The Preserve
Wyatt Prunty

Having said no to every good inquiry,
These stretch above starched verities
On that great swim bladder called alcohol
While, poised like cuddle fish against the tank's
Thick glass, each gapes over his drink
Pausing as if . . . but looking out on what
He steadily refuses any fathom . . .
Shoppers measuring terse afternoons
That here, in this brief tide pool of reserve,
Are followed with diluted envy.

The best of this subset are at the front,
Testing the tinted glass against a light
That in their stalled expressions appears
To strike as something indigestible
But which they monitor in a silence
Matching the refrigerated depths
That hold still more—some mildly sweetened,
Others weathering past recognition
Of the season when they felt themselves lifted
Suddenly, and for the first time held aloft
As if judged, then left to grow and thicken.

Such preserved remains suggest another's hand,
And these at the least are the gatherings
Or something overzealous, heard perhaps
The way a distracted Adam must have heard
The unrequited voice that gave him leave
As suddenly as he could think to leave,
Speaking, in fact, only what he wanted . . .
A leveled habitat in which he might
Raise, divide, and goggle as possessively

As these do here, when someone catches an eye,
Looking across that barren area
Restricted to two famous species—
The ones who didn't hesitate and these,
Who fleeing will always turn their heads,
Watching the way they would not go
Until they cross the stoop of this
Cool dive, having purchased something cold
And depressing but audible inside
Where they can always stop the clock,
Order another round, and close the whole place down.

The Sun Is Still Here
Kathleen Raine

In mid-morning
William Blake's sun
Brilliant in the sky
Over World's End shone
In love and wisdom
Withheld from none.
I could not look upon
But knew the presence
Of a million angels
Travelling on beams
Of dazzling glory.
How otherwise
Than as all we see
Can we be shown
Compassion and mercy?
Invisible realms
But in these visible
Heavens where clouds pass,
Birds fly,
Earth where the trees are rooted
And the grass?

Anapest, Dactyl, Trochee, Iamb
Charles Gullans

The arbitrary limit of a foot,
When I accept its shape, becomes the form
Of thought and then of words. A canvas edge
Is limit, too, the boundary of intent,
The field of vision that the paint defines
With volume, color, mass, and vivid line
As they delineate the farthest reach
Of painterly perception by their means.
A birthday is a boundary of sorts.
And all things have beginning and their ends,
As all things come and go. And so sleep ends,
And wakefulness begins in measured words,
Which turn to measured phrase. A door is shut,
Or it is open to the morning sun.
You speak or you are silent. Poems end
As surely as they are begun. They say,
"This and no more; if there were more to come,
I would be different in each and all

Of my internal measures of my speech,
And every line would have a different weight
And fall upon your ears with different sound.
Another form would blossom in your mind,
And other rhythms beat within your heart."

Prose into Poetry: D. H. Lawrence's
The Rainbow

Ashley Brown

The immediate subject of this paper is a famous novel by a man who also has a reputation as a poet. It would be tempting to spend some time on Lawrence's verse, but I intend to direct my attention to certain qualities of his prose in this one novel and then go off in several unexpected but very poetic directions. Lawrence had some influence on poets who were temperamentally different from himself, but the influence seems to have come through his fiction.

The relationship between prose and poetry is rather close in English literary history, especially since the beginning of the nineteenth century. The poet-novelists who immediately come to mind include Scott, Emily Brontë, Meredith, Hardy, and of course Lawrence. There is a corresponding line of American writers from Melville to Robert Penn Warren. Then there are novelists who did not really succeed as poets, for instance Stephen Crane and Faulkner. These are all romantic or postromantic figures, and they remind us that the romantic movement in English poetry had a great influence on the novel, as one can see by turning from Jane Austen, with her late-Augustan sensibility, to the Brontës or even Dickens. But I think that the prose-poetry relationship also has something to do with the English language, which often invites the prose writer to pause and explore its resonance, its many shades of meaning, its suggestiveness. In French, which I often use as a kind of foil to English, and which is another great language for novel-writing, I don't find a line of writers similar to the one that I just traced among the British and Americans. Indeed the only French writer who has a great reputation as both poet and novelist is Victor Hugo. Stendhal, with his cultivation of a style based on the Code Napoleon, is probably closer to the norm of the French novelists who have carried on a certain kind of tradition ever since the seventeenth century. And French poets, as I know them, seldom approach the kind of prose usage characteristic of American poets as different as Whitman, William Carlos Williams, and Elizabeth Bishop. No wonder that at a certain point in the development of modern French poetry, more than a century ago, the prose-poem was invented, the form that would completely liberate the poet from the usual restraints of verse. Very few English or American poets have used this, for reasons that I have already suggested.

Like the other English writers from Scott to Hardy, Lawrence started out as a poet and then turned to fiction. There is no need here to describe his rapid development as a novelist from *The White Peacock* of 1911 to *Sons and Lovers* of 1913. He was an impatient artist, unlike his contemporary Joyce, and at times one hesitates to judge him as an artist at all. Some of his admirers used to think of him more as a prophet. But he had his own ideas about what he wanted the novel to do; he was no longer interested, he said, in "the old stable ego—of the character." And if his characters sometimes seem like floating states of mind, we must respect his intentions. More than most novelists, he relies on a lyrical and symbolic rendition of the action; it is useless to apply the usual criteria of plot-making to his fiction. Perhaps in the end his travel books are the most successful—*Mornings in Mexico*, *Sea and Sardinia*, and *Etruscan Places*, books where he responds directly to landscapes and people and does not have to invent.

All the same, *The Rainbow* is a very original contribution to English fiction, uneven though I think it is, and a brief presentation of it is in order before I move on to my special emphasis on its poetry. Around 1913, after he had published *Sons and Lovers*, Lawrence began to think of a large family chronicle that was to be called *The Sisters*. This was to be the story of three generations of a family named Brangwen in the Midlands, which of course was Lawrence's native region. He wrote very rapidly, changed the title to *The Wedding Ring*, then to *The Rainbow*, and presently he broke up the manuscript into two novels, *The Rainbow* as we now have it, and *Women in Love*, its successor. *The Rainbow* was published in September 1915, and by November it was seized by the police and prosecuted for obscenity. Most people read it after 1920.

The plan of the book is rather loose. We have a prosperous agricultural family, the Brangwens, at some point in the mid-nineteenth century. Lawrence deliberately suppresses dates, as though to suggest that the community lingers on from the timeless era of the Middle Ages. We are aware of the encroachments of the industrial era that is symbolized by the canal and the railroad that are run through the countryside, but the usual events of history—the wars and reigns of important monarchs—are only dimly felt in this remote place. The Brangwen of this generation, Tom, meets Lydia Lensky, a young Polish widow, and their courtship and marriage form the center of the first part of the novel. The marriage is a balancing between alien forces, as Lawrence would say, and its equilibrium corresponds to some lingering vitality in the community where it takes place. But the family situation is not simple. Lydia's young daughter, Anna, whom Tom loves more than his own son, resists his affection. She is far more assertive than her mother. Though she is brought up in the midst of the Brangwens and speaks no Polish, we sense that even when she is a child she will establish her own terms of behavior. Eventually she is "Anna Victrix," which is the title of a long chapter. She marries Will Brangwen, Tom's nephew. Will, a far more complicated person than his uncle, is a failed artist who is passionately drawn to Lincoln Cathedral in the vicinity. If we wanted to make out a case for Lawrence as a poet in prose, we could do no better than point to the famous chapter called "The Cathedral," from which I quote briefly, just to demonstrate certain qualities of style:

Between east and west, between dawn and sunset, the church lay like a seed in silence, dark before germination, silenced after death. Containing birth and death, potential with all the noise and transition of life, the cathedral remained hushed, a great, involved seed, whereof the flower would be radiant life inconceivable, but whose beginning and whose end were the circle of silence. Spanned round with rainbow, the jewelled gloom folded music upon silence, light upon darkness, fecundity upon death, as a seed folds leaf upon leaf and silence upon the root and the flower, hushing up the secret of all between its parts, the death out of which it fell, the life into which it has dropped, the immortality it involves, and the death it will embrace again.[1]

There is, one might say, a self-consciousness about the religious experience here that is peculiarly modern, even though the rhythms of the prose are descended from the poetic books of the Bible. Will Brangwen is a true follower of John Ruskin. His marriage to the independent Anna is far more precarious than that of his uncle and her mother, and meanwhile the community from which they all draw their strength is declining.

Half of the novel—perhaps too much of it—is devoted to the

girlhood and youth of Ursula, the oldest of Will and Anna's children. She is of course even more English and more a Brangwen than her mother; she is also a child of the twentieth century and lacks the certainties of belief that her ancestors, English or Polish, had. The moral issues become more abstract and strident as the past recedes from memory. Neither the grandmother Lydia nor the mother Anna can really help Ursula as she goes out in the world. She is a member of Lawrence's own generation, and her problems are in many ways his. In *Women in Love* she is drawn to Birkin, who is a version of Lawrence himself. At the end of *The Rainbow,* however, only she is left, with an extraordinary vision of promise that I shall presently take up.

Lawrence, according to his own account, is more interested in the "primal forces" that are prior to character than to character itself. If we accept the idea that the novel is the literary form most directly concerned with human conduct, then Lawrence must seem a rather unwilling novelist; he uses the form because it is so available. But he is certainly preoccupied with states of feeling that are very human indeed, and the structure of *The Rainbow,* like that of *Women in Love,* has something of the effect of a musical composition at times, cyclical or at any rate repetitive. Francis Fergusson, who wrote the best general essay on Lawrence that I know, said that "If you go to Lawrence with a great deal of free and undefined emotion, he will orchestrate it for you; he will provide sensuous molds for your emotion to flow into."[2] But Fergusson pointed out in this same essay, which was written in 1933, only three years after Lawrence's death, that "His influence on other writers is different. Whether they agree with him or not, they find him a source or beginning, fertile in problems and nearly devoid of solutions; and they tend to elaborate or crystallize the raw materials of pure perception that he gives them."[3] (Fergusson's essay, "D. H. Lawrence's Sensibility," never collected, appeared in *Hound & Horn* in 1933). In the rest of this paper I shall follow Fergusson's suggestion and take up three passages in *The Rainbow* where Lawrence has provided a source for poems by writers whom we all know.

My first example occurs in the second chapter. Tom Brangwen has settled down with Lydia and little Anna, who "was a sore problem to Brangwen and to all the people at the Marsh."

She made playmates of the creatures of the farmyard, talking to them, telling them the stories she had from her mother, counseling and correcting them. Brangwen found her at the gate leading to the paddock and the duckpond. She was peering through the bars and shouting to the stately white geese that stood in a curving line:

> "You're not to call at people when they want to come. You must not do it."
>
> The heavy, balanced birds looked at the fierce little face and the fleece of keen hair thrust between the bars, and they raised their heads and swayed off, producing the long, can-canking, protesting noise of geese, rocking their ship-like, beautiful white bodies beyond the gate.
>
> "You're naughty, you're naughty," cried Anna, tears of dismay and vexation in her eyes. And she stamped her slipper.
>
> "Why, what are they doing?" said Brangwen.
>
> "They won't let me come in," she said, turning her flushed little face to him.
>
> "Yi, they will. You can go in if you want to," and he pushed open the gate for her.
>
> She stood irresolute, looking at the group of bluey-white geese standing monumental under the grey, cold day.
>
> "Go on," he said.
>
> She marched valiantly a few steps in. Her little body started convulsively at the sudden, derisive can-cank-ank of the geese. A blankness spread over her. The geese trailed away with uplifted heads under the low grey sky.
>
> "They don't know you," said Brangwen. "You should tell 'em what your name is."
>
> "They're *naughty* to shout at me," she flashed.[4]

This, I think, is Lawrence at his best: a vivid quick response to a scene, uncomplicated by theory. Now I turn to "Bells for John Whiteside's Daughter" by John Crowe Ransom; this dates from 1924:

> There was such speed in her little body,
> And such lightness in her footfall,
> It is no wonder her brown study
> Astonishes us all.
>
> Her wars were bruited in our high window.
> We looked among orchard trees and beyond,
> Where she took arms against her shadow,
> Or harried unto the pond
>
> The lazy geese, like a snow cloud
> Dripping their snow on the green grass,

> Tricking and stopping, sleepy and proud
> Who cried in goose, Alas,
>
> For the tireless heart within the little
> Lady with rod that made them rise
> From their noon apple-dreams and scuttle
> Goose-fashion under the skies!
>
> But now go the bells, and we are ready,
> In one house we are sternly stopped
> To say we are vexed at her brown study,
> Lying so primly propped.[5]

I could not state when Ransom read *The Rainbow*—probably in 1924, when the American publisher Seltzer reissued the novel— but he was certainly aware of Lawrence and once referred to his "brilliant and fitful" power of language. Suffice it to say that the central image in his poem is remarkably like that in the novel, and indeed several phrases are identical, but Ransom does not sound like Lawrence. He has other poems that rework passages from Hopkins or Stevens or Henry James, and they still are Ransom. The chief difference here—the way in which Ransom "elaborates . . . the raw materials of pure perception"—can be seen in the framework that he creates in the first and last stanzas. The little girl is suddenly dead, for reasons unexplained, but the image of her annoying vitality remains. The framework puts the experience into perspective, and there Ransom, as the finest southern poet of his generation, speaks out through the community, in fact shows his southernness. In a sense the Old South was organized by the public voices of the preacher and the politician, and in this poem, as in others by Ransom, one can catch a distillation of the old manner: "But now go the bells, and we are ready." The poem has a steady focus that the prose passage lacks; the facts of death and life illuminate each other.

Two years before Ransom first published his poem, T. S. Eliot brought out *The Waste Land*. As everyone knows, this is a prime example of art being made out of other art. The famous notes to the poem, which some readers find helpful, are in fact inadequate and even misleading. Some of the sources on which Eliot drew most extensively are not mentioned at all. A case in point is *The Rainbow*. Chapter 13 (which is called "The Man's World") has Ursula as a young schoolteacher, uncertain about her private life and her prospects for a career. Suddenly she receives a summons to appear at the Education Office of Kingston-on-Thames, which is a suburb of London, and if her interview is successful she will probably be offered a post there. This unexpected news starts her reverie:

> . . . as the afternoon wore away, the sweetness of the dream returned again. Kingston-on-Thames—there was such sound of dignity to her. The shadow of history and the glamour of stately progress enveloped her. The palaces would be old and darkened, the place of kings obscured. Yet it was a place of kings for her—Richard and Henry and Wolsey and Queen Elizabeth. She divined great lawns with noble trees, and terraces whose steps the water washed softly, where the swans sometimes came to earth. Still she must see the stately, gorgeous barge of the Queen float down, the crimson carpet put upon the landing stairs, the gentlemen in their purple velvet cloaks, bareheaded, standing in the sunshine grouped on either side waiting.
> "Sweet Thames, run softly till I end my song."[6]

We can be quite sure that Eliot had been reading *The Rainbow* when he was composing *The Waste Land* late in 1921. He did not acknowledge this till a decade later. In *The Criterion*, the issue for July 1931, he mentioned some "marvellous passages" of narrative in Lawrence's books, among them the episode involving Ursula in *The Rainbow*.[7] It may be that Eliot was even more affected by this part of the novel than he suggested. Ursula's quest for love and its attendant sexual encounters are the main concern of her life at this point. The part of *The Waste Land* where Eliot uses Lawrence, "The Fire Sermon," is wholly concerned with this theme, and reading it through after reading Lawrence one sees how close the two writers can be. After Pound insisted that Eliot reject the original opening of "The Fire Sermon," a brilliant but rather coarse parody of *The Rape of the Lock*, Eliot composed the following, obviously set going by Lawrence, as a substitute. We now realize that it is deeply personal.

> The river's tent is broken: the last fingers of leaf
> Clutch and sink into the wet bank. The wind
> Crosses the brown land, unheard. The nymphs are departed.
> Sweet Thames, run softly, till I end my song.
> The river bears no empty bottles, sandwich papers,
> Silk handkerchiefs, cardboard boxes, cigarette ends
> Or other testimony of summer nights. The nymphs are departed.
> And their friends, the loitering heirs of city directors;
> Departed, have left no addresses.[8]

This euphonious "Spenserian" passage is capped by the line from Spenser himself, but that is rudely countered by the debris of the modern scene, and thus we get a double focus, the past juxtaposed with the present, a procedure that is entirely typical of Eliot's modernist poetry. One hundred lines later he returns to Ursula's vision of the queen on her barge:

> Elizabeth and Leicester
> Beating oars
> The stern was formed
> A gilded shell
> Red and gold
> The brisk swell
> Rippled both shores
> Southwest wind
> Carried down stream.[9]

Here we have the complete transmutation of prose into poetry. Eliot's extraordinary rhythmic sense has worked up the image into something that approximates the movement of the river itself. I might remark, somewhat parenthetically, that in the preceding stanza he has created the same movement out of the opening paragraphs of Conrad's *Heart of Darkness*, which is set on the Thames estuary. This entire section of "The Fire Sermon" echoes, at least in its rhythms, the Wagnerian quotation in the early part of *The Waste Land:*

> *Frisch weht der Wind*
> *Der Heimat zu*
> *Mein Irisch Kind*
> *Wo weilest du?*[10]

Eliot's juxtaposition of past and present is sometimes said to be a criticism of the modern scene through an evocation of ancient glories, but anyone with some historical sense should see that the image of Elizabeth and Leicester is a kind of sham, a show put on for the populace, luxury without love. Ursula is the sentimentalist; her evocation of the past indeed makes her life in the Midlands seem a drab affair; she is only dissatisfied.

At the end of the novel Ursula, who has been deserted by her lover, merges her private illness with a general malaise: the beautiful hills of the Midlands ruined by indiscriminate coal-mining, the dreadful new houses for the working class, a "dry, brittle, terrible corruption" that extends to the inhabitants themselves. And then she sees the rainbow, the symbol that resolves the novel; the fictional point of view widens:

The arc bended and strengthened itself till it arched indomitable, making great architecture of light and colour and the space of heaven, its pedestals luminous in the corruption of new houses on the low hill, its arch the top of heaven.

And the rainbow stood on the earth. She knew that the sordid people who crept hard-scaled and separate on the face of the world's corruption were living still, that the rainbow was arched in their blood and would quiver to life in their spirit, that they would cast off their horny covering of disintegration, that new, clean bodies would issue to a new germination, to a new growth, rising to the light and the wind and the clean rain of heaven. She saw in the rainbow the earth's new architecture, the old, brittle corruption of houses and factories swept away, the world built up in a living fabric of Truth, fitting to the overarching heaven.[11]

This final paragraph of the novel has Ursula, the completely liberated individual, accepting a vision of unlimited promise. It is far more precarious than her father's vision of the cathedral, which it seems to repeat; one would suppose it is very transitory, like the rainbow itself. Again I turn to a poet—Auden—who was moved by Lawrence's prose, at least at one time. His first book ends with a sonnet in couplets, that is somewhat complicated in style; it has the nervous energy typical of the early Auden:

> Sir, no man's enemy, forgiving all
> But will his negative inversion, be prodigal:
> Send to us power and light, a sovereign touch
> Curing the intolerable neural itch,
> The exhaustion of weaning, the liar's quinsy,
> And the distortions of ingrown virginity.
> Prohibit sharply the rehearsed response
> And gradually correct the coward's stance;
> Cover in time with beams those in retreat
> That, spotted, they turn though the reverse were great.
> Publish each healer that in city lives
> Or country houses at the end of drives;
> Harrow the house of the dead; look shining at
> New styles of architecture, a change of heart.[12]

In Auden's first book, the *Poems* of 1930, this appears as simply Poem 30, the final poem in the collection. I need not go into the details of its style, with its opening phrase borrowed from Hopkins, its elliptical syntax, its interesting conversion of Freudian terminology. The final line seems to be the crux: "New styles of architecture, a change of heart." This is surely taken over from the last sentence in Lawrence's novel. At first glance Lawrence would not seem to be Auden's kind of writer, any more than he is Ransom's or Eliot's, but in 1930 Auden did subscribe to an ethic in which Lawrence was rather important. In Poem 22 of the same book Lawrence is referred to as a "healer" along with Blake and Homer Lane, an American psychologist who had worked in London, and the poet even says, somewhat jocularly, that "Lawrence was brought down by smut-hounds." The last line of Poem 30 was very famous during the 1930s; it appealed, I suppose, to an audience who shared Auden's youthful exuberance and quasipolitical sympathies. But the poet grew to dislike it. He retained the poem as late as 1945 in the *Collected Poems*, where he called it "Petition." Then he began to drop it from his collections, and in the foreword to the 1966 edition of the *Collected Shorter Poems* he writes: "I once expressed a desire for 'New styles of architecture'; but I have never liked modern architecture. I prefer *old* styles, and one must be honest even about one's prejudices." I think, however, that the poem remains one of Auden's finest early things; its formulation of a certain state of mind and perhaps a certain social condition is memorable. And I suggest that the cumulative effect of *The Rainbow* lies back of the climactic line. This is a perfect example of prose into poetry and also an example of what Francis Fergusson says Lawrence's works are: "invitations to try to realize something."

Notes

1. D. H. Lawrence, *The Rainbow* (New York: Modern Library, n.d.), 189.
2. Francis Fergusson, "D. H. Lawrence's Sensibility," *Hound & Horn* 6 (April–June 1933): 458.
3. Ibid., 462.
4. Lawrence, *The Rainbow*, 60–61.
5. John Crowe Ransom, *Selected Poems* (New York: Knopf, 1945), 8.
6. Lawrence, *The Rainbow*, 342.
7. T. S. Eliot, review of *Son of Women: The Story of D. H. Lawrence* by John Middleton Murray, *The Criterion* 10 (July 1931): 770.
8. T. S. Eliot, *Collected Poems, 1909–1935* (New York: Harcourt Brace, 1936), 78.
9. Ibid., 82–82.
10. Ibid., 70.
11. Lawrence, *The Rainbow*, 467.
12. W. H. Auden, *Poems* (London: Faber and Faber, 1933), 89.

The Kensington Quartets
M. C. Bradbrook

Eliot's original title, *The Kensington Quartets,* locates his poems where he lived in the 1930s and early 1940s, near to his church, Saint Stephen's, Gloucester Road, which drew him at first to Chesterfield Gardens, then to the presbytery, Church House, from 1934–37; then to a flat with the vicar, Eric Cheetham, in the nearby Emperor's Gate at No. 11. From here, when the war broke out, he enrolled as an air raid warden at the local post, but in September 1940 moved to Shamley Green, near Guildford. Coming up to London, he firewatched two nights a week in Russell Square in a flat above the office of Faber and Faber, sleeping either there or with the Fabers at Hampstead, or at his club, the Oxford and Cambridge, while continuing at Saint Stephen's as churchwarden, whence he could take the Piccadilly Line from Gloucester Road to Russell Square. In the London of *Four Quartets,* the Underground as Inferno counterpoints the scenes in country places from which the poems take their names—although except for "The Dry Salvages," Eliot's connections were slight, with only one visit each to Burnt Norton, East Coker, and Little Gidding. Each marked a staging post where in the journey through time he encountered the timeless. He once thought in his ribald voice to use an epigraph from Dicken's "Time is a rum thing ain't it?"

The Waste Land was mainly set in London, as Empson observed; but in *Four Quartets,* the Timeless was woven through the pattern laid in the daily life in London, where Eliot received the Sacrament every day; where, in the words of Institution, "Do this in remembrance of me," the worshiper is taken into the upper room centuries ago, where the same Presence is now and forever there, in a moment in time that altered all time to come.

> The dripping blood our only drink,
> The bloody flesh our only food.
> In spite of which we like to think

> That we are sound, substantial flesh and blood
>
> ("East Coker," IV)

Eliot did not wish Christian implications to be overt, but at this point he reveals them.

Again, in spite of this, we call this Friday Good. In the unpublished lecture at Edinburgh in 1937, now in the Houghton Library at Harvard, Eliot said that Shakespeare,

> when I am in a sensitive enough mood . . . makes me see *through* the ordinary classified emotions of our active life into a world of emotion and feeling beyond, of which I am ordinarily not aware. What he makes me feel is not so much that his characters are creatures like myself, but that I am a creature like his characters, taking part, like them in the common action, of which I am for the most part unaware.[1]

The two plays preceding *Four Quartets, Murder in the Cathedral* (1934) and *The Family Reunion* (1939), illustrate this strongly but not as strongly as *The Cocktail Party*, which followed (1949).

Eliot returned to lyric, since drama was interrupted by the war, to start with an expansion of "Burnt Norton" (1935), itself expanded from a speech originally designed for the Second Priest after the exit of the Second Tempter.[2] Eliot closed *The Criterion* just before the outbreak of hostilities in 1939, and *The Family Reunion* had closed after five weeks. In February 1940, during the "phony war," he quickly wrote "East Coker" and equally quickly in January 1941 "The Dry Salvages," but "Little Gidding" proved more difficult and did not appear till after some gestation, in October 1942, the series being first published on 11 May 1943 in the United States. Eliot felt, as he had of *The Waste Land*, that the conclusion was the best: "the second is better than the first, the third is better than the second, and the fourth is best of all."[3]

Eliot interweaves his inner life, or inner journey till "a mysterious pattern of reality appears as from a palimpsest."[4] Social, religious, theological material, the topographical, and the historic with words of other writers provide the instruments on which the themes are played. The quartets are prefaced with two Greek quotations, the first of which says "Although the Word is common to all, most men live as each had a private wisdom of his own" (Heraclitus). He had allowed that the readers' version of a poem may be different from the poet's; he even said it might be better (*The Music of Poetry*, 1942). For every reader of *Four Quartets*, some one theme may predominate. I shall begin with the last and the best poem, "Little Gidding," because the place is part of my own experience. Little Gidding is just down the road from Cambridge to Peterborough (Eliot may have visited it from Magdalene) and—four years after Eliot—I served as an air raid warden in the district he had served, although it was the V2 or flying bomb that hit London in 1944 and not the German Air Force. This relates me to section IIb, for these are the very streets I trod, though not in patrol, for my duty was in a cellar with the communications unit. Here I heard the horn sounding the All Clear at the ending of interminable night, but there was no ghost among the clattering machines to fade upon the blowing of the horn. My own memories imply that Eliot's solitary patrol is an inner vision imposed upon a setting, not a typical or even a possible event, but one built on many layers.

My head warden, a splendid bus conductor named Dagger, cried in anguish when one crump came very close, "Oh, there goes the Albert Memorial!" (evidently his particular shrine), but picking up the telephone, hastily added with relief, "No, it's only the Royal Geographical Society!"

Kensington was where Eliot first met Pound and Yeats in 1914; from his prison at Pisa, Pound was later to write:

> What thou lovest well remains
>   the rest is dross.
> What thou lov'st well shall not be reft from thee
> What thou lov'st well is thy true heritage
>
> and the Serpentine will look just the same
> and the gulls be as neat on the pond
> and the sunken garden unchanged
> and God knows what else is left of our London
>   my London, your London.

(Cantos 81 and 80)

Pound's little three-cornered house was in Church Walk, next to Saint Mary Abbot's and also near a flat round the corner in Holland Park Chambers, where he lived after his marriage to Dorothy Shakespeare, daughter of Yeat's friend Olivia Shakespeare. On 10 January 1957, after marrying Valerie Fletcher Eliot returned to Church Walk for his wedding breakfast, as this was now the house of the officiating priest at Saint Barnabas, the church in which he found Jules Laforgue had also been married.

Besides Kensington there is only a brief glimpse in *Four Quartets* of the City where Eliot worked from 1917 to 1925 as an

employee in Lloyds Bank. As Pound was working for Yeats (on
Noh drama), the familiar compound ghost of "Little Gidding" IIb,
Dante and Yeats, included one of Pound's chief interests, shared
with Eliot, as a native of Eliot's Kensington. (In his later years
Eliot and Valerie lived just south of Kensington High Street, in
Kensington Court Gardens.)

Until the end of the second world war Kensington was still like
a village, an enclave within London, while now the whole place
feels like a vast air terminal—there is even one in the High Street.
In 1942–45, when I lived in Prince of Wales Terrace, Kensington,
Church Street was still "our London," beautified by little antique
shops, small Italian restaurants (Ciccio's for me), and secondhand
bookshops. Every day I walked past Saint Stephen's, Gloucester
Road, to my bus for the Board of Trade's offices, but I thought it
was a Roman Catholic Church because its notice board men-
tioned only Low Mass, High Mass, or Confessions and did not
include the name of the churchwarden. I believe some people
went to church just to see Eliot handing round the offertory plate.

For Eliot there were already many layers of memory in the core
of the Royal Borough, and the beginning of the second world war
must have felt to him a dreadful mirror image of the first. The
"descent" in "East Coker" III echoes both Milton and Sir Edward
Gray ("the lights are going out all over Europe")

> O dark dark dark. They all go into the dark.
> The vacant interstellar spaces, the vacant into the vacant,
> The captains, merchant bankers, eminent men of letters,
> The generous patrons of art, the statesmen and the rulers,
> Distinguished civil servants, chairmen of many committees,
> Industrial lords and petty contractors, all go into the dark.

This is not an empty roll but very like the membership of the
Moot, except that the roll is not that of Christians; "Clerisy" was a
condition of belonging to the Moot, which Eliot joined after the
Oxford Conference in 1937.[5] It is reminiscent of "Difficulties of a
Statesman."

In September 1939 the first signals of hostilities were the eerie
darkness of railway stations, streets and ports, the timid hand-
torches, the blue light at nodal points.

Darkness is a theme of *Four Quartets*, beginning in "Burnt
Norton" with "a dim world" but "not darkness purifying the
soul," which belongs to the mystics' Dark Night of the Soul.

> Descend lower, descend only
> Into the world of perpetual solitude,
> World not world, but that which is not world,
> Internal darkness, deprivation
> And destitution of all property
>
> ("Burnt Norton," III)

This in "East Coker" is welcomed when "the darkness shall be the light":

> let the dark come upon you
> Which shall be the darkness of God.
>
> ("East Coker," III)

In "The Dry Salvages," the solitude "between midnight and dawn, when the past is all deception, The future futureless" is for anxious worried women on shore, while at sea voices are heard "at nightfall, in the rigging and the aerial" (I, III). In "Little Gidding" the fires of hell fade

> After the dark dove with the flickering tongue
> Had passed below the horizon of his homing
>
> (II)

In the uncertain hour of waning dusk, recreated in *terza rime* of Dante's form, comes the voice "both intimate and unidentifiable":

> So I assumed a double part, and cried
> And heard another's voice cry: "What, are *you* here?"
>
> (II)

The original version was "Are you here, Ser Brunetto?" Brunetto Latini (*Inferno*, Canto 15) had long haunted Eliot's poetry; but here too was Yeats who "left his body on a distant shore" in January 1939, and perhaps Swift, whom Yeats had raised as a ghost so powerfully in the *Words Upon the Window Pane* with the irony of "the gifts reserved for age"[6] and "the laceration of laughter at what ceases to amuse" ("saeva indignatio ulterius cor lacerare"). This is the later Yeats, not the one Eliot first met in Kensington, and the only place in *Four Quartets* where irony, so pervasive in the earlier Eliot, emerges; it is not directed outwards, but towards the self. In this confessional poem there is nothing about the enemy without, only that within:

> Of things ill done and done to others' harm
> Which once you took for exercise of virtue.
>
> ("Little Gidding," IIb)

Eliot's family motto *(Tacuit et facit)* meant that it was not decent to evoke this recantation during the hubbub in his centenary year about his alleged anti-Semitism. While he was struggling with "Little Gidding," Eliot went to Sweden with George Bell, bishop of Chichester, who met there Deitrich Bonhoeffer, German pastor and martyr, who was to be imprisoned and later hanged by Hitler (the English Foreign Secretary ignored the message that Bell took). The Moot, the religious group that Eliot belonged to from 1937, was largely led by Karl Mannheim, professor at the London School of Economics, a Jew who had fled from Germany in 1933. Eliot's outbursts against Jewish financiers belong only to the years 1917–25, when he worked on foreign correspondence at Lloyds Bank; the only name directly mentioned, in "A Cooking Egg," was Sir Alfred Mond, head of ICI and of German Jewish extraction; he is contrasted with Sir Philip Sidney. Other names are imaginary, but Eliot did not repress or obliterate this poetry as he did for the animosity of *After Strange Gods*.

From that earlier period evoked it is Yeats and not the anti-Semitic Pound who appears; but this is not the Kensington of the second world war. There is nothing of the Norwegian navy in "The Dry Salvages," although they dominated the scene (it was they who rescued me from my one "incident" after a V2 landed on the de Vere Hotel). The British-Norwegian Institute, however, received a lecture from Eliot, and he wrote for their literary magazine, *The Norseman*.

Later Donald Davie felt some fury at "The Dry Salvages," surprising Helen Gardner, for instance.[7] But Davie had been a young naval officer with the convoys to Murmansk through the Barents Sea in winter, while Eliot was recalling the Massachusetts sea he had sailed as a boy, although it was the Battle of the Atlantic, Britain's most testing moment, which aroused him. Rear-Admiral Samuel Eliot Morison, USN, who knew this coast, wrote, "These lines and indeed all that follow, ring a bell in any sailor's heart."[8] Not in Donald Davie's heart, who, like myself, felt the distance from the direct impact of that time. It can be seen in Dover Wilson's edition of *King Henry V* with its dedication to Wavell, "star of England in her darkest hour," and in Olivier's film of *King Henry V*, shot at Powercourt in County Wicklow. Those who did not know Dover Wilson's life (including his efforts in South Africa) can angrily react, as did Terence Hawkes in *That Shakespearean Rag* (1986), for the Heritage does not conclude with one generation.

Eliot's direct war verses were written for an exhibition of photographs in New York, shown shortly after Dunkirk, as an appeal from his new to his old countrymen. These foreshadow some of the themes he was to use in "Little Gidding," refined and blended with others. In *Collected Poems 1909–1962* he notes:

> *Defence of the Islands* cannot pretend to be verse, but its date—just after the evacuation from Dunkirk—and occasion have for me a significance which makes me wish to preserve it. . . .
>
> Let these memorials of built stone—music's enduring instrument, of many centuries of patient cultivation of the earth, of English verse
>
> be joined with the memory of this defence of the islands
>
> and the memory of those appointed to the grey ships—battleship, merchantman, trawler—contributing their share to the ages' pavement of British bone on the sea floor
>
> and of those who, in man's newest form of gamble with death, fight the power of darkness in air and fire
>
> and of those who have followed their forebears to Flanders and France, those undefeated in defeat, unalterable in triumph, changing nothing of their ancestors' ways but the weapons
>
> and those again for whom the paths of glory are the lanes and the streets of Britain:
>
> to say, to the past and the future generations of our kin and of our speech, that we took up our positions, in obedience to instructions.

These last lines, evoking the Spartans at Thermopylae, had appeared more negatively in "Gerontion," perhaps in memory of Jean Verdenal, who "was mixed with the mud of Gallipoli" in that earlier war.

> I was neither at the hot gates
> Nor fought in the warm rain

Eliot encountered one air attack while at Faber and Faber's, which he recalls in

> Ash on an old man's sleeve
> Is all the ash the burnt roses leave.
> Dust in the air suspended
> Marks the place where a story ended.
>
> ("Little Gidding," II)

The roses of the garden that appear so often in Eliot's poetry are already dusty on a bowl of rose leaves in "Burnt Norton" (where he was accompanied on his only visit by Emily Hale, "figlia che piange" of earlier times and to whom he had sent roses). Dust got into everything when the bombs fell, it was our souvenir; pages in my Bible and my Yeats still show it.

Eliot accordingly first took up his position near to Saint Stephen's, Gloucester Road, which still survives in its dull early Victorian stolidity. It does not appear in this poem, however, but is replaced by the little chapel built by Nicholas Ferrar, friend of Lancelot Andrewes, representing that tradition of seventeenth-century devotion to which Eliot at first gave adherence more than fifteen years before. It appears before the firewatching scene in the difficult section II; but is equally unimpressive.

> when you leave the rough road
> And turn behind the pig-stye to the dull facade
> And the tombstone.
>
> ("Little Gidding," I)

The tomb is Nicholas Ferrar's, also a friend of George Herbert, who founded the Community at Little Gidding, which was broken up by Cromwell's army—its brass font was lately recovered from the nearby horse pond. Eliot placed tombstones in the last three quartets: "East Coker's" never entered the village, but goes from a field outside to the graveyard where Eliot now lies buried. "The Dry Salvages," filled with memories of the dead at sea, ends

> We, content at the last
> If our temporal reversion nourish
> (Not too far from the yew-tree)
> The life of significant soil.
>
> ("Dry Salvages," V)

The yew trees of the English churchyards provided the wood for weaponry in earlier times. In "Little Gidding" death is pervasive,

> a step to the block, to the fire, down the sea's throat
> Or to an illegible stone: and that is where we start.
>
> ("Little Gidding," V)

Eliot had visited Little Gidding on "a lovely day at the end of May" in 1936, when the hedges would have been white "with voluptuary sweetness," but the visit in the poem is in December since the winter is the fourth of the four seasons in the quartets. Fire the fourth element, after air, earth, water:

> Midwinter spring is its own season
>
> .   .   .   .
>
> . . . the short day is brightest, with frost and fire,
> The brief sun flames the ice, on pond and ditches,
> In windless cold that is the heart's heat,
> Reflecting in a watery mirror
> A glare that is blindness in the early afternoon.
>
> ("Little Gidding," I)

Eliot "faded" summer into winter, as he "faded" Lancashire or the Scottish coast into Cape Ann, Saint Stephen's into Little Gidding, Yeats into Brunetto. History can be freedom for the poet. A pentecostal fire burns in its history, shines at the chapel in its forlorn state, as ruined as London churches; but

> You are not here to verify,
> Instruct yourself, or inform curiosity
> Or carry report. You are here to kneel
> Where prayer has been valid.
>
> ("Little Gidding," I)

Like Pascal's "Feu!" the scene is *within*. At Little Gidding, the Presence shines "the spring time, but not in time's covenant" in tongues of fire "beyond the language of the living": as had been written in "The Dry Salvages" V, the point of intersection of the timeless with time, is an occupation for the saint. The Community here is now "not in the scheme in generation," the purpose "altered in fulfillment." It is beyond death, though death must first be passed (but the moment of death is every moment, "Dry Salvages" III). History is now and England but

> There are other places
> Which are also the world's end, some at the sea jaws,
> Or over a dark lake, in a desert or a city—
>
> ("Little Gidding," I)

When I was being rowed over a lake in Berlin soon after the war, the young student shipped his oars and said in a cutting voice, "There are many RAF planes at the bottom of this lake." I took the thrust silently but said inwardly to myself, "And thank heaven my brother's Wellington was not one of them."

The Community at Little Gidding was engaged in sacraments and prayer. The psalms were recited daily. Men and women, even children took part. This "Protestant Nunnery" may have provided a precedent for Eliot for the Moot, which came to existence in a different form in 1937. In a letter to me Dr. Kathleen Bliss wrote,

> The first idea had been to constitute themselves into an Order on the lines of Coleridge's Clerisy, and T. S. Eliot contributed an early paper on the Clerisy. It was taken to pieces in his gently devastating way by Karl Mannheim on Elites. Anyway, we finally came back from going public, and settled for being a group of friends who submitted their thoughts in written papers for criticism. J. H. O's wide reading and deafness made him an excellent chairman and Eric Fenn's minutes are superb. Eliot was one of the "collaborators" named on p. 1 of the *Christian Newsletter,* and was a pretty regular member of the Editorial Board which met in the Board Room of W. H. Smith and Sons at the corner of Kingsway and Portugal Street. I have very happy memories of these meetings. The Newsletter had a very wide influence— through it, many people were helped through the war; there were scores of discussion groups all over the country and the forces (led by Chaplains). Robert Runcie told me that it was a major influence on his decision to be ordained. . . . Eliot told me that doing something for youth was the only constructive response to the general gloom which we felt and shared much more keenly than may most others, as he saw what was about to crash down.

Dr. Bliss asserts that the fruit was seen in the universities, where later other groups of the same kind sprang up; and in the Butler Education Act of 1944, the Moot had many figures from public life—there is a list in Kojecky's book—and it closed after the death of Karl Mannheim. She dissents from the account given by Ackroyd in his *Life.* J. H. Oldham, whose *Life* she wrote, was chairman of the World Council of Churches in Geneva after the war and was thoroughly ecumenical. Although in 1943 Eliot denounced the unification of the churches of South India, in which Kathleen Bliss had played a part, his mood in the early 1940s was in general far more generous than the convert's harshness of the 1930s; and if he remained an attendant at Saint Stephen's, his friends included a wider spectrum. As he now recalled the religious wars of the seventeenth century,

> These men, and those whose opposed them
> And those whom they opposed

> Accept the constitution of silence
> And are folded in a single party.
>
> ("Little Gidding," III)

The men were Charles I, Laud, and Milton, whom he recalled were "united in the strife which divided them." Eliot's poem itself revived the Community at Little Gidding, for in 1947, he and Alan Maycock set up the Friends of Little Gidding, from which grew the Community of Christ the Sower, a group of lay people who now reside in houses formed out of the pigstyes and farm buildings. Some members work outside, others run a small farm and manage the domestic life there, holding a weekly ecumenical celebration of the Lord's Supper, daily prayers, and the study of scripture, as in the seventeenth century. Friends can join and visitors are welcome.[9] So Eliot's activity remains in the place as a living force.

When he returned to Kensington after the war, Eliot did not go back to church lodgings but shared a flat with John Hayward from 1946 to his marriage in 1957. This decision indicates a strong theme in the consort of the Quartets, that of poetry in its historic perspective and as the concern of his deepest activity, just as Christianity gave him his deepest experience. "The language of the tribe" was for him an instrument both of his faith and of social concern.

Attachment and detachment, which "flourish in the same hedgerow," and "growing between them, indifference," take us back to "East Coker" with its open field, to "liberation / From the future as well as the past" ("Little Gidding," III) and that glimpse of the blue heaven reflected in the mud beside the pungent wild garlic in "Burnt Norton" III—"Garlic and sapphires in the mud / Clot the bedded axle-tree"—which derives from Mallarmé's "Tonnerre et rubis aux moyeux," where the wheels and the sexual excitement combine in a universal vision.[10]

In each of the *Four Quartets* section V expresses the theme of the language itself, but in the last quartet this theme is slight, compared with its weight in the other three. In section III of "Little Gidding" Eliot uses a voice from the fourteenth century, that of the anchorite Julian of Norwich,

> Sin is Behovely, but
> All shall be well, and
> All manner of thing shall be well,

to be re-echoed in the conclusion. We have reached the place where history is not servitude but freedom, so that places and faces "become renewed, transfigured, in another pattern" ("Little Gidding," III).

In the lyrics of "Little Gidding" (II and IV) symbols are transformed paradoxically so that "the way up and the way down are the same," as the epigraph from Heraclitus says. Pentecost and the infernal fire are brought together: when "the dark dove with the flickering tongue / Had passed below the horizon of his homing" (II), we find "The dove descending breaks the air / With flame of incandescent terror" (IV) as the Presence witnessed at Christ's baptism (Matthew 3) proclaims, "This is my Son, my beloved," proclaiming also the cross and the resurrection. As in the Transformation on the road to Jerusalem (Mark 9), the Presence unites this man with the power behind the universe and transfigures the whole creation through the death of "the intolerable shirt of flame."

Both Dante and Yeats had worn their own "intolerable shirt of flame"; in the Greek tragedy, Herakles died in the poisoned shirt sent by his wife, but on his funeral pyre he was stellified by his father, Zeus (recently Christopher Ricks recalled Herakles' shirt of flame but omitted the stellification).

For Eliot baptism had been a death, as he said in the "Journey of the Magi," and for any Christian, baptism is to be signed with the cross and so with Christ's death. So we are left with

> the choice of pyre or pyre—
> To be redeemed from fire by fire.
>
> ("Little Gidding," IV)

As Deitrich Bonhoeffer, denouncer of "Cheap grace," knew, it was

> A condition of complete simplicity
> (Costing not less than everything)
>
> ("Little Gidding," IV)

During the "phony war," "East Coker" recorded this ("O dark dark dark")—Gethsemane was agony before Golgotha—"Let's get it over," said Jesus to Judas at the Last Supper. Even "Burnt Norton," written in the year Hitler invaded the Rhineland, is stamped with foreboding, for by that date the war was inevitable, indeed it had been seen by General Ludendorf in *The Coming War*, from which Eliot had taken the catalogue of armaments in

"Difficulties of a Statesman" (1931). In "Burnt Norton" (III) the
London Underground is the world of the spiritually dead:

> Driven on the wind that sweeps the gloomy hills of London,
> Hampstead and Clerkenwell, Campden and Putney,
> Highgate, Primrose and Ludgate. Not here
> Not here the darkness, in this twittering world.

Primrose and Ludgate are within the City itself, the earlier vision
of *The Waste Land*. This wind from the Dantesque depth blows
before and after time. The other hills are north of the City, where
at that time Eliot had lived with Vivien, in Marylebone and
Clarence Gate; in her mental hospital she was now farther north.
In "East Coker," the Underground stops between stations—that
is, at the beginning of the second world war. The most individual
confession of "halting" is that of the writer:

> So here I am, in the middle way, having had twenty years—
> Twenty years largely wasted, the years of *l'entre deux guerres*—
> Trying to learn to use words, and every attempt
> Is a wholly new start, and a different kind of failure.

("East Coker," V)

The vision from Mallarmé, with the coarse garlic smell, the
reflection of the empyrean in the mud, and the re-echoing in the
bloodstream of the deep rhythm of the whole universe of stars,
unites in a musical composition ("Burnt Norton" II): but we have
already heard that "Only through time time is conquered"
("Burnt Norton" II). In the last poem, "the drawing of this Love
and the voice of this Calling" is through the Love that devised the
torment and whoever endures it in human form; "take, eat" is the
repetition of the words of that historic moment in time.

In *Four Quartets* there are not different characters, speaking in
different voices as in *The Waste Land*, but rather Eliot in different
phases of his life: with his first love, Emily Hale, at Burnt Norton;
with his ancestors in the churchyard at East Coker, where now he
lies (we never get into the actual village of East Coker); his youth
at Cape Ann; at Little Gidding, ancestor of Saint Stephen's, dating
from the age of the English church that Eliot studied most deeply
but echoing the devotion of the fourteenth-century mystic Julian:
the shirt of flame is now a crown

> And all shall be well and
> All manner of thing shall be well

> When the tongues of flame are in-folded
> Into the crowned knot of fire
> And the fire and the rose are one.
>
> ("Little Gidding," V)

The flat symbol is that of a prayer before a crucifix. As the old peasant said when the Curé d'Ars asked him what he did while sitting so long before the crucifix at church, "I sits and looks at him, and he looks at me."

For Eliot moments of illumination in verse came by "prayer, observance, discipline, thought and action":

> For most of us, this is the aim
> Never here to be realised;
> Who are only undefeated
> Because we have gone on trying
>
> ("The Dry Salvages," V)

Eliot's last word on Little Gidding came twenty years later, in his booklet on George Herbert (1962), the last work he ever wrote. On his deathbed Herbert had sent his poems to Nicholas Ferrar of Little Gidding, who was responsible for their appearance in 1633 in a superb edition printed by the Cambridge University Press from the sign of the Angel on Market Hill; for Herbert had asked Ferrar to burn them unless he thought they would be of some use to "any dejected poor soul." Eliot thought *The Temple* "a record of the spiritual struggles of a man of intellectual power and emotional intensity who gave great toil to perfection of his verses," "a man of delicate physical health who had known much illness," whose close relation to his predecessor as poet, John Donne, led Eliot to close examination of the fine shades in Herbert's use of words. He urges that it is not necessary to accept Herbert's beliefs in order to enjoy his poetry and that enjoyment must come before we can hope to penetrate the poet's mind and find "the fluctuations of emotion between despair and bliss, between agitation and serenity, and the discipline of suffering which leads to peace of spirit!" It is also himself he delineates, as Yeats fades into Brunetto. Eliot's multiple vision springs from a palimpsest to a holograph, as Brooker and Bentley have recently shown in *The Waste Land*.

Notes

1. Ronald Bush, *T. S. Eliot: A Study in Character and Style* (New York: Oxford University Press, 1984), 165.

2. Helen Gardner, *The Composition of 'Four Quartets'* (London: Faber, 1978), 39.

3. Ibid., 4.

4. Bush, *T. S. Eliot*, 165.

5. Roger Kojecky, *T. S. Eliot's Social Criticism* (London: Faber, 1971).

6. Bush, *T. S. Eliot*, 235.

7. Gardner, 'Four Quartets,' 4.

8. As quoted by Helen Gardner, 'Four Quartets,' 51, from *The American Neptune*, 1965.

9. The Community, Little Gidding, Huntingdon PE17 5RJ.

10. Translated by Roger Fry, 1936, and printed by Gardner, 'Four Quartets,' with one howler, "sun" for "sin" in line 6.

11. Jewel Spears Brooker and Joseph Bentley, *"The Waste Land": Modernism and the Limits of Interpretation* (Amherst: University of Massachusetts Press, 1989).

Know Thyself

On Revising the English Dictionary
R. L. Barth

When, after long work, Scaliger beheld
His dictionary finished, he felt compelled,
Bored with the slight performance and outraged
At useless study and the trifles paged,
To groan aloud: "This punishment upon
All convicts: make them write a lexicon!"
  How just that sublime, learned, and shrewd man,
Fitted for more important volumes than
A dictionary, should indeed repent
Years lost that had been, once were, better spent
With ancient poets, generals; with the wise
And virtuous; with empire and what lies
Behind the movements of the universe!
  Exempla deceive us. Listen to the curse
Of little scholars who, rashly, compare
Their works, themselves to you. Pedants, beware:
Know yourselves and potentiality!
Greatest of men, it was not granted me
In scholarship or ire to equal you—
Whether because of my dull blood or through
Long idleness or a weak intellect.
  Hard at your sterile work, you could detect
Wisdom beyond words' rough terrain; when done,
She took you to her regions; and you won
Art's praise, heard once discordant tongues surround
You, who led them from exile, with harmonious sound.
  I am my own man, now that I am free
Of this long work; and yet a deep ennui
Awaits me. Soon black, sullen ease will come,
Harsher than duty, with the tedium

Of easy living. Worries spring from worries,
And a brash company of problems hurries
Behind to harass me with cares on cares.
My empty mind conjures its own nightmares.
How noisy pleasures and late meals invite,
Now quiet places. Impatient of the night
And fearing day, I vainly call on sleep.
Anxious, I hurry everything—or keep
Circling to see if somewhere a wide lane
Will open on a better life, in vain!
What can I do? I meditate each scheme
In vain, till I am forced to one last theme:
Know myself better and, at last, confess
A squalid heart and mind whose power is less.
If learning does not aid materially,
The mind must waste away in penury:
As Phidias, with master's hand and heart.
Lacked skill to chisel thin air into art.
    Still, wherever I go, when I act,
My poverty and poor mind hold me back.
Surveying its works now, the heart is blind
To wealth accumulated by the mind;
And, counting the slow years, never delights
In past accomplishments. The heart indicts
Itself, rejecting honors and the gains
Of a good life; but viewing its domains,
Dreads the huge regions, silent in the night,
Where inane forms and shadows spin in flight.
    Now, what remains? Does a vast darkness wait
These old bones? Should I turn myself to great,
Weighty works? Or if this is too much, dare I
Take up at last—another dictionary?
          —from the Latin of Samuel Johnson (1709–84)

In the Greenwood
Clive Wilmer

When Michael Ryan in that forest glade—
Armed and flak-jacketed, his camouflage
Not disentangled quite from the green shade—
Let out the first spurt of his huge discharge,

He invoked Emptiness: in these dull days
Prince of this land and Regent for the King,
Who broods in exile on our ancient ways
And the green woods of the meandering.

Now, as the echoes die, I hear a man
My countrymen once dreamt of wind his horn—
A note of warning from a vanished wood;

He, gentle yet pugnacious, jovial
And stubbornly endearing, gave up all
His right and fortune to the common good.

On 19 August 1987 a young woman was shot dead in Savernake Forest in the
South of England. The killer was a twenty-seven-year-old gun-collector named
Michael Ryan; he had no obvious motive, though a sexual interest has been
generally inferred. Ryan then turned on the people of the nearby small town of
Hungerford, killing fifteen of them, including his own mother, before commit-
ting suicide.

Bird Watching
David Middleton

For Don Stanford

> *O learn to open the creatures*
> —Richard Baxter

i.
You held those birds so firmly in your mind
Setting them free in song, in poems that defined

A chasm too profound ever to cross:
You marked the abyss as gain, accepted loss.

And yet how well you knew them all the same,
Your "oriole's thin dividing flame,"

Your thrush weaving through the woods' deepening green,
Your sea gull storm-blown out of the sunlight's sheen,

Abstractions from the senses that became
The symbols that were latent in each name.

ii.
This spring in a quiet turn of the garden path
I put out elderberries and a bath

Attracting to my daughter's great delight
Some local birds that came to trust the site.

Now mockingbirds, black grackles, raucous jays
Gathering scattered seeds then flying away

Grace our feeding-station where they wing
Quick-eyed with purpose, alighting to sing

Across the noted chasm to a mind
So different in degree, so like in kind.

The Humanities: Liberator of Mind and Spirit

Cleanth Brooks

> Nothing but liberty can draw men forth from the isolation into which their independence naturally drives them—can compel them to associate together, in order to come to a common understanding, to debate, and to compromise together on their joint concerns. Liberty alone can free them from money-worship, and divert them from their petty, every-day business cares, to teach them and make them feel that there is a country above and beside them. It alone awakens more energetic and higher passions than the love of ease, provides ambition with nobler aims than the acquisition of wealth, and yields the light which reveals, in clear outline, the virtues and the vices of mankind.
>
> —Alexis de Tocqueville, from the preface to *The Old Regime and the Revolution*, trans. John Bonner (1856)

From the very beginning of the United States, *liberty* and *freedom* have been the great watchwords. A few years ago we were voicing them even more frequently than usual, as we rededicated the Statue of Liberty in New York Harbor. Phrases like "The land of the free and the home of the brave" and "Sweet land of liberty" were fervently—but, I suspect, often thoughtlessly—sung. And why not, most of us would ask. *Freedom* and *liberty* do not require special cogitation. Everyone knows what those words mean.

What does the Statue of Liberty stand for? Emma Willard's famous poem speaks of Liberty standing by the "golden door" as if inviting the "huddled masses" of Europe to enter into prosperity; and freedom from poverty is a worthy goal, though not easy to achieve. But is this the only liberty for which she stands?

The official description of the lady describes her as "enlightening the world." I would like to think that her torch is meant to provide an enlightenment of mind and spirit as well as the way to political liberty and economic prosperity. I would even argue that true political liberty involves a liberation of the mind. Since the statue's brazen lips cannot form human speech, it is no use asking her what kind of liberty she represents. But by the same argument, she cannot say me nay if I contend that the enlightenment she would shed on this country involves a liberation of mind and spirit.

All of which brings me to the liberal arts and what they represent—or should represent. Why are they called liberal arts at all? Why is welding, for example, though enormously useful, not regarded as a liberal art? Or auto mechanics? Or business systems?

The traditional liberal arts—studies such as literature, history, and philosophy—can indeed trace their distinguishing name back to the same Latin adjective that we find in *liberty* and *liberate*. But what is the relation of freedom to the liberal arts? Is the term *liberal* as applied to them merely fanciful? No. These studies were originally called liberal because the ancient world regarded them as the proper education for free men as opposed to an education for slaves. See the *Oxford English Dictionary*, meaning no. 1.

I think it fair to say that average citizens have no idea of why certain arts were ever called "liberal," and today they certainly see no connection between them and freedom. They are more than likely to think of the so-called liberal arts as in themselves quite useless, education refinements, mere luxuries, acquisitions nice to have if readily affordable, but far from essential. No wonder that more and more of our citizens think of college itself as a sort of superior training school that gets its students ready for a job.

Recently one of our members of Congress was quoted in the *New York Times* as saying that he meant to choose not only his daughter's college for her, but her curriculum. He wanted her to enroll in courses that would ensure her a job—not such things as the study of literature and history. *He* evidently saw no connection between her education and her life as a free person. In fairness to the congressman, I am sure he is far from alone in holding such opinions.

On the other hand, Thomas Jefferson, that notable Founding Father of our country, did see a connection. His own education included the liberal arts, and he wanted even those citizens who supported themselves by the use of the plow and the spade, or the carpenter's or mechanic's tools, to have at least the rudiments of an education befitting free men. For if all men were created equal, as he had asserted in the Declaration of Independence, they had to be able to read, write, and reason if they were also allowed to vote. Ignorant voters would make poor decisions. Such voters make poor decisions today.

You may fairly object that I have not yet met head on the question raised earlier: what is the actual connection between the liberal arts and freedom? Why is it fitting and necessary that a free person be skilled in the liberal arts? In short, from just what do the liberal arts free us? Am I implying here that these arts are also liberating arts?

I do imply that. Think about the matter for a moment. Each of us is born into a certain narrow environment, into a particular nook or cranny among the millions to be found on this planet, and born into one thin stratum of time. For most of us it will amount to some seventy years or fewer, whereas human history as recorded in one way or another stretches back over thousands of years. To be freed from such narrow constrictions on our vision of what lies all about us and behind and beyond us is a matter of great consequence in itself. When we regard space and time not simply as abstractions but as constituting the great arena in which various kinds of human beings have tried to realize themselves; when we are able—at least vicariously—to enter into the world of Homer's bronze-age warriors or the world of the Mayan civilizations or that of our forefathers two hundred years ago, our own lives become richer, more spacious, multidimensional. If we do not in the process become somewhat wiser, it will be because we are incapable of learning from those thousands of examples of success and failure enacted earlier on this planet.

I want to emphasize the importance of our liberation into the full range of history. It is here that the liberal arts come into something like their true importance. Shorn of historical associations, travel itself loses most of its attraction. Even the finest cathedral becomes to many a bored and weary tourist simply another famous edifice to be ticked off his list as having been "seen," and each new castle becomes indistinguishable from the last.

It may seem odd, however, that I, a good provincial, should stress so heavily the importance of surmounting the narrow particularities of the place and time of our birth and childhood. I do not advocate an education that pulls us up by the roots. In my opinion, we have today entirely too many rootless people roving around this country, people lacking local and even family ties. That kind of mobility can be unsettling and unhealthy.

I am sure that literature in this country would suffer terribly if we lost our sense of belonging to a special place and to a particular era. Though a southerner, I have now lived for many years in Connecticut. My end of that state is jammed with writers of all sorts. But it is amusing to notice how few are native to the state and how the rest of them continue to produce novels and stories set in their own native regions. Apparently most of us need a fixed point of reference to which we have to relate the rest of our experience. William Faulkner is an apt example. In spite of his criticism of the shortcomings of his native South, he could not, and confessedly did not want to, escape it. It gave him a vantage point from which to judge general experience.

This compatibility of a genuine provincialism with a total world view provides me with an opportunity to make an important point about the liberal arts. They do not seek to eliminate our individuality, but to discipline it. They do not ask us to give up our inner beings in favor of some enlightened substitute *new* self. On the contrary, we are persuaded to do no more than measure our values and beliefs against others; not necessarily to give up our own, but to reshape and modify them in the light of other experiences; at the very least to take into account the values of other cultures.

Earlier I interpreted the liberal arts as not merely arts appropriate to the education of free people, but considered them as possessed of a liberating power in themselves. Such is apparently the way in which St. John's College at Annapolis, one of the nation's most interesting liberal arts colleges, views them. Indeed, the motto of that institution represents a succinct and pithy statement of what those arts seek to do. It consists of a string of interlocking Latin puns: *Liberos libris librisque liberamus.* If your Latin is as rusty as mine, you may be grateful for a little help from the Latin dictionary. *Liberos* means children, specifically the children of free men, children who are to be educated to become free adults. The first *libris* is the ablative plural of *liber,* a book. The second *libris* is the ablative plural of *libra,* a pair of balances or scales for weighing objects. *Liberamus* is easy: it means "we liberate." A literal translation of the whole would read: We free the children of free men by means of books and balances. But I prefer to translate more freely still and in a manner more nearly in the spirit of the college motto: "We make young people truly free by means of books and scientific instruments." I should explain here that the exact sciences can also be taught as liberal arts, as apparently is the aim at St. John's College. But they are not always taught in this spirit elsewhere. (I must go on to concede that too often literature and history are not taught in that spirit either.) Any subject matter can be allowed to degenerate into a mere pile of information. Important as information is, it has to be interpreted. Raw information cannot organize itself into meaningful patterns. As mere information, facts are inert.

Yet in years in which we plan to do special honor to Liberty as she holds up her torch, enlightening the world, more and more college students turn away from the liberating arts to those studies that they believe will ensure their getting good jobs. Obviously they do not see the choice as between gaining a good job or a liberated mind. Nor do their parents, who may have made hard sacrifices to see them through college. In modern America they are likely to see the choice as between essentials and frills—between things you have to have and things that you can do without.

I could argue that the liberal arts provide what is actually the best basic training for any job of consequence. A highly successful industrialist has told me that he will not hire a person, whatever his technical skills, who lacks a liberal education. A technician who works in a large clinic where I am a patient has told me that the physician in charge insists that his technicians also be, as she put it, "reading and writing people."

I could also argue that there is enough time in our systems for both, that if the primary and secondary schools did their jobs satisfactorily, then the years required to move from the first grade up through four years of college are enough to provide a reasonable introduction into the liberal arts and also to train students more specifically for particular vocations.

As it is, too many colleges and universities have to admit students who are not really prepared to do college work. It is absurd, for example, to have to provide courses in remedial reading and call them college work, or to teach students how to write lucid and well-organized English prose. An ability to read and write competently is a necessary requirement for good citizenship. I might add to these attainments the learning of the rudiments of logic so that one can detect falsities and defects in one's own or another person's reasoning. To ask less than these requirements makes a mockery of what we like to call higher education.

Yet important as such liberation from narrow concerns and limited horizons may be, I am aware that for many modern

Americans what I have said so far in an advocacy of the liberal arts may not constitute a very telling argument. Many a young man or woman feels himself or herself in possession of all the freedom needed for happiness. Besides, once you acquire plenty of money, you will have the means to buy everything a truly good life requires. Actually, a great many people do not want any more liberty. Was there ever such an age as this for seeking help in making decisions: help from the marriage counselor, the job counselor, and the psychiatrist? Was there ever such a plethora of how-to-improve-oneself books on sale?

So I propose another line of defense for the liberal arts. I do not guarantee its effectiveness, but it at least engages the issues about which the average citizen wants to be convinced. Besides, the relative novelty of my line of defense may be appealing.

My argument involves still another way of viewing the liberal arts. They are the arts that deal, not with means but with ends, not with how best to accomplish some purpose but with what is and what is not worth accomplishing. A tool or a machine, which is a more complicated tool, exists in the realm of means. A spade, for example, which is effective for removing earth, is a good spade whether one uses it to prepare a flower bed or to dig a grave. A jet plane's effectiveness as a means for transporting people or materials rapidly from one place to another is not a good machine only when it brings a heart transplant in time to save a dying patient but a bad machine when it delivers an atomic bomb. The purpose it serves does not affect its value *as pure means*.

The applied science and technology that we have a right to be so proud of serve to produce more powerful and effective machines and give the modern age the ability to accomplish ends and purposes unthinkable to the earlier world. It is a magnificent accomplishment, but its value to humankind is ultimately no greater than the worth of the ends it is asked to implement. Moreover, whereas it is not easy to choose ends, it is comparatively easy to choose effective means. We have developed excellent ways of testing which means are better than others; consequently, we can usually choose with confidence the best machines. But the choice of ultimate ends is another matter entirely. Sometimes individuals, until their lives are essentially over, cannot be sure that they have made the right choices as to how to live their lives. If they discover that they have made the wrong choice, the discovery often comes too late.

Another difficulty is that we are presented with so many options from which to choose our ends—no wonder that some of us are a long time in choosing. Yet, on reflection, it is worse to believe that we have few options, especially if our notion of what life offers is so narrow that we overlook possibilities that we had not known were ours to attempt.

Yet even if the liberal arts do not necessarily provide easy answers as to what our ultimate goals are to be, their importance should be plain. They do deal with the whole realm of purposes and values as the technological training does not, and they are the proper complement to our present intense study of means (I had almost said our American obsession with technological means). If ends are ultimately as important as means, as surely they are, then for a proper education the liberal arts are not mere luxury but essential.

Yet because their place in American culture is so regularly misunderstood, it is usually assumed that this matter of values and ends can be left to take care of itself. Leaving this matter to take care of itself means in reality that our choice of ends too often depends on the lure of money or what counts as "success," and, politically, to the rhetoric of demagogues, tribal urges, and gut reactions. But if we have to depend on tribal instincts and gut reactions, the technological person becomes a very dangerous animal, and to no one more dangerous than to itself.

We have to recognize that the layer of civilization that overlays humanity is very thin and brittle. The terrible events of the twentieth century provide plenty of examples. Early in our century the poet W. B. Yeats wrote that he sensed a growing murderousness in the world. Subsequent events were to vindicate him fully.

Yet can proper values and goals be taught—and more to the point, taught by the liberal arts? There is no easy affirmative answer. I have already observed that there exist no objective tests in the scientific sense to "prove" that this goal is better than that one; yet we Americans demand positive answers and always want them in a hurry.

The liberal arts, however, do offer some features that ought to be attractive to us in our present situation. George Santayana's celebrated remark that those who will not heed the lessons of history are condemned to repeat the mistakes of their predecessors hits home.

For example, ours is not the first time in history that two superpowers confronted each other. Rome and Persia found that neither could knock the other out. There had to be some sort of accommodation. In the twentieth century the British Empire came to feel itself overextended and took what it thought the proper action, or rather, series of actions, to accomplish the necessary retraction. Two centuries ago a popular cause like the French Revolution released powerful forces that shook all Europe and so set up problems that had to be dealt with. Compare Communist doctrine today. The American government is not the first to have to decide whether to support or dump unpopular tyrants who either were or professed to be friendly to it. Experience is a hard school but fools will learn in no other; the wise, however, will be willing to learn from the experience of others.

No one expects that history will spoonfeed us the proper remedies for present woes. But a knowledge of what has happened might give perspective. The dismaying matter is to discover how little of real substance average American students know about even their own national history. Ask them. You might get some surprises.

If history has no ready-made remedies to offer for present problems, one quickly learns to expect none at all from literature; and yet there are advantages in this very lack. A reading of the great literature of the past and some of the best literature of the twentieth century presents, instead of admonitions and generalizations about human purposes and values, a whole spread of options. It traces the different courses followed by various people, narrates what happened to them, and, most important of all, tells how the protagonist faced up to the situation.

Such literature describes both success and failure, courage and cowardice, wisdom and folly. In authentic literature the action is not rounded off with a flat moralization. We are allowed—even compelled—to form our own judgment and shape our own attitude. That is a useful discipline.

Thus we have to participate imaginatively in the action. If we are completely passive readers, inert and nonparticipating, we shall miss what literature has to offer. The spiritual food that genuine literature provides requires chewing and digesting. It is not junk food, though inauthentic literature indubitably is.

Since authentic literature does not preach to us, its mode is ultimately dramatic. It portrays human beings in action, experiencing their various temptations, and enduring, for better or worse, the consequences of their choices. In saying its mode is ultimately dramatic, I am not limiting myself to drama. I include fiction and poetry, even lyric poetry, for in the tiniest lyric someone is always speaking to someone, if only to oneself, out of a special situation.

A fine sermon is admirable—one hears too few of them—and I enjoy a good editorial. But I do not want literary artists to preach to me or to argue a case with me. Rather, I want them to admit me into the world that they have created and to allow me to observe what happens in that world. If they have any wisdom to impart to me about what is good or true or beautiful, I can best appropriate it in that way.

But I feel the need of some concrete examples here, and I believe I can find some excellent examples in poems written in their later years by three poets of the twentieth century. In the poems from which I shall be quoting, these poets glance back at their own lives and those of others and meditate on what constitutes a good life, well lived.

My first poem is by Yeats. It is in fact from a suite of poems, the general title of which is *Vacillation*. Yeats had learned that all of us are pulled now this way and now that by opposing needs and ambitions. Let me say that the great poets do not deal in vague moonshine. They are profound realists. As T. S. Eliot once wrote, we express our ideals in our prose, but in our poetry, it must be reality.

In the third section of *Vacillation* from which I shall quote, Yeats notes some of the various courses that people are tempted to take: to acquire wealth, to strive to realize a great ambition, or simply to live every moment of life to its fullest. He reviews these possibilities for his reader thus:

> Get all the gold and silver that you can.
> Satisfy ambition, animate
> The trivial days and ram them with the sun.

That is to say, make each day that would in itself be simply another day intensely meaningful by filling it to overflowing with the light and energy of the sun, Yeats's favorite symbol of vitality. Yeats is doubtless remembering here Walter Pater's celebrated aphorism: "To burn with [a] hard and gemlike flame, to maintain this ecstasy, is success in life." But Yeats wants to go Pater one better by substituting for Pater's rather delicate and "arty" image one more masculine and robust.

Yeats does not commit himself to any one of these three choices. What he goes on to say is this: whichever of these, or any

other alternatives you choose, you still may not have achieved
complete success in life. For he writes:

> And yet upon these maxims meditate:
> All women dote upon an idle man
> Although their children need a rich estate;
> No man has ever lived that had enough
> Of children's gratitude or woman's love.

Suppose you end your life as a wealthy but tired businessman
and forget how to be a lover. Or suppose you elect to be the "idle
man" who refuses to allow the lover to dwindle into the mere
husband, continuing all the little loverlike attentions, but ending
up for your pains as the ridiculously out-of-date and shabby-
genteel antiquated gallant. In either case you might feel you had
badly failed.

Yet Yeats does not end his meditation on a note of damned if
you do and damned if you don't. Whatever the decision you
make, he seems to be saying here, it is an important one, nothing
less than a life-and-death decision. As warrant for my interpreta-
tion here, consider the closing lines of this section of his poem.

> Begin the preparation for your death
> And from the fortieth winter of that thought
> Test every work of intellect or faith,
> And everything that your own hands have wrought.
> And call those works extravagance of breath
> That are not suited for such men as come
> Proud, open-eyed, and laughing to the tomb.

Laughing all the way to the tomb rather than laughing all the
way to the bank will scarcely be alluring to the Yuppie genera-
tion, and yet some men and women, including Yeats himself,
have chosen so well what they wanted from life that they could
accept their deaths as an apt and satisfying conclusion.

Robert Frost's poem "Provide, Provide" is also a poem about
choosing a good life and a satisfactory death, but Frost seems to
be in no doubt at all as to what a young man or woman should do.
The poem pretends to be triggered by the fate of a former movie
queen. She has lost her looks and her fortune, either by squan-
dering it or having been tricked out of it. Now a poor old crone,
she ekes out her living with "pail and rag" as a scrub woman. The
poet says, in effect: take heed. Do not let that happen to you.

> If need be occupy a throne
> Where nobody can call you crone.

The latter reference is not entirely fanciful. The beautiful Grace Kelly did in fact, after her Hollywood career, come to occupy a throne, though that of a principality rather than of a kingdom. But the poet gives no special hint that he was thinking of her.

In the closing stanzas of this short poem Frost drives home the admonition contained in the title of his poem:

> No memory of having starred
> Atones for later disregard
> Or keeps the end from being hard.
>
> Better to go down dignified
> With boughten friendship at your side
> Than none at all. Provide, provide!

Yet this closing image of a deathbed comforted by purchased friendship, reinforced as it is by the use of the New England dialect form "boughten," puts the sensitive reader on the alert. Surely, the poet himself has not been taken in by this shabby second-best departure from life, and so the reader goes through the poem again. Sure enough, there it is, tucked almost out of sight in the body of the poem, these three lines:

> Some have relied on what they knew;
> Others on being simply true.
> What worked for them might work for you.

If the choices of the sage and the saint are those that Frost really hopes his reader will adopt, he is employing here anything but the hard sell to recommend them. These two alternatives are put differently, almost absent-mindedly, as if the poet were saying: oh, by the way, I suppose that I should mention some other ways of leading one's life. But I'm not sure that you'd be interested, and anyway, though they worked for others, I can't guarantee that they would work for you.

Jesus Christ was not the only one to cry out, "Let him who hath ears to hear, hear." The authentic artist mutters it under his breath in all that he writes. This is why the literary artist, instead of writing an essay on ethics, usually tells us a story.

Robert Penn Warren provides plenty of examples. For the better part of his lifetime, in writing about the choices we make in the great issues, he very often gives us an anecdote or describes a character or tells us a story.

His fine suite of poems about the life of John James Audubon is a case in point. That great naturalist was fired by a passionate interest in the birds and mammals of North America. It was a passion that enabled him to surmount physical discomfort, the dangers of the American wilderness, social indignities, and embarrassing poverty. Warren sees Audubon as thoroughly human, but nevertheless a man utterly devoted to knowledge, but to knowledge of a certain kind; not as a commodity to be marketed or a device for gaining prestige and power, but knowledge for its own lovely sake. His passion for it amounted to a disinterested love.

Space permits me to give only a few scattered passages: the first is on Audubon's dreams of what he hoped to be.

> His life, at the end, seemed—even the anguish—simple.
> Simple, at least, in that it had to be,
> Simply, what it was, as he was.
> In the end, himself and not what
> He had known he ought to be. The blessedness!
>
> To wake in some dawn and see,
> As though like a rifle barrel, lined up
> Like sights, the self that was, the self
>
>   that is, and there,
> Far off but in range, completing that alignment, your fate.

Audubon, like the rest of us, had his pride, a pride often wounded. As the poet puts it later in the poem, Audubon was seated

> Below the salt, in rich houses, he sat, and knew insult.
> In the lobbies and couloirs of greatness he dangled,
> And was not unacquainted with contumely.

Yet how could men of power be expected to treat a mere schoolmaster even if one used the more dignified term and called him a tutor?

But Audubon's passion for the birds he was painting sustained him, and Warren tries to make his reader see the wonder of those creatures as they must have appeared to Audubon's own eyes.

> Their footless dance
> Is of the beautiful liability of their nature.
> Their eyes are round, boldly convex, bright as a jewel,
> And merciless. They do not know
> Compassion, and if they did,
> We should not be worthy of it. They fly
> In air that glitters like fluent crystal
> And is hard as perfectly transparent iron, they cleave it
> With no effort. They cry
> In a tongue multitudinous, often like music.

The section of the poem in which this passage occurs bears the significant title "Love and Knowledge." It is indeed a significant coupling of terms, for knowledge pursued as an Audubon pursued it is in fact a form of love.

I am confident of Warren's meaning here. I remember once, long ago, bringing up Bertrand Russell's definition of science as "power knowledge"; and I remember Warren's reminding me that Russell had also, and in the same context, called all knowledge pursued for its own sake "love knowledge." Audubon's wish to know all about his birds was an instance of such love knowledge.

In making this distinction I return once more to the nature of a liberal education as opposed to utilitarian skills. As human beings, of course, we need both: we need to know the best means to accomplish our ends, but we need to choose our ends by meditating both rationally and passionately on what the truly valuable things in life are. In sum, the liberal arts deal in love knowledge and with the nature of the good life itself.

How and why Audubon chose to live the life he did is the theme of Warren's magnificent poem. The poem beautifully renders how his passion did give him so good a life that he must have felt that the mishaps, hardships, and indignities that he had endured had been fully redeemed. Warren does not say this in so many words, but the closing section of the poem makes it clear.

In this closing section there are no references to Audubon at all, but to an evening in Warren's own boyhood when he stood by a dirt road in Kentucky and listened to the cries of the wild geese overhead as they flew northward on their spring migration. It was a dark night. He could not see them, but their calling was enough.

Warren does not tell us that his heart was deeply stirred or that he shared for a moment at least Audubon's passion. He does not need to tell us. Instead, he ends his poem with the following cryptic lines:

Tell me a story.

In this century, and moment, for mania,
Tell me a story.

Make it a story of great distances, and starlight.

The name of the story will be Time,
But you must not pronounce its name.
Tell me a story of deep delight.

And so the poem ends, some readers would say, enigmatically, but we need not be too deeply baffled. Warren himself has just finished telling the reader a story that he obviously believes to be a story of deep delight, Audubon's own story. In a time of mania, such stories are worthy of telling. Why does Warren say that the story's name will be time? It is because the delight he is concerned with does not involve a rejection of time and history. The poet is not relying on an easy transcendence of time. We have to accept the burden of time and history—not disavow it—if we are to share in Audubon's or Warren's deep delight.

Then why does the poet enjoin us not to pronounce the name of Time? Frankly, I don't know. But I am not afraid to make a guess: we must avoid abstractions, such as the monstrous entity Time spelled with a capital T. Time is not off in some Platonic realm. It is part of us. It has allowed us our lives and our chances to find this deep delight in our beautiful but perplexing world.

Time and history will not prevent our finding our true passion. It was Audubon's love of this temporal beauty and wonder that gave him his vocation. Unless we can find our true vocations, all the technical know-how in the world will hardly make our life story one of deep delight.

But I must not moralize overmuch here. Warren has been careful to refrain from all moralizing. As I remarked earlier, our genuine artists usually prefer not to provide their wisdom in neat tamper-proof, labeled bottles. Instead, they tell us a story. But what storytellers the best of them are, and how much they have to tell us—provided we are willing to listen and know how to listen.

The Amateur Professor
Roy Fuller

Such is Oxford's prestige that the title of "Professor," fortuitously acquired for five years, lingers on to this day. I never much liked to employ it myself even in office, and when I joined the Board of Governors of the BBC in 1972, the end of my Oxford career in sight (my last lecture was during the 1972 Michaelmas term), I asked the director-general's office not to use the handle. It was too late: labels with "Professor" had been printed to stick on the great envelopes full of bumf that were to arrive for the next seven or so years. Besides, I think the BBC found it difficult to believe that anyone appointed to the Board might be a plain "Mr."

I suppose I solved the problems of the Oxford professorship as well as most outsiders. I was helped by the presence there of my son and his family, and the fact that not long after election I gave up my fulltime lawyer's job. Cecil Day Lewis sometimes took a railway day-return ticket to deliver his termly lecture, and one cannot blame him, having regard to the stipend paid. I was occasionally asked what I would do to improve the usefulness of the office—poet in residence the sort of thing suggested, the stipend perhaps augmented by the Arts Council. Certainly now I think the office well left alone, being a curious anomaly, typically English. Anyone desiring it, or willing to stand, will have reasons—duty, publicity, discoveries to impart—and will contribute, however strangely, to the long history of the chair.

Without the spur of the office I would never have produced a single, let alone two, books of criticism. Some of the things in *Owls and Artificers* and *Professors and Gods* I am glad to have perpetuated in print, perhaps especially the business about syllabic verse in a lecture called "An Artifice of Versification." As I wrote in a postscript to the lecture, part of it derived from an already extant lecture and review. When in 1969 I was rearranging and adding to this material I was conscious of Elizabeth Daryush as a poet who had used syllabics, but merely mentioned her as such. Then, as the time for the delivery of the lecture approached, I was seized with guilt at not having investigated her further. She had been born, a daughter of Robert Bridges, the year before my mother, in 1887—early enough for her arrival to have been commented on by Gerard Manley Hopkins—so was then aged eighty-two. I was uncertain whether she would be willing to suffer, or be capable of responding to, an enquiry from a stranger about verse technique—perhaps, indeed, whether or not she was still in the land of the living. Accordingly, I wrote to the second Lord Bridges (Robert's grandson), who had just succeeded his father to the barony, probably addressing my letter to the House of Lords, for I was not acquainted with him. I received an encouraging reply, so I wrote to Mrs. Daryush at Stockwell, Boars Hill, Oxford, where Lord Bridges said she was still living. I trust it will be of interest to reproduce that first exchange of letters in October 1969.

Dear Mrs Daryush,

I hope you will forgive me for troubling you with this letter. As the current Oxford Professor of Poetry I am lecturing on 6 November about syllabic verse. I was led to the subject by a talk I gave some time ago to the Royal Society of Literature about my own experience of the metre and a review of Marianne Moore's *Collected Poems* I did for the *Times Literary Supplement*. I'm not an academic and I don't really think of myself as a critic, but for the forthcoming lecture I was led deeper into the subject than I'd been before. In my first draft of the lecture I merely mentioned you as one of the poets of our time who have experimented with syllabic counts, but then I felt guilty at not having made a more thorough investigation. I have to confess that at that moment I thought your experiments were mainly confined to combining a regular syllabic count with regular stress. But from your note to *The Last Man* I have been led to *Verse, Fourth Book*—and then, of course, to a closer look at your poetry and the belated realisation that it often embodies "true" syllabic practice. I've now revised the lecture in several places and hope I've done justice to the clear and penetrating things you said about syllabics in the Thirties. The point of this letter is to ask you two things:

1. I guess in my lecture that your syllabics were inspired by your father's investigations into Milton's blank verse and his own experiments in classical metres. Is this a fair statement?

2. I say that I haven't been able to discover any overt links between you and Miss Moore. Were you ever in communication; and did you know her work before your own experiments; and if so, were you influenced by it?

Please do not bother to reply to this if it is a burden, though I think your answers would illuminate an obscure bit of literary history! I've been greatly impressed with everything you say about syllabics: you have confirmed, with greater precision, the opinions I'd formed about several practical points in which I differ from Miss Moore.

Two things embarrass me now about this letter: the underlying assumption that someone in her eighties might be gaga or at least have lost interest in art; and its referring to a considerable corpus of verse as "experimental." But Mrs. Daryush promptly and fully replied. I may say that despite its reference to her sight, the letter is written with a steel nib in an italic hand reminiscent, if lacking the beauty, of her father's—a fine specimen of which I was to see a few years later when as a governor of the BBC I visited its written archive, where among other literary treasures had been laid out for my inspection a holograph script of a Robert Bridges radio talk.

Dear Mr Fuller,

Many thanks for your letter. In answer to your first question:—it is hardly correct to say that my syllabic ventures wre "inspired by" my father's "investigations into Milton's blank verse, and his own experiments in classical metres". I now realise that my inclination towards this form goes back a very long way. In my second collection (1916) a distinctly childish production which I have since suppressed, there are obvious signs of it. I remember my father asking me, with regard to a piece in this book which he particularly liked, "What is this new metre?" and my reply of "only syllables". (But perhaps you need not repeat this in your lecture). However, my approach, in direct contrast to his own, has never been deliberately technical. What rules I have arrived at are the result of an often almost unconscious analysis of my dissatisfaction, or otherwise, with what I have already (again half subconsciously) written. And despite his often expressed opinion, by which I have no doubt been influenced, that the traditional "accentual syllabics" were, as he put it, "played out", and his life-long interest in technical possibilities, I think that perhaps he never quite appreciated the full implication of a whole-hearted surrender to the syllabic principle—as, for instance, in the use of unaccented rhymes, and the strict avoidance of all ambiguity in the matter of elision.

Owing to failing eyesight, my knowledge of modern verse is minimal—Marianne Moore is little more than a name to me—apart from one or two casual perusals in anthologies I know nothing of her work.

If at any time you should be in Oxford and would care to visit me here, it would be a great pleasure to meet you, and to discuss these matters at greater length than is possible in a letter. I have some recent, unpublished work, which might possibly be of interest to you.

I took up Mrs. Daryush's invitation when I went to Oxford to deliver my lecture of that Trinity term, "An Artifice of Versification." "Stockwell," as she precisely told me in a further letter, was the last house "on the Ridgeway on the left. To find the Ridgeway you go first to Ripon Hall, a castle-like place on the top of Boar's Hill—and take the middle road of the cross-roads just after it."

I had never before been to Boar's Hill, and at Stockwell (somehow prefigured by the Daryushes' pink-printed, private-pressy writing-paper), found myself in the vanished world of Bridges, Masefield, the young Robert Graves—a large house but rather spartan; a courteous reception from the owners; provision of good coffee; literary talk. I came away with the manuscript of her new book of poems! She had once been published by the Oxford University Press, but they had abandoned her in the late thirties, and she had brought out her last book privately. I knew Jon Stallworthy quite well, who was then working for the press, and I approached him to ask if there was any hope of their taking her on again. He was not sanguine, though sportingly read the manuscript (Mrs. Daryush had offered to get it typed, but because of her eyesight it would have taken some time to correct the resulting typescript).

Jon's verdict was adverse, but in the end Michael Schmidt of the Carcanet Press brought the book out. Those were the days when Carcanet was run more modestly than now, from Pin Farm, a rural setting difficult to get to by car, entangled as it was by main roads on the outskirts of Oxford. But even then Michael was practical and enthusiastic about bringing into print (or back into print) the unfashionable (as well as promoting new authors), though one had no conception of the substantial and remarkable publisher he would become. About what was called, with typical austerity, *Verses Seventh Book*, he wrote to me: "The Daryush goes to press today. . . . I have read the book closely now, and can say frankly that I don't like it at all! I see the point of publishing it as an historical piece more than anything else." However he went on to publish a *Selected Poems* in 1972 and a *Collected Poems* in 1976, the latter with an introduction by Donald Davie, far more comprehensive than the similar office I had performed for *Verses Seventh Book*. Michael also visited and made friends with the Daryushes: I never myself went back, though Mrs. Daryush had issued an open invitation: my usual combination of diffidence and failure of duty (however dutiful in some areas I might appear). But I did in 1970 put her in touch with the *Southern Review*, the great literary quarterly from Louisiana State University, where at that time Professor Donald E. Stanford was an editor; and poetry of hers appeared there—three of her last poems after her death in her ninetieth year on 7 April 1977. I knew Don would be sympathetic—as his mentor Yvor Winters had been in the thirties—not only because of his expertise in English prosody but also because he was then in the process of becoming the leading authority on Robert Bridges and the Bridges circle, it being left to him by unenterprising English academics to bring out an edition of Bridges's letters. I might also add that the disloyalty of the marooning of Elizabeth Daryush by the Oxford University Press in the thirties is only exceeded by their allowing the *Poetical Works* of her father in the Oxford Standard Authors series to go out of print in the eighties.

Where All the Ladders Start
Lindon Stall

Old bottles, bone-dreams, elegiac ghosts
Sunk into anecdotes or moss-holes: these
The Irish know, the bogey-bottomed hosts
To stout-tongued, hero-headed mockeries.
God's chosen connoisseurs, His cellarers
Of dispossession snug within the heart's
Me fecits, kin of Miledh, clan of words,
Who troll the cultic hidey-holes of art,
Some elf-mound otherworld of fairy forts
Whose glamour-knotted pits outCaesar all
The Barbar Imperators—scrobes retorqued
To *scribo*, England wisped to Glannagalt.
Cold cozies, cock-'em-ups, the eloquence
Of strangers: these are our inheritance.

Fountain in the City
Timothy Steele

The water climbed in a white crest, and fell,
Plashy and heavy, to a metal shell
Forever in a state of overflow
And then went dripping to the pool below.

The square had, otherwise, a leafless tree,
And litter's swirling, sad agility;
And densely-packed surrounding buildings made
The place, save at mid-day, a cheerless shade.

The homeless slumped on benches. Some would range
Out to a bus-stop, where they'd search for change
(The mood of these excursion dazed and lax)
In coin-return cups of newspaper racks.

To pass the square at evening was to feel
The tension and the weight of stone and steel.
Striking a building's many-windowed face,
The sunset would glare redly back through space.

Yet still the cast-up flow would splash and spill,
As if with an anomalous, great good will
Which all the world surrounding it had lost
But which no deprivation could exhaust.

Three Menus for Don Stanford
Raymond Oliver

1. Plain

Don, when I write for you to overhear,
I sense a steady, rock-ribbed presence near,
A break-water to my poetic surges—
Spontaneous overflows of salty urges—
That turns the mere slosh of the ill-defined
To leaping, light-shot patterns in the mind.

"Style is the man." No, style is what I try,
As man, to give my clothes. As artist I,
Alas, must also *make* my coat and tie.

The best cakes are compact
And terse, like ladentorte,
As is the best and hardest
Verse. Is it merely taste
I'm talking? Yes; my "mere"
is *merus*—pure, essential.

Cesario Verde, 1855–1886

"Less green, more Caesar!", went the witticism
At the expense of poet Caesar Green
Whose gift was not for suave imperialism
But for the verdant shaping of the seen.

"Life is a feast." The poet, scrounging, tries

To shape the leavings into poem pies
(Even if no one's nourished, no one dies.)

—Ah, *the meaning of life.* Is it invented,
Given, or like a sidewalk penny, found?
—However gotten, it has not relented
From keeping, as I go, my eyes on the Ground.

During the search for God, as I disjoint
My thoughts and feelings, twisting to see, to find,
I sense that back of the radars of my mind
A needle spins, hovers, trying to point.

"God is within"; but what
Or who in me is God?
Easy to see what's not,
Like plucking petals off
A daisy down to the stock—
And there the plucking stops;
The "eye of day" is gone.
The eye of night looks on.

Old Song

Tudo passa, tudo passara;
Nada fica, nada ficara.
Everything passes, everything will pass;
Nothing remains, and nothing will remain.

On Holy Spirit Day, they set the mass
To fireworks to make the meaning plain
Of this old song; figures of smoke arise,
Born of big bangs, and march along the air
Compact and upright. What a brave surprise
They keep their forms so long, these forms we wear.

I remember the everyday
Of 'fifty-three—so far away

Now, it might be legend or dreamed;
But then how commonplace it seemed.
Memory, memory! See how strange
Is *now,* if we remember change!

Could it be that desire—
Not its degree or shaping,
Just desire—is the same
From one of us to the next
Exactly as the flame
From each match to the next
Is fully the same fire?

I can recall just how at nine
I projected myself at fifty—
To now. Projected a clean line
(Expecting nothing blurred or shifty)
To where the man recalls the child
And nothing need be reconciled.

In this eternal Now
Through which the moments course
We take our stand; but how
Stem the increasing force
Of particles of time
As they accelerate?
Perhaps by mimicking rhyme
We might secure our state,
Binding present to past;
And in a measured way
Assign to life amassed
Values and weight, as stay.

2. Slightly Richer

Bretanha, Azores, like parent Brittany,
Faces westward over a northern sea;
So does Brittany's distant parent, Wales.

Their greenness is the grace of winter gales;
Their inwardness, of ocean clouds and mist.
Surf is a Celtic fringe that urges: persist,
Resist by paradox when too hard pressed,
By tricks, like *orienting* towards the *west.*

Aquamarine, those glassy banks of water
Below the surf-reticulations marking
A border: color of the sea yielding
To land; its blue effort to meet with green.

Scrapings of sky, those clouds, ploughed up
By some celestial edge that throws
Shavings and curls of white as it goes.

Windmill

Its walls of whitewash suit
The salt of the island air,
And noon, and the blue glare
Of sky; but mostly they suit
The surging windwash stress
Of windmill in the airswell,
White against colorless.

In Latin countries *time's* the same as *weather:*
Seasonal, sensory, and mostly pleasure.
Such countries too are Catholic, where time
Turns on the year of God, and bread and wine
(Seasonal, sensory) prepare salvation,
Greatest of pleasures. Admirable, these nations.

Even as ostentation it's ornate,
This Rococco ecclesiastical
Of twisty shapes, especially in gold,
Of rapt mothers and wriggling babies (Jesus,
Angels)—faith is no steady inwardness,
It's all the God-folk squiggling up the walls!

Portuguese sausage:
Anthology
Of pig-parts, satur-
Nalia, *satura*
But not to mock
The hog, whose stuffings
Jumbled in gut,
All but the grunt,
Are honest numbles—
No Orphic offal
Or offering,
But snout-to-pizzle
Anatomy
For puzzlebuffs,
And goods for the guts
Of Portuguese
And such as me.

Lemon or lime,
In supplementing
Maracuja,
Imposes limit:
Sweetness yields—
So far, no farther!—
To citrous strictness.
Good fences make
Good drinks for neighbors.

How apt that speech as old, melodious,
And strange to English, yet so close, As Welsh
Should cling to valleys and hills, like moss to rocks
And ancient trees, where birds, *adar,* that look
English are still *llatai,* the poets' spokesmen,
Flying with secret sayings in a language,
Old and melodious, recorded once—
With meters as intricate as any twitter—
By Dafydd and Aneurin and Taliesin.

A crackling winter in this citadel
For quiet selves, brooding on paper birth,

Speech in the air as Welsh as snow is fresh
Scurry of pens on paper, sleet on panes:
"St Deiniol's Residential Library"
Is the address, in Wales the well-imagined.

3. A Healthy Balance

All our memorials in classic marble,
Marmoreal indeed, sepulchral temples,
Monumental sculpture and mausoleums—
This *classical* of politics and death
Cries for plain relief, for the living *Greek:*
A brush of olive oil on rough white bread,
Some pungent feta, salty little olives
As hard as almonds, and for warmth and color
Wine that blossoms like an Aegean sunset.

Presidential Privilege

That meeting? Oh, he wasn't there
Or if he was he can't recall.
In any case he doesn't care.
Perfect indifference pardons all.

Victorian Hotel, Stockbridge, Berkshires

The marble mantle-piece's
Knicknacks of tinted glass,
Jumble of nineties gimcracks,
All souvenirs of fairs
And courtships far off now,
Lose their intrusive, nervous
Poignance in light of sundown
Spent at length in this wicker
Chair on the wide veranda.

In dogs, *being* is going on;
It feels like something to be a dog,

Though only speechless dog knows what.
Or doesn't know but feels; yet not
"Feeling like a dog" but being one,
As hidden in itself as God.

Salvation, brave Franciscans, help
Salvage us soldiers of the Cross!
We're crisping in the fat of hell,
Sausages in satanic pans;
He's walked about the world and found
Whom to devour. But you, with Jesus
And Francis and seven hundred years
of fasting: teach us Christian rich
To lose the fat we're frying in!

With that appassionata of rain
That smacks the streets, the Gulf has opened
To take Cafe du Monde. But I
And a cup of coffee hold each other.

*   *   *   *   *   *   *   *

Seeking an English fresh as April's lettuce,
As Shakespeare when Elizabethans listened,
Or Herrick when he set his verse to birdsong,
Leads me to places where the language tarries
In telling tales, giving advice, describing,
To *pirouette*—suddenly fine of figure
Beneath the workclothes given shape for a moment.

The Exiles
John Finlay

1.

The battle took place early fall between
The red men and the whites. But it was brief.
Before the unknown magic of the rifle,
The red men, panic-struck and terrified,
Collapsed and fell apart, and when their chief
Was shot, their power ebbed totally away.
The whole tribe then was rounded up; the old,
The women and the children, all of them,
Uprooted from their land and local god
Were herded west to eke out foreign life.

2.

Time passed, perhaps a week. One afternoon
I felt an eerie crawling on my skin
As when we sense someone unseen close by.
I was outside. I raised my eyes to see
An Indian woman standing in the yard,
Who had been separated from the tribe
And now was wandering in search of it.
A child hung from her back in woven straw.
Her sudden presence startled me; she seemed
Uncanny till I saw she was of flesh.
Warm sunlight cast her shadow on the ground.
She didn't make one sound, but cupped a hand
And raised it to her mouth. I went inside
And brought back food for her, along with milk.
She slowly ate and drank to make them last,
Then swung in front of her the strawed papoose,
And took her child and nursed him on her breast.

She rested there on our porch a little while
And left as silently as she had come.

3.

For some time on the woman lived in me;
I followed her inside my taken mind.
Those nights unsheltered and exposed, the bed
Of leaves on ground too damp and cold by dawn,
The long hard night, the two would have endured
So closely joined I thought of them as one.
I wondered if she found their tribe or if
She and her child were killed by animals or men
So that they lie unburied on wild earth.
The wolves and rattlesnakes she would have faced
Both on the open ground and in the woods.
But if the worst occurred; it was the life
I saw and felt, not death, which stayed with me.
And though some years have passed, I yet can feel
The sunlight of that afternoon in fall
When she consumed the food and fed her child.
I see the exiled pair, the woman's strong
And toughened face, the strangely silent child's
Leaning rearward from his mother's back,
Gazing toward the home he now will never have.

The Classic Mind Restored: The Achievement of Donald Stanford—Poet, Editor, Mentor

David Middleton

1

Donald Stanford was an active poet from the early 1930s through the middle 1950s. Though the body of work is small—about thirty-six published poems—it contains a number of well-crafted, intelligent, and beautifully lyrical pieces that should be preserved. Many of these poems first appeared in some of the most distinguished literary journals and other magazines of the thirties. These include *Hound & Horn*, of which Yvor Winters was western editor, and *The Magazine* (1933–35), Howard Baker's successor journal to Winters's famous mimeographed magazine *The Gyroscope* (1929–30). In his essay "The Gyroscope" in the Yvor Winters issue of *The Southern Review* (1981), Howard Baker quotes from Winters's "Statement of Purpose" to *The Gyroscope*. There Winters says that the aim of the quarterly will be an "approximation of a classical state of mind." Baker acknowledges that his own *The Magazine* was "an actual offshoot of *The Gyroscope* . . . with continuing vital assists from Winters." Although Stanford arrived too late to contribute to *The Gyroscope*, he did publish seven poems in *The Magazine*; and in the anthology *Trial Balances* (1935), which printed the poems of young poets "balanced" by critical remarks from older poets, poems by J. V. Cunningham and Donald Stanford appeared under the rubric "Two Gyroscope Poets," an appellation true in spirit, if not, in Stanford's case, in fact.

Other anthologies in which Stanford's poems appeared include *Ten Introductions* (1934, four poems), Winters's *Twelve Poets of the Pacific* (1937, nine poems), and the celebratory anthology for Winters, *Laurel, Archaic, Rude* (1966, one poem). Twenty-six of Stanford's poems were published in his first collection, *New England Earth and Other Poems* (1941, with a fore-word by Yvor Winters). *The Traveler* (1955), richly printed on Harry Duncan's famous Cummington Press, selected eight poems from the 1941 collection and added five more. *The Cartesian Lawnmower and Other Poems* (1984) brought together fourteen of the best poems from the two previous books and added two uncollected pieces. The poems "Lizard King Here" and the second "Valentine" poem remain uncollected.

The pervasive influence of Winters on Stanford reveals itself in "Letter from Widener Library" in the *New England Earth* volume, originally printed in *The Harvard Advocate* as "Letter to Yvor Winters: On Re-reading 'The Journey,' Widener Library, 1933." In this poem, Stanford, who, like Winters, defines himself as a philosophical dualist and a reluctant theist, contrasts the "eternal thought" embodied in the fruits of scholarship and great poetry contained within the library's walls to the sprawling ivy outside, to political and sexual scandals of the age, and to the limitations of youth—rage, lust, and the "blundering body." Stanford praises Winters for having distilled "truth and virtue" in the "tired lines" of "The Journey," a poem that presents and defines the brutal life of a western mining town. As Stanford says in the final lines of his poem, only by reading the "fuller lives" of greater men, as preserved especially in poems whose language adjusts feeling to meaning, do we escape from the narrow limits of the self: "The Concept saves us when our forms decline." One might compare Winters's essay "The Extension and Reintegration of the Human Spirit . . ." (1929), read by Stanford before he met Winters. Speaking of the "monstrous discipline" of the modern artist who must create a "moral godhead" and a new "dynamic synthesis" of the facts of modern life, Winters stresses that such an artist sees "thought [as] . . . the core of experience" and in his work "leaves that state of mind completed behind him for others to enter." Illustrating these ideas, "Letter to Yvor Winters," a poem written in a library by a young poet praising scholarship, thought, classic poetry, and a beloved mentor, is an exact portrait of Donald Stanford in his literary life.

From 1935 to 1967, Winters found occasion to comment on Stanford's verse. In his remarks in *Trial Balances* (1935), Winters notes flaws in the work of the twenty-two-year-old poet. These include a failure to master fully the subject matter, some erratic thinking, and occasionally overly rhetorical and awkward diction. Balancing these flaws are Stanford's virtues: sound feeling, lyrical sweetness, formal craftsmanship, and an exquisite ear "more sensitive" than Cunningham's. Winters concludes by calling "Noon at Neebish" "one of the finest purely descriptive poems in recent years" and by judging Stanford as having written some of "the best poetry thus far produced by the American and English poets in their twenties."

Two years later, in 1937, Winters edited his famous *Twelve Poets of the Pacific*. In his brief foreword, Winters defines these poets as a group, known to one another, and with the common aims of clarity of conception, the expression of rightly motivated feeling, and purity of style devoid both of personal mannerisms and of cultivated personal weaknesses. Of Stanford, Winters writes that although his greatest flaw is too great facility, he has written such poems as "The Sea Gull," which "deserves a permanent and distinguished place in the body of our literature, and will eventually find it." In his critique of modern experimentalist poetry, *Primitivism and Decadence* (1937), Winters classifies Stanford as a member of "The Reactionary Generation" of poets—"reactionary" being a literary and not a political term. Later, in his *Anatomy of Nonsense* (1947), Winters defends the university as "the intellectual and spiritual center of our world" and lists Stanford as·one of the "best" younger scholar-poets who had made their home in the university. Winters singles out "The Grand Mesa," "The Meadowlark," "The Bee," "The Sea Gull," "Summer Scene," and "The Thrush" as Stanford's finest poems. Last, in *Forms of Discovery* (1967), completed as he was dying of cancer, Winters reaffirms that although "Stanford's poems are few in number . . . the best of them are excellent," and to favorite poems listed earlier he adds "The Cartesian Lawnmower."

In addition to these comments, Winters wrote a substantial foreword to Stanford's *New England Earth and Other Poems*. Calling Stanford "one of the finest poets of our time," Winters finds in Stanford's poetry an effort "to retrieve a classical sensibility" by retracing "the path by which that sensibility was lost." Strewn along the path are various influences from "the complexity of Donne and the suavity of Dryden" through neo-classical generalizations and late-eighteenth-century romantic hyperbole to a concern with "the disintegration of the spirit" in the modern period. The result of Stanford's "deliberate effort to master himself and to find his personal bearings with relationship to history" is, according to Winters, "a poetry civilized, and deceptive in that its claims are far more modest than its scope." Winters notes Stanford's growing preference for brief nature poems celebrating the loveliness and everchangingness of the physical world. In these later poems, Winters finds, "a beauty which I, at any rate, cannot expel from my mind."

"Sonnet on Graduation: Stanford University, 1933" praises the hard discipline of schooling as a proper cultivation of the mind and feelings. Truth may bloom out of reason and lie in part beyond it, but reason leads to knowledge and gives our lives direction, just as a rose must be tended from seed to blossom. The knowledge reason gives is hard yet necessary for the poet. In "For the Audience," for instance, the poet finds in the sound of the night wind blowing through the trees the paradox of "marriage" and "singleness," of a union of things (wind/trees) that brings harmony (music) yet dilution (the wind is slowed by the trees), and of an isolation that is pure yet desolate (the unchecked wind or death-still trees). Hearing his own poems as nothing but an empty field's wind-rattled stones, the poet asks, "How should I dare construe experience?" Stanford's cautious modesty before the complexity of experience finds its dramatic opposite in "Rhesus," a poem about a giant who wades into the sea (experience) and drowns. Cast in the form of a classical myth, this poem, Stanford has confessed, refers to the life of Hart Crane, the romantic poet who committed suicide by drowning. Purged of historical detail and generalized as myth, the poem presents the case of the romantic who, having discarded reason, immerses himself unthinkingly in pure sensuous experience and is absorbed within it to the point of death. However heroic Rhesus may be, and Stanford concedes his bravery, the giant, both in his size and in his action, exceeds the limits of the human and is lost.

A number of Stanford's poems deal with limit, restraint, and moderation in another context, that of love. "A Valentine" contrasts the "evading wraith" of untested love to "love beyond experiment," symbolized by a sculptor's statue of love. Artful, proven, faithful love allows the lovers to face life with confidence, skill, and grace: "Court changing life with paced persistent breath / Not vainly forward nor yet lax in hope." The last stanza, addressed by the poet to his beloved, is beautifully written: "Fix my desires, that in your sensuous skill, / As marble grows what carver's dreams intend, / I see immovable my fleeting will / And am in seeing what I comprehend." This ideal union of the lover and the loved does not presuppose the complete absorption of one by the other, as Rhesus is absorbed by the sea. In "Monologue," for example, the poet knows that the pleasure of his love's kiss is not for him fully to possess: "I taste, but cannot

keep or give, for all / That kiss's brimming sweet belongs to you."
He dreams of sexual union on the wedding night—sighs, arms,
breasts, cheeks, eyes—"More blinding charms than man would
care to gaze on"—and knows "All these are yours and only partly
mine." Similarly, in "Wedding Wine," the newlyweds drink their
wine "in formal toast," yet know that unlike "mingling nature"
they possess separate identities that can never be simply one.
This ultimate separateness of the self, indeed, is not an evil thing,
for, as the poet says, "Without this difference we could never
love." Difference, however, can lead to problems as in "Reflec-
tions on Fear," a poem in which a white rose and its table-top
reflection are the "twin images" and "separate reveries" of two
persons whose only relation seems to be through the illusory
surfaces and reflections of themselves. Finally, in the bitter and
disillusioned poem "For Hate," the poet, disappointed in love,
yearns for "black ice" in place of blood. Passion is an octopus
pulling the tranquil poet down into time's whirlpool. Coupling
flies, drunk with lust, and thick-thighed cows show the poet that
"Love should be watched," for love is "a capering thing" devoid
of the steadiness of hate. Nevertheless, these darker poems aside,
Stanford, in "A Valentine," "Monologue," and "Wedding Wine,"
has written three of the most positive, mature, tender, and clear-
eyed poems on love that I have ever read.

Other poems in *New England Earth* represent a growing sense
of the beautiful, everchanging, mysterious otherness of the land-
scape, a landscape both rich in history and far more ancient than
history. The title poem, "New England Earth," finds Stanford
meditating on his Puritan inheritance. Stanford's father was orig-
inally a Baptist, his mother a Congregationalist. Stanford was
raised a Congregationalist but since college has been, like Win-
ters, a reluctant theist, or, at times, even an agnostic. Stanford has
said, "I love New England but not its religion." In the title poem,
the children of New England are "winter sown" and they reap
cultural harvest "ere the season go." In this eternal wintry pallor,
the poet asks "What sighs, what tears for one unfruitful mound?"
I take the (burial) mound as the poet's metaphor for his own life
at the time. He asks "death's soil" to be "your sometime son," and
he seems to accept his Puritan heritage as an ineradicable part of
his being. Still, Stanford is no historical determinist. He seems to
tell himself (and maybe New England as well): "Go till the field
with forward memory. / When in the present future work is done /
Time and ill fortune shall defeated be." Another New England
poem is "Country Church" (the Baptist Church in Rowe, Massa-

chusetts). In the church windows, painted clouds hold their dew for "paradisal fields, unharvested." Meanwhile, farmers sing hymns that rise heavenward from fields that they cannot forsake except on Sundays, whose "heaven is holiday." The farmers' religion seems here a pleasant illusion, psychic compensation, or at best a truth utterly divorced from their hard weekday lives. On Monday, a cock in the churchyard, "crowing with local amplitude," calls the farmers back to the hard labor of working the soil.

A more personal poem on the same subject as "Country Church" is "Spring." The first three quatrains present a vernal world of grass and birds and leaves, a place of sensuous beauty and joy parallel to the poet's own youth: "My spring and summer are together here." Yet thoughts of God darken the mood of these lines. Nature is a "brief garden" now but also "a great desert," a land "snatched from heaven" and "saved from what is His," for God here is apart from and other than the world of matter. God's absence from the world leaves the poet "bright with doubt" and, like any rebellious youth, fleeing the Father's "sheltering hand." In the last, chilling stanza, the spring of youth becomes the winter of age with its cold and hard theology. Fearful, remote, inscrutable, and dark—God seems to be a fusion of the deity of Calvin and the bleakly indiffrent platonic One: "In fear I shall embrace Him when I'm old, / His eye is darkness and His palm is cold, / His dreadful visage He will never show, / I shall not know Him, yea, but I shall know." These are powerful, haunting lines. "Spring" moves quickly from the joyous spring and summer of youth to the stark theology of winter and age. "Sonnet in Autumn," a lovely performance, meditates on the consequences of spring and summer as these appear in fall, or, on the human side of the analogy, how the poet's green passion of spring hardens in summer then expends itself in the sad reaping of autumn. Thinking of the winter to come, the poet asks, "What barren season keeps there yet in store?" The answer, given in the couplet, is stoic and adult: "Yet as the sapling deepens with the snow, / Plundered of grief and joy I still must grow."

Not all of Stanford's nature poems are set in Massachusetts. Two important poems that recall eighteenth-century loco-descriptive pastorals, "The Grand Mesa" and "Noon at Neebish," make use of, in turn, Colorado and an island (Neebish) in Lake Munuscong on the Michigan side of the Canadian border. A cursory reading might leave the impression (which even Winters seemed to have formed) that these are nothing more than lovely descriptive pieces; in fact, both poems approach *postsymbolist* methods in the use of controlled association to convey important ideas. Stanford visited Colorado in 1934, and "The Grand Mesa" is one result of that visit. The mesa, a volcanic mountain with steep sides and a level top, exists between two inhuman extremes: above, the sun of noon, and below, the ever-shifting chaos of the desert sand. The mesa is a pastoral haven, a middle world between extremes, where human life and natural life can flourish. The "sylvan lakes," banked by the cool foliage of the spruce, yield a rich catch to fishermen by day. By night, the lovers, "in sacred talk," stroll amid the balsams or sail through moonlit waters in canoes. The mesa is "a hallowed place, where all things seem to grow / For human ecstasies!" Then, looking below, the poet sees the inhuman absolutes of sun and sand, locked in mutual self-reflection, and concludes:

> Fierce is the heart whose godless beat withstands
> The ravages of wrinkled desert lands,
> Whose threatening rapture like a trumpet blows
> Through all time's vacancies, although it knows
> Down where the swift infrequent traffic turns
> Through speechless eons Colorado burns.

The vast pre-human emptiness of geologic time is all but overwhelming. The desert below the mesa and the ocean strode by Rhesus are at one.

Like "The Grand Mesa," "Noon at Neebish" is a descriptive poem and something more. This poem came from the summer of 1933 when Stanford accompanied Janet Lewis Winters on a visit to her parents to act as babysitter for Mrs. Winters's daughter. Whether or not he had his eye always on the child, Stanford surely took in many details from this lovely place, for his poem is full of them. Yet there are clues in the descriptive language pointing toward a theme only hinted at even in the final stanza. The theme seems to be that the natural world is a spectacle of ever-changing surfaces and depths rising from and collapsing into, out of, and ultimately against some final metaphysical ground. At noon, the clouds seem "foam," "shadows" of daisies disappear into the stalks, and the waxwing merges into the "mellowing hay," his "red heart hidden" beneath the "red spurt" of color on his wing. The cows, with granite bones and "muscle of brute stolidness," have "outward forms" half-sunk in the "deepening turf," their earthly origin. A wind turns the water from blue to green, then whitens its peaking waves. Even a solid-looking stallion, brilliantly described, covers his flanks in "a shower of mane" as he stamps in a "surf" of grass. A red squirrel, too, jumps so fast from bough to bough that he seems "a moment of swimming fur." This watery, shadowy island-world of shifting depths and surfaces recalls its origin in the posited pure matter without form of the primal ocean of chaos. In the poem's final stanza, the sun remains, behind all changes, a moving image of the immaterial noon of the absolute: "Through rest or motion the noon walks the same, / With tread resistant to each thaw and freeze, / Bringing sweet summer with her drowsy claim / And sometimes winter with her icy breeze."

The poems so far considered, from "New England Earth" through "Noon at Neebish," show a gradual diminishment in the use of dense, strained, and occasionally obscure metaphysical conceits in favor of descriptions of the natural world that either contain implicit meaning or else are interwoven with or followed by more or less explicit statements of meaning. The later poems in *New England Earth* and the new poems added in *The Traveler* refine the technique of landscape description charged with meaning in beautiful 8–12 line lyrics. But "The Cartesian Lawnmover" (not in these collections) seems to me an almost perfect fusion of the earlier metaphysical wit and the later allegorical nature lyrics. The poem is a demonstration of Stanford's philosophical dualism. In the act of mowing, the lawnmower (the rational mind) encounters and attempts to reduce to its own order the physical world (the grass and weeds). This physical world is irrational and disorderly—"wandering vast unbounded"—and thus "perplexes" the logical mind (the machine). The nominalist/universalist philosophical dilemma is neatly summed up in lines that tell how the poet mows "Till each particular blade or spike / In essence different looks alike." The mind necessarily orders the particulars of the world into general categories yet seems to do so only at the cost of some distortion. The poem closes with a distinction between "grass" (tractable nature) and "weeds" (intractable nature). Encountering a tough patch of weeds, the lawnmower wheezes and pops "Until at last the tense machine / Is merged with an intenser green." The poem seems to say that mind can understand and order nature (the grasss) to its own ends, but only to a certain extent. Some final undistilled element in nature (the weeds) eludes the mind and frustrates its categories of thought.

The troubling relationship between mind and world is the subject of a number of the late brief nature lyrics. "Vacation

Harvest" tells of two harvests, that of nature, represented by salmon spawning in their pool, and the harvest of the mind bent to the page, ground down into its flour by time. It is this intellectual harvest that is most satisfying to man: ". . . Here, here is grown / The heart's joy, discretely sown, / That few have gathered in." Still, a few men venture far from the cultivated fields of nature and the mind, as in the haunting lyric "The Old Woods." There, as an angler fishes "where man seldom comes," the sounds of the "dry cicada" and the owl mark the ancient passage of daytime into night. The animals, flowers, and trees will repeat their lives, generation after generation, but "the angler shrunk and cold / Will sleep in shadows then." The unique human identity finds no rebirth in the natural cycles of creation and decay.

Similarly, in "The Intruder," the inscrutable otherness of animal life is presented to the mind in the strange form of a glowing jelly fish, "a creature soft as air / That pulsed in primal sleep." The poet's wish was to walk along at night by the sea, to be at peace and to contemplate among the more familiar configurations of the world. Instead, he is intruded upon by this luminous, unknowable thing, "a phosphorescent flare / In time's crepuscular deep." The jelly fish, the poet says, will be held in the mind tonight as a symbol, but the morning tide will find in place of the pulsant sea-thing "a powder beached and white." The senses thus present to the mind an image from nature; this image becomes a symbol, takes on mysterious meaning, as the mind tries to find significance in the subrational, the beautiful, the strange. At night this tentative communion may seem possible, but the harsh light of reason (the full glare of the sun) rejects this as illusion. The sense that nature is elusive of final human understanding is also present in "The Thrush." In the woods where the thrush lives, every tree is a "screen / Of brilliant and illusive green," grass has "sealed" the earth, and the woods are "veiled from human eyes." The bird lives out its life passing freely, easily, and safely through a world in which the human cannot finally be at home.

As in "The Thrush," so in the lovely "Summer Scene" and the quietly somber poem "The Bee," Stanford sensitively responds to natural life. Influences here include Stanford's love of the landscape of his native Massachusetts, his father the botanist, and his love of Emily Dickinson's nature poems. "Summer Scene" first describes the flight of the goldfinch (stanza 1), then the later flight of the oriole (stanza 2). The poem may seem merely descriptive. But the goldfinch, moving through "silence" and "the immobile deep," and the later oriole, coursing "through the emptiness," present in just eight lines the philosophical speculations of "Noon at Neebish," or, as stated here, "life changes yet remains the same." Stanford seems fascinated by the possibility of the existence of some metaphysical ground against which, through which, out of, and into which phenomena of the restless world of matter are ever passing. "The Bee," which I quote entire, is a profound though simple lyric on a universal theme, the passing of time and of the seasons:

> No more through summer's haze I see,
> In sunlight like a flash of spume,
> The resolute and angry bee
> Emerging from a flood of bloom.
>
> The bee is quiet in her hive.
> The earth is colorless and bare.
> The veins of every leaf alive
> Have stiffened in the altered air.

The last line, echoing Dickinson, is a haunting conclusion to a poem utterly clear and absolutely true. The bee has changed her behavior by instinct as the seasons change, but it is the poet alone, who, in the barer clarities of the fall, actually comprehends that the passage of time leads, as with the leaves, to death.

Three other brief nature lyrics, "The Meadowlark," "Bird Call," and "Bayou," address a theme of the earlier poems—passion and its consequence. In "The Meadowlark" the poet speaks of the desert as a place of absolutes, threatening to the human: "Eternal silence dulls the ear, / Eternal brightness seals the eye." Here in the desert nothing lives except "the rare / Illusion of the lark in air." The "fiery bird" and "lust" are equated as soul-stirring visions whose realization is no longer possible, existing in the desert-dry brain only as "eternal dream." Similarly, in "Bayou," a late poem set in south Louisiana, the poet speaks of a heart purified by loss. Like the oak tree, brilliantly described as "a pleached / Excrescence drowned in moss," the poet finds protection from painful experience by looking for beauty only within: "Relinquish all that's fair! / And seek for your delight / Far in the soul's dark night / The image pure and bare." Here, the poet's classical control of disturbingly romantic emotion is extreme. Likewise, in "Bird Call," the problematic nature of passion and its aftermath is examined. It is April, yet winter is lingering; the smell of decaying matter scents the wind. The poet is terrified when "through the open window bare / That glistens in the icy air" a bird call, probably a mating call, is heard. Within a room, the mounting firelight crests with the lovers' passions, which, like the coals, "congealing at the very heart / . . . settle in the ashy cold / Encrusted with putrescent mold."

Two final poems express those qualities of Stanford's poetic style and those ideas that I find most appealing in his work. "The Falls" describes the chaotic plunge of waters that then rise up "suffused with light." Just so, we may immerse ourselves in experience—nature, evil, the subconscious mind—and come back strengthened and purified: "So may the violent mind / Rise from the depths of hell / Illumined and refined." Finally, I quote the poem "For a Book of Elizabethan Madrigal Verse":

> Our tongue could ill afford
> While we new accents seek
> The loss of beauty stored
> In Latin and in Greek,
>
> But most in English rhyme
> Where England's balmy days
> Breathe to the end of time
> In pure melodious phrase.

Here, crystalized in eight lines, is Stanford's mature poetic theory, his allegiance to traditional poetic forms and the Western intellectual past as opposed to the "new accents" of the *vers librists* who often have no use for history. Unlike Ezra Pound, but like Winters, Stanford argues that the poet should use as his model the *English* lyric, especially the Elizabethan lyric, the ever-serviceable short poem often written in the plain style. "Illumined and refined," "In pure melodious phrase": these lines sum up the virtues of Stanford's poetry and the poetry he praises most highly in his own criticism. Stanford has surely written a few of the century's loveliest brief lyrics. They should not be forgotten.

2

The most incredible story of the origin and history of the original series of *The Southern Review* (1935–42) has been told by Thomas Cutrer in his 1984 book, *Parnassus on the Mississippi: The Southern Review and the Baton Rouge Literary Community, 1935–1945*, and in the 1988 compendium of papers and addresses given at the 1985 celebration at Louisiana State University of the fiftieth anniversary of the LSU Press and *The Southern Review* (*The Southern Review and the Modern Literature*, LSU Press). In the heady atmosphere of Huey Long's Louisiana, money was found to start a literary quarterly under the editorship of Charles W. Pipkin, Robert Penn Warren, and Cleanth Brooks. In the seven years before administrative corruption and mismanagement led to a reform administration that, in the midst of a world war, withdrew funds from the quarterly and caused its demise, *The Southern Review* established itself as one of the leading literary quarterlies in English. Containing the work not only of established southern writers such as John Crowe Ransom, Allen Tate, Donald Davidson, and Katherine Anne Porter, the review was also largely responsible for making the early reputation of Eudora Welty and for giving many unknown, forgotten, and other beginning writers their first break. However, *The Southern Review* was never merely a regional journal; the editors published works by English and Continental writers and, of course, works by American writers who lived outside the South.

In addition to their demanding editorial responsibilities, Brooks and Warren wrote many of the essays, reviews, textbooks, and, in Warren's case, the poems and fiction that would soon make them famous. The presence of *The Southern Review* and its editors at LSU also attracted to Baton Rouge, at one time or another, writers and editors such as Katherine Anne Porter, Robert Lowell, Jean Stafford, Peter Taylor, Richard Weaver, Albert Erskine, and John Palmer, among others. By the end of the 1940s, however, Brooks and Warren had left, *The Southern Review* was dead, and an astonishing literary period seemed gone forever, as unrepeatable as the Southern Literary Renascence in which it played an important part.

The definitive account of the new series of *The Southern Review*, which began with the winter issue of 1965, will probably not be written for some time to come. Nevertheless, no account of Donald Stanford's literary life would be complete without some mention of his role in the revival of the review and his contribution to the review as editor, along with Lewis P. Simpson, from 1963 until Stanford's retirement in 1983. When Stanford came to LSU in 1949 and again when he returned permanently in 1953, he suggested to Thomas Kirby, chairman of the English Department, and to others that *The Southern Review* should be revived. In the early 1960s John Hunter vowed that if he ever became president of LSU he would start up the review again. As Stanford has said, "he was as good as his word." After some discussion, Donald Stanford and Lewis P. Simpson were appointed in 1963 as coeditors, thus reflecting the Brooks-Warren partnership. However, in the case of Stanford and Simpson, each editor was usually fully responsible for the contents of a single issue. Thus, longtime readers of *The Southern Review* often refer to a "Stanford issue" or a "Simpson issue" of the journal. Undeterred by the Kennedy assassination on 22 November 1963, Stanford kept his commitment to fly to New Haven to consult with Brooks and Warren about the revival of the review. Brooks and Warren suggested an anniversary issue and assisted Stanford in planning the issue and in securing seventeen contributors from the original series. Securing these earlier contributors was a great help, Stanford recalls, in getting the new review off to a good start. Of course, Stanford's own connections, through Yvor Winters, with most of America's outstanding formalist poets and a number of major critics were important as well. Stanford also credits assistant (later associate) editor Rima Drell Reck and business manager Patt Roberson for working hard, especially on the earlier issues.

As Stanford remarks in an interview with the *Texas Quarterly* (1984), from 1963 to 1968, he, Simpson, and Reck met monthly to choose manuscripts, the final choice resting with Stanford and Simpson, and, since the coeditors planned separate issues, each contributor had, in Stanford's words, "two shots" at acceptance. Following the format of the original review, Stanford published essays, poems, stories, and reviews, usually in that order. Thus, the review is a true literary quarterly whose essays and reviews Stanford calls "creative criticism," the underlying principles of which are often exemplified in the poems and stories printed in the same issue. Stanford has said of *The Southern Review* "we [were] pretty conservative . . . we were conservative and semi-cosmopolitan in outlook—not purely regional." This balance between an interest in southern literature and an interest in the national and international scenes also provides continuity between the new series of *The Southern Review* and the old.

As to his editorial policies, Stanford has stated in the unpublished paper "Some Problems in Publication" (1981) that his policy was not quite as rigid as that of Allen Tate who said, "it is the function of a literary quarterly to give the reader not what he wants but what he ought to have." In partial contrast Stanford says that as editor he tried "to distinguish between my own personal taste and the tastes of sensitive and intelligent readers which may differ from mine but which deserve representation." Regular readers and contributors may be curious to know a few other facts about the review, which Stanford has provided. Average circulation was around 3,000 during his tenure, but even that respectable figure did not prevent a switch to cheaper paper due to a doubling of printing costs between 1973 and 1981. As to contents, all reviews and half the essays were commissioned, but poetry and fiction were never commissioned.

What is Stanford most pleased to have published in *The Southern Review*? In the *Texas Quarterly* interview, he mentions the "New Formalism" in poetry and cites as examples members of the Winters group, the Cambridge poets of the 1960s, and his own group of graduate-student/poets at LSU in the 1970s. In addition Stanford is particularly proud of the special issues of *The Southern Review* that he compiled and edited. These include the anniversary issue (summer 1965), Robert Frost (autumn 1966), England, Ireland [Yeats], and the Commonwealth (summer 1969), Eric Voegelin (winter 1971), Caroline Gordon (spring 1971), Wallace Stevens (summer 1971), the twenties and the thirties (winter 1973), the special poetry issue (spring 1975), Wallace Stevens centennial issue (fall 1979), and Yvor Winters (autumn 1981). The first Stevens issue sold out quickly; the Voegelin issue, the most popular of all, sold out, was reprinted, and sold out again.

Stanford has compiled a list of contributors whom he brought in to the new series of the review and also a list of the issues he edited, including a few in which he and Simpson shared the space. Because the numbers of *The Southern Review* from 1965 to 1983 are usually either "Stanford issues" or "Simpson issues," it may be helpful to print here the census of Stanford issues and a list of contributors brought in by Stanford. The census is: 1965 (nos. 1,2,3,4); 1966 (1,2,3,4); 1967 (1,2,3,4); 1968 (1, and half of no. 3); 1969 (1,2,3,); 1970 (1, and two-thirds of both 2 and 3); 1971 (1,2,3,4); 1972 (half of 1 and two-thirds of 2); 1973 (1, half of 2, and both 3 and 4); 1972 (2); 1975 (2,3,4); 1976 (2); 1977 (1,3,4); 1978 (1,2); 1979 (1,3,4); 1980 (2); 1981 (1,3,4); 1982 (2); 1983 (1,3). Contributors brought in to *The Southern Review* include Howard Baker, F. W. Bateson, Ben Belitt, Bernard Bergonzi, Harold Bloom, Edgar Bowers, Kay Boyle, Cleanth Brooks, Kenneth Burke, Malcolm Cowley, J. V. Cunningham, Elizabeth Daryush,

Donald Davidson, Donald Davie, James Dickey, Denis Donoghue, Richard Eberhart, James T. Farrell, Northrop Frye, Roy Fuller, John Gardner, Nadine Gordimer, Caroline Gordon, Shirley Grau, Albert Guerard, Thom Gunn, Robert Heilman, David Hoffman, Graham Hough, Irving Howe, Randall Jarrell, Matthew Josephson, Hugh Kenner, Maxine Kumin, Max Lerner, David Levin, Janet Lewis, David Lodge, Harold Loeb, Mary McCarthy, W. S. Merwin, N. Scott Momaday, Pablo Neruda, Joyce Carol Oates, Thomas Parkinson, Katherine Anne Porter, Reynolds Price, Kathleen Raine, John Crowe Ransom, W. W. Robson, Theodore Roethke, Louis Simpson, J. B. Singer, William Stafford, Ann Stanford, Timothy Steele, Wallace Stegner, Allen Tate, Anne Tyler, Eric Voegelin, Robert Penn Warren, René Wellek, Eudora Welty, and Yvor Winters. Stanford is also proud to have published some of his own graduate students. These include Everett Emerson, John Finlay, Julie L'Enfant, George Lensing, David Middleton, Ronald Moran, Richard J. O'Dea, Wyatt Prunty, and Lindon Stall.

The number of notable fiction writers on the list makes this survey an appropriate place to mention that Stanford has published quite a few essays and reviews on fiction writers whom he admires. These include Henry James, Caroline Gordon, Albert Guerard, and Janet Lewis. In fact, Stanford's own contribution to the original series of *The Southern Review* was an omnibus review of fiction (he still has all the books, he says!) entitled "*The Beloved Returns* and Other Recent Fiction" (1941). In this review, Stanford's opinion of *The Hamlet* as "Faulkner's latest explosion in a cesspool" with characters "completely phoney" and "insensitive and stupid" both defines Stanford's own classicism and demonstrates the catholicity of Brooks and Warren as editors. In addition to his essays and reviews on fiction, Stanford was honored in 1985 to introduce Eudora Welty at Louisiana State University during the fiftieth-anniversary celebration of *The Southern Review*. In his introductory remarks, Stanford said: "In her essays and in her autobiography Eudora Welty shows great rspect for authors and for the art of writing. She takes her craft seriously and has studied its rules and theories carefully. But she is also in love with it."

In "The Function of the Literary Quarterly" (1936), Allen Tate defended the quarterly as crucial to serious literary criticism that "instructs the reader in three fundamentals of mounting importance: the exercise of taste, the pursuit of standards of intellectual judgment, and the acquisition of self-knowledge." And in his essay entitled "The Present Function of Literary Quarterlies" (1961), Monroe K. Spears said that in our increasingly subliterate world the quarterly has "the responsibility of maintaining literature as a unifying center for the culture." The original *Southern Review* (1935–42), he added, "was the first full-fledged example of the form, and a brilliantly successful one."

Now that the new series of *The Southern Review* has enjoyed a lifespan over three times as long as that of the original review and now that with the retirement of Stanford and Simpson the review is still a going concern under James Olney and Dave Smith (Fred Hobson's replacement), it is perhaps not premature to suggest that, like its illustrious predecessor, the present review is a most distinguished member of that small body of true literary quarterlies (not a few located in the South) on whose continued thriving existence the polity of letters so heavily, and, increasingly, so desperately depends. In that enterprise, Donald Stanford has had a major part, especially in having published so many works that, in various ways, participate in the recovery of the classic sensibility.

3

My debt to Don Stanford began seven years before we ever met. I started writing poetry in 1964 at the age of fifteen. My earliest influences were, after Robert Frost, mainly the English romantics, especially Wordsworth and Shelley, poets whose works I read and came to love through the enthusiasm of a typically long-suffering, underpaid Louisiana high-school English teacher and Anglophile, Marilyn Gibson. Soon, however, I was frequenting the Paperback Book Store in Shreveport and spending my allowance on selected editions of the poems of T. S. Eliot, e. e. cummings, Carl Sandburg, Walt Whitman, and Ezra Pound. My brief, Frost-inspired apprenticeship to traditional poetry gave way to the writing of obscure, symbol-ridden amalgamations of half-understood sections of *The Cantos* and *The Waste Land*. In the winter of 1964–65, my mother—a well-read former teacher— and my father—a teacher, principal, artist, and sometime poet— showed me a flier for *The Southern Review*, about to be revived in its new series beginning with the winter 1965 issue. My father said that he had already sent in a subscription in my name. So, at age fifteen, I became an original subscriber to the new series of *The Southern Review*. I remember little about the issues I received from 1965 until my graduation from Louisiana Tech University in 1971. I do remember always reading the poetry first, then the reviews, skimming the essays, and never reading the fiction. (I still do the same today, I'm afraid!) I vividly recall the smell and texture of the richly printed pages and the pleasure I felt running my fingers over the imprinted letters of the words of the poems so beautifully presented with lots of white space. I could hardly understand the essays, although I do remember reading Winters on T. Sturge Moore, the British poet on whom I would work, at Stanford's suggestion, nearly twenty years later. I also remember feeling that I could never, never hope to write a poem good enough to be printed in *The Southern Review* and laid to rest in those rich white pages.

During my undergraduate days at Tech (1967–71), I was a disciple of the modernists. Eliot's *Collected Poems* was my King James Bible and the lyrics of the rock poets (Bob Dylan and others) were my hymns. In 1968, after reading some of his poems in *The Tech Talk* (the campus newspaper that in those days actually had a regular poetry page!), I met Lindon Stall, my lifelong friend and one of the most technically skilled poets I have ever known. We shared the same tastes in poetry and song and, over a three-year period, provided one another with that essential supportive yet critical audience that fosters the young poet. A year older than I, Lindon preceded me to graduate school at LSU in 1970. There, in 1970–71, he met the extraordinarily talented Alabama poet John Finlay, who had come to LSU to do graduate work under Stanford because of Stanford's connection to Yvor Winters. I think Lindon underwent a poetic conversion experience of sorts, judging from the letters I received back at Tech, and by the time I arrived at LSU in June 1971 to begin my own graduate career, he had abandoned free verse and had begun an apprenticeship in formalist verse under Finlay's influence outside of class and under Stanford's direction in class, in tutorials, and in more informal discussions. At first I resisted the arguments against free verse and even recall writing a long poem (ironically, in couplets) attacking Winters, Cunningham, and Bowers (of whom I knew virtually nothing at the time). Eventually, however, Stanford, Finlay, Stall, and the works of the Winters group led me to abandon free verse for verse written in traditional forms.

Stanford has often recalled showing some of his early poems to Winters in 1932–33 and Winters's harsh criticism of them all, even one accepted for *Poetry* by Harriet Monroe. I, too, got the

"Winters treatment" in the fall of 1971 when I brashly exhibited to Stanford the best of my undergraduate work. He dismissed it all except for one stanza in one poem about birds (sparrows, I think), a subject on which he has written such lovely brief lyrics. I was almost crushed, but the faint praise of that single stanza kept me going. (Did he *really* even like *that*, I now wonder, or was it his weakness for birds?) Somewhat later, in the fall of 1972, I worked up the courage not only to come to Stanford's editorial office to show him some new poems but also to submit them formally to *The Southern Review*. He liked these poems better than the first ones he had seen—at least they were not in obscure Eliotic free verse—but he rejected them all for the review. Having just served what I thought had been a more than adequate apprenticeship to formalist verse of twelve whole months or so, I was visibly miffed at the rejection. Sensing this, Stanford said something that I have never forgotten: "David, when I judge your work I am judging it against the best poems of Tate, our greatest southern poet." It took a while for that remark to sink in, but I think I am right in believing that this was Stanford's way of saying that he was taking me seriously as a poet. I do not, incidentally, wish to leave the impression that Stanford wanted to make me, Stall, Finlay, or slightly later, Wyatt Prunty, into little disciples of Yvor Winters. I distinctly remember accompanying Lindon Stall into Stanford's office upon the occasion of Lindon's showing Stanford his new poem, "Of Demosthenes." Stanford said to Lindon: "You've mastered Winters's style; now go find one of your own." (Lindon jokes today, "I did, but he didn't like it"!) In time, all four of Stanford's poet-students of the 1970s—Finlay, Stall, Prunty, and I—appeared in *The Southern Review* as poets, reviewers, and, in some cases, as essayists. Overwhelmed with the sense of responsibility, I think I worked harder on my five-page review of Dylan Thomas studies (my first appearance in the review, in 1974) than I did on my 770-page dissertation on that poet five years later. When Stanford finally took a poem from me for the review, I felt the literary equivalent of saving grace and relished my small place in those distinguished pages. (At that time, by the way, the review still provided offprints, beautifully done, that served almost as slim pamphlets of two or three poems.)

The more I studied poetry with Donald Stanford the more aware I became of the significance (at least for me and at that time) of a "Stanford issue" of *The Southern Review*. In my graduate student office on the third floor of Allen Hall, I could hardly wait for the appearance of the next such issue. I can still recall being profoundly moved on first reading new poems by Helen Pinkerton Trimpi, Janet Lewis, Edgar Bowers, and John Finlay in the review. When I learned that Stanford had sent a copy of Helen Pinkerton Trimpi's essay on Edgar Bowers to Bowers himself for comment and that Bowers had returned the essay with notations, I found occasion to slip into Stanford's editorial office to get a peek at the profoundly philosophical essay and what I then took as oracular marginalia by the great poet himself. In short, the presence of *The Southern Review* and Donald Stanford at LSU during my years there in the 1970s made a difference in my poetic life, and surely in that of others, which cannot be measured. For me, at that time, LSU was the only place in the world I wanted to be.

All that would seem enough, but there is a little more yet to add. Stanford believes that the best poet, ideally, should be a critic and a scholar as well. As a major professor, Stanford was unfailingly helpful, always available, constantly reminding his students to face up to the general exams and to keep going on the dissertation, always ready to write yet another letter of recommendation for a possible job, and suggesting places to publish besides the review. His classes in modern poetry, the New England tradition, Yeats, and Henry James always yielded fat notebooks of useful biographical-critical commentary that could be profitably reviewed for the general exams. Stanford's professional reliability extended, in my case, to good advice about taking a job. Through fortuitous circumstances, I was offered a one-year, full-time appointment at a small college near Baton Rouge. Fearing that if I left LSU with my dissertation unwritten, I would become another permanent ABD, I hesitated about taking the job. This was during the bleakest job years of the 1970s, and Stanford, who had endured the much worse years of the Depression of the 1930s, had no qualms about giving advice: "Take the job." I did, I finished the dissertation, and I am a full professor at the same small college today. It was good advice.

Finally, I must mention social life with the Stanfords—not only Don but his lovely wife, Maryanna, whose gourmet skills and exquisite taste have displayed themselves in formal dinners and in sherry-and-buffet parties for many years. Graduate students were relatively poor in the 1970s: I remember pooling quarters with John Finlay one Saturday night in Tigertown to see if we could come up with the $1.05 it took to buy a six-pack of the cheapest beer. We were not to receive our monthly graduate assistantship checks (about $180 or so) until Monday, but on Sunday the Stanfords were having a sherry party for his students and a few professors. Famished and temporarily impoverished graduate students bellied up to the buffet table and, as quickly as good manners allowed, devoured Maryanna's gourmet goodies both from delight in our hostess's cooking skills and from sheer hunger. At other times, just for the poetry boys, there were beer-and-pretzel parties at which Don would play his recordings of Valéry and Allen Tate reading their poetry and we would talk shop for a while as fellow poets. In England, where Maryanna serves as Don's research assistant, the Stanfords introduced my wife, Francine, and me to the wonders of tea at Harrod's, Bloody Marys at the Grenadier, After Eights at any play, and dinner at Don's club, the Athenaeum. The image of me sunk deep in a leather chair and surrounded by the Athenaeum library's high walls of leather-bound books, drinking port and talking as friends to "Don" and "Maryanna" would have seemed incredible to my fifteen-year-old self, who, in 1965, barely managed to tear himself away from Beatles records and thoughts of girls long enough to examine volume 1, number 1, of the new series of *The Southern Review.*

It is difficult to sum up the life of a man such as Donald Stanford in a single sentence, but I must try. A New Englander, a Californian, a resident southerner, admirer of the best in the British tradition, both realist and optimist, and a gentleman refined—Donald Stanford, in my view, has achieved, both in his life and his work, a restoration of the classic mind.

Bibliography of Works by Stanford in Chronological Arrangement

Books, Chapters, Anthologies

In *Ten Introductions: A Collection of Modern Verse*, edited by Genevieve Taggard and Dudley Fitts, 89–92. New York: Arrow Editions, 1934. "A Valentine," "For the Audience," "Country Church."

In *Trial Balances*, edited by Ann Winslow, 113–15. New York: Macmillan Co., 1935. "A Valentine," "Spring, 1934," "Sonnet on Graduation," "Noon at Neebish." [Commentary by Yvor Winters.]

In *Twelve Poets of the Pacific*, edited by Yvor Winters, 115–23. New York: New Directions, 1937. "A Valentine," "New England Earth," "Spring, 1934," "Noon at Neebish," "Birthday Card," "Rhesus," "The Meadowlark," "The Sea Gull," "The Grand Mesa."

New England Earth [poems]. San Francisco: Colt Press, 1941.

The Traveler [poems]. Rowe, Mass.: Cummington Press, 1955.

Editor of *The Poems of Edward Taylor*. New Haven: Yale University Press, 1960.

    1963: abridged paperback edition with new introduction by Stanford

    1971: hardback edition selected for inclusion in the Library of American Civilization by *Encyclopedia Britannica*

    1977: new paperback edition of the 1960 hardback edition

    1989: abridged paperback edition reprinted by the University of North Carolina Press

"The Puritan Poet as Preacher—An Edward Taylor Sermon." In *Studies in American Literature*, edited by Waldo McNeir, 1–10. Baton Rouge: Louisiana State University Press, 1961.

Editor of *A Transcript of Edward Taylor's Metrical History of Christianity*. Cleveland: Micro Photo, 1962; reprinted by Books on Demand. Ann Arbor, Mich.: University Microfilms International, 1977. [Poem of 21,500 lines.]

Editor of *Nine Essays in Modern Literature*. Baton Rouge: Louisiana State University Press, 1965.

Edward Taylor. Minneapolis: University of Minnesota Press, 1965. Reprinted 1972 by Scribners for Dictionary of American Biography series.

In *Laurel, Archaic, Rude: A Collection of Poems Presented to Yvor Winters on His Retirement by the Stanford English Department*. Stanford: English Dept., Stanford University, 1966. "The Grand Mesa."

"Edward Taylor." In *Major Writers of Early American Literature*, edited by Everett Emerson, 59–61. Madison: University of Wisconsin Press, 1972.

Editor of *Selected Poems of Robert Bridges*. Cheadle Hulme, Cheshire: Carcanet Press, 1974.

Editor of *Selected Poems of S. Foster Damon*. Omaha, Neb.: Cummington Press, Abattoir Editions, 1974.

In The Classic Mode: The Achievement of Robert Bridges. Newark: University of Delaware Press, 1978.

Preface to *My Personal Conception of Religion* by Isaac Bashevis Singer. Lafayette: University of Southwestern Louisiana, 1982.

Editor of *The Selected Letters of Robert Bridges*, 2 vols. Newark: University of Delaware Press, 1983–84.

Revolution and Convention in Modern Poetry: Studies in Ezra Pound, T. S. Eliot, Wallace Stevens, E. A. Robinson, and Yvor Winters. Newark: University of Delaware Press, 1983.

Editor of *British Poets, 1880–1914*. Dictionary of Literary Biography, vol. 19. Detroit: Gale Research Co., 1983.

Editor of *British Poets, 1914–1945*. Dictionary of Literary Biography, vol. 20. Detroit: Gale Research Co., 1983.

Editor of *John Masefield: Letters to Margaret Bridges (1915–1919)*. Manchester: Carcanet Press, 1984.

Editor of *John Masefield: Selected Poems*. Manchester: Carcanet Press, 1984.

The Cartesian Lawnmower and Other Poems. Florence, Ky.: Barth Press, 1984.

"Bridges and Hopkins: The Problem of Influence." In *Hopkins Among the Poets: Studies in Modern Responses to Gerard Manley Hopkins*, edited by Richard F. Giles, 1–6. Hamilton, Ont.: International Hopkins Assoc., 1985.

Editor (with Lewis P. Simpson, James Olney, and Jo Gulledge) of *Selected Stories from the Southern Review, 1965–1985*. Baton Rouge: Louisiana State University Press, 1988.

In *A Garland for John Finlay*, edited by David Middleton. Thibodaux, La.: Blue Heron Press, 1990. "For a Book of Elizabethan Madrigal Verse."

JOURNAL ARTICLES

"The Classicism of Yvor Winters." *Kenyon Review* 3 (Spring 1941): 257–59.

"Edward Taylor and the Lord's Supper." *American Literature* 27 (May 1955): 172–78.

"Two Notes on T. S. Eliot." *Twentieth-Century Literature* 1 (October 1955): 133–34.

"A Note on Yvor Winters." *Talisman* 9 (Summer/Autumn 1956): 38–46.

"More Sacramental Meditations by Edward Taylor." *Yale University Library Gazette* 31 (October 1956): 61–75.

"Nineteen Unpublished Poems by Edward Taylor." *American Literature* 29 (March 1957): 18–46.

"The Giant Bones of Clavarack, New York: A Curious Extract from the Manuscript of Edward Taylor." *New York History* 40 (January 1959): 47–61.

"The Earliest Poems of Edward Taylor." *American Literature* 32 (May 1960): 136–51.

"The Language and the Truth." *Sequoia* (special Yvor Winters issue) 6 (Winter 1961): 20–23.

"The Parentage of Edward Taylor." *American Literature* 33 (May 1961): 215–21.

"Edward Taylor's Metrical History of Christianity." *American Literature* 33 (November 1961): 279–95.

"This Difficult Individual, Ezra Pound." *South Atlantic Quarterly* 61 (Spring 1962): 290–91.

"The Continuity of American Poetry." *South Atlantic Quarterly* 61 (Summer 1962): 424–25.

"Edward Taylor's Spiritual Relation." *American Literature* 35 (January 1964): 467–75.

"The Latin Poems of 'Edward Taylor.'" *Yale University Library Gazette* 40 (October 1965): 75–81. [With Professor Leo M. Kaiser.]

"Edward Taylor's Treatise Concerning the Lord's Supper." *American Literature* 39 (March 1967): 112–13.

"Yvor Winters: 1900–1968." *Southern Review* 4 (Summer 1968): 861–63.

"Classicism and the Modern Poet." *Southern Review* 5 (Spring 1969): 475–500.

"Foreword, W. B. Yeats: Critical Perspectives." *Southern Review* 5 (Summer 1969): 831–32.

"Robert Bridges on His Poems and Plays: Unpublished Letters by Robert Bridges to Samuel Butler." *Philological Quarterly* 50 (April 1971): 281–91.

"Out of that Source of Time: The Poetry of Allen Tate." *Southern Review* 7 (April 1971): xvii–xxiii.

"Robert Bridges and Samuel Butler on Shakespeare's Sonnets: An Exchange of Letters." *Shakespeare Quarterly* 22 (Autumn 1971): 329–35.

"Robert Bridges and the Free Verse Rebellion." *Journal of Modern Literature* 2 (September 1971): 19–32.

"Foster Damon's Dream Frontiers," *Southern Review* 7 (Winter 1971): xv–xx.

"Caroline Gordon: From Penhally to A Narrow Heart." *Southern Review* 7 (Spring 1971): xv–xx.

"Two Notes on Edward Taylor." *Early American Literature* 6 (Spring 1971): 89–90.

"An Introductory Note" [Wallace Stevens and the Romantic Heritage]. *Southern Review* 7 (Summer 1971): xxvi.

"Edward Taylor versus 'The Young Cockerill' Benjamin Ruggles." *New England Quarterly* 44 (September 1971): 459–68.

"A Prefatory Note" [to Eric Voegelin's essay on *The Turn of the Screw*]. *Southern Review* 7 (Winter 1971): 3–5.

"Marianne Moore, 1887–1972." *Southern Review* 8 (Spring 1972): xi–xiii.

"S. Foster Damon, 1893–1971," *Southern Review* 8 (Spring 1972): xiii–xv.

"Thoughts on the Pound Era." *Southern Review* 9 (Winter 1973): xiii–xv.

"Edward Taylor and the 'Hermophrodite' Poems of John Cleveland." *Early American Literature* 8 (Spring 1973): 59–61.

"Eudora Welty and the Pulitzer Prize." *Southern Review* 9 (Autumn 1973): xx–xxiii.

"The Short, Short Poem." *Southern Review* 9 (Summer 1973): xix–xxiii.

"W. H. Auden." *Southern Review* 9 (Autumn 1973): xix–xx.

"The Poetry of James Agee: The Art of Recovery." *Southern Review* 19 (Spring 1974): xvi–xix.

"Roy Fuller's Oxford Poetry Lectures." *Southern Review* 11 (Spring 1975): xiii–xiv.

"On Poetry Readings." *Southern Review* 11 (Summer 1975): xvii–xix.

"The Imagination of Death in the Poetry of Philip Pain, Edward Taylor, and George Herbert." *Studies in the Literary Imagination* 9 (Fall 1976): 53–67.

"Elizabeth Daryush (1887–1977) and Ezra Pound (1885–1972)." *Southern Review* 13 (Autumn 1977): 641–45.

"Edwin Arlington Robinson's 'The Wandering Jew.'" *Tulane Studies in English* 23 (1978): 95–108.

"A Footnote to Flux^2." *Southern Review* 15 (Autumn 1979): 769–70.

"Katherine Anne Porter." *Southern Review* 17 (Winter 1981): 1–2.

"Caroline Gordon." *Southern Review* 17 (Summer 1981): 459–60.

"Yvor Winters in the Academic Bower." *Southern Review* 17 (Autumn 1981): 711–15.

"Robert Bridges, Poet-Typographer." *Fine Print* 9 (January 1983): 7–9.

"An Interview with Donald Stanford" by Donald Coers. *Texas Review* 5 (Spring/Summer 1984): 7–19.

"The First Mrs. Eliot." *Library Chronicle of the University of Texas at Austin*, (n. s., no. 40 (Fall 1987): 89–111.

"From the Letters of Elizabeth Bishop, 1933–1934." *Verse* 4 (November 1987): 19–27.

"Ann Stanford (1916–1987)." *Southern Review* 23 (Autumn 1987): 965–66.

"*The Poems of Edward Taylor*: The Making of the Yale Edition," *Studies in Puritan American Spirituality* 1 (1990): 3–12.

Book Reviews

"*The Beloved Returns* and Other Recent Fiction." *Southern Review* 6 (Winter 1941): 610–28. [Thomas Mann, *The Beloved Returns*; and twenty-seven other novels.]

"An Unusual First Book." *Poetry* 59 (March 1942): 340–43. [Anna Maria Armi, *Poems*.]

"Mr. Winters' Recent Criticism." *Poetry* 91 (March 1958): 393–95. [Yvor Winters, *The Function of Criticism*.]

Review. *American Literature* 34 (November 1962): 412. [Norman S. Grabo, *Edward Taylor*.]

Review. *American Literature* 35 (May 1963): 242–43. [Norman S. Grabo, ed., *Edward Taylor's Christographia*.]

"The Well-Kept Life: The Letters of Wallace Stevens." *Southern Review* 3 (Summer 1967): 757–73. [*Letters of Wallace Stevens: Selected and Edited by Holly Stevens*.]

Review. *American Literature* 43 (May 1971): 301–2. [Richard Allen Blessing, *Wallace Stevens' Whole Harmonium*.]

"Stevens' Selected Poems." *Southern Review* 7 (Summer 1971): xxiii–xxiv. [Holly Stevens, ed., *The Palm at the End of the Mind: Selected Poems and a Play by Wallace Stevens.*]

"Thompson's Frost and Bailey's Hardy." *Southern Review* 7 (Autumn 1971): xvii–xxi. [Lawrance Thompson, *Robert Frost: The Years of Triumph*; J. O. Bailey, *The Poetry of Thomas Hardy: A Handbook and Commentary.*]

"Edward Taylor: An Annotated Bibliography, 1668–1970." *Early American Literature* 7 (Fall 1972); 200–201. [Constance J. Gefvert, *Edward Taylor: An Annotated Bibliography, 1668–1970.*]

"The Fiction of Caroline Gordon: A Reissue." *Southern Review* (Spring 1972): 458. [A note on the Cooper Square Publisher's reissue of Caroline Gordon's eight volumes of fiction.]

"*The Glory of Hera* by Caroline Gordon." *Michigan Quarterly Review* 12 (Winter 1973): 89–90.

Review. *Journal of Modern Literature* 3 (February 1974): 576–78. [John Cody, *After Great Pain: The Inner Life of Emily Dickinson*; John Evangelist Walsh, *The Hidden Life of Emily Dickinson: A Biography.*]

"Georgia on My Mind." *Hudson Review* 28 (Winter 1975–76): 629–36. [C. Vann Woodward, *Tom Watson—Agrarian Rebel*, and ten other books on Georgia.]

"The Puritan Origins of the American Self." *Early American Literature* 11 (Spring 1976): 107–9. [Sacvan Bercovitch, *The Puritan Origins of the American Self.*]

Review. *American Literature* 51 (May 1979): 285–87. [Thomas Parkinson, *Hart Crane and Yvor Winters: Their Literary Correspondence*; Robert Combs, *Vision of the Voyage: Hart Crane and the Psychology of Romanticism.*]

Review. *Early American Literature* 15 (Winter 1980/81): 280–81. [Barbara Lewalski, *Protestant Poetics and the Seventeenth-Century Religious Lyric.*]

Review. *Alabama Review* 34 (July 1981): 223–25. [Richard Beale Davis, *A Southern Colonial Bookshelf: Reading in the Eighteenth Century.*]

Review. *Yeats Annual No. 1* (London: Macmillan Co., 1982): 237–43. [Patrick J. Keane, *A Wild Civility: Interactions in the Poetry and Thought of Robert Graves.*]

Review. *William and Mary Quarterly* 39 (Summer 1982): 542–45. [Daniel Hoffman, *Brotherly Love.*]

"Formality and Restraint." *Southern Review* 19 (Winter 1983): 169–72. [Recent books of poetry in the formalist tradition.]

"The Best of Bynner." *Hudson Review* 36 (Summer 1983): 389–98. [*The Works of Witter Bynner*, 5 vols.]

Review. *South Central Review* 1 (Winter 1984): 100–103. [T. Sturge Moore, *Twenty-three Poems*, edited by David Middleton.]

Review. *Yeats: An Annual of Critical and Textual Studies*, Vol. 2 (Ithaca: Cornell University Press): 279–86. [A. E. Dyson, *Yeats, Eliot, and R. S. Thomas: Riding the Echo.*]

"The Independent Voice of Roy Fuller." *Sewanee Review* 94 (Winter 1986): xix–xxi. [Roy Fuller, *New and Collected Poems 1934–1984.*]

"Adventures Among the Absolutes: Four Contemporary Volumes of Poetry." *Michigan Quarterly Review* 25 (Summer 1986): 607–15. [Helen Pinkerton,

Poems 1946–1976; Rosanna Warren, *Each Leaf Shines Separate*; Molly Pea-
cock, *Raw Heaven*; Richard Tillinghurst, *Our Flag Was Still There*.]

Review. *National Forum* 68 (Fall 1987): 46–48. [Timothy Steele, *Sapphics
Against Anger and Other Poems*; Rodney Jones, *The Unborn*; Rita Dove,
Thomas and Beulah.]

"Milosz, Davie, Fuller and the Lyric," *Southern Review* 23 (Summer 1987):
736–40. [Donald Davie, *Czeslaw Milosz and the Insufficiency of the Lyric*;
Roy Fuller, *Consolations*.]

"Review-Essay on *The Complete Notebooks of Henry James*." *Henry James
Review* 8 (Spring 1987): 221–26. [*The Complete Notebooks of Henry James*,
edited by Leon Edel and Lyall H. Powers.]

"Masefield Reconsidered." *Sewanee Review* 97 (Winter 1989): vi–xii. [June
Dwyer, *John Masefield*.]

"Caroline Gordon: An Uprooted Agrarian." *Sewanee Review* 97 (Autumn 1989).
[Veronica Makowsky, *Caroline Gordon: A Biography*: Ann Waldron, *Close
Connections: Caroline Gordon and the Southern Renaissance*.]

"Missing Measures," *Southern Review* 26 (Summer 1990): 708–14. [Timothy
Steele, *Missing Measures: Modern Poetry and the Revolt Against Meter*.]

Review, *Early American Literature* 25 (Summer 1990): 211–13. [John Gatta,
Gracious Laughter: The Meditative Wit of Edward Taylor.]

Poems in Magazines

"Lizard King Here." *Poetry* 42 (August 1933): 263.

"Three Poems: 'For Hate,' 'For the Audience,' 'Reflections on Fear,' " *Hound &
Horn* 6 (Summer 1933): 590–91.

"Two Poems: 'On a Child Lost in the Woods,' 'Sonnet in Autumn.' " *The
Magazine: A Literary Journal* 1 (December 1933): 5–6.

"Sonnet on Graduation." *The Magazine: A Literary Journal* 1 (January 1934):
66.

"A Valentine." *The Magazine: A Literary Journal* 1 (February 1934): 95.

"Country Church." *Harvard Advocate* 120 (March 1934): 7.

"New England Earth." *The Magazine: A Literary Journal* 1 (April 1934): 148.

"Letter to Yvor Winters." *Harvard Advocate* 120 (April 1934): 9.

"Wedding Wine." *The Magazine: A Literary Journal* 1 (May 1934): 196.

"Noon at Neebish." *Hound & Horn* 7 (Summer 1934): 658–59.

"A Valentine" [number two]. *The Magazine: A Journal of Contemporary Writing*
2 (July–August 1934): 25–26.

"Spring, 1934." *New Republic* 80 (7 November 1934): 360.

"The Grand Mesa." *The Magazine: A Journal of Contemporary Writing* 2
(March–April 1935): 235.

"Birthday Card." *Commonweal* 22 (14 June 1935): 177.

"The Meadowlark." *New Republic* 84 (9 October 1935): 234.

"Tussle." *Talisman* 8 (Winter 1955–Spring 1956): 55.

"The Bee" and "The Thrush." *Duke University Archive* 74 (December 1961): 14–15.

Encyclopedia Articles

"Edward Taylor." *Collier's Encyclopedia* (1962).

"Edward Taylor." *The Concise Encyclopedia of English and American Poets and Poetry* (1963).

"Caroline Gordon" and "Albert Guerard." *Contemporary Novelists* (1972).

"Robert Bridges." *Reader's Encyclopedia of English Literature* (1975).

"Edward Taylor" and "Yvor Winters." *Writers of the English Language* (1979).

"John Masefield's Plays." *Dictionary of Literary Biography, Modern British Playwrights* (1982).

"Robert Bridges," "John Masefield," and "W. S. Blunt." *Dictionary of Literary Biography, Modern British Poets* (1983).

"Edward Taylor." *Dictionary of Literary Biography, Colonial American Literature* (1984).

"Donald Davie." *Dictionary of Literary Biography, Modern British Poets Since World War II* (1984).

"Janet Lewis." *Dictionary of Literary Biography Yearbook* (1987).

"Edward Taylor," "Yvor Winters," "Taylor's 'God's Determinations,' and "Wallace Stevens' 'Sunday Morning,'" *Reference Guide to American Literature* (1988).

"Robert Bridges," *Dictionary of Literary Biography; Modern British Essayists* (1990).

Contributors

Percy G. Adams is the author of *Travel Literature and the Evolution of the Novel* and *Graces of Harmony: Alliteration, Assonance and Consonance in Eighteenth Century Poetry*, which are among his best-known books.

R. L. Barth, as owner of the R. L. Barth Press, has been active in publishing contemporary "formalist" poetry. He is author of *A Soldier's Time: Vietnam War Poems*.

Maclin Bocock, winner of a PEN Syndicated Fiction Award in 1987, has contributed short stories to the *Southern Review*.

Edgar Bowers, who was awarded the Bollingen Prize and the Harriet Monroe Poetry Prize in 1989, has recently published *For Louis Pasteur*.

M. C. Bradbrook, former Mistress of Girton College, Cambridge, is the author of *Artists and Society in Shakespeare*, *Themes and Conventions in Elizabethan Tragedy*, and many other books on Elizabethan and Jacobean literature.

Cleanth Brooks, a founding editor of the *Southern Review*, is well known for his *The Well-Wrought Urn*; *William Faulkner: The Yoknapatawpha Country*; *William Faulkner: Toward Yoknapatawpha and Beyond*, and many other volumes of criticism.

Ashley Brown's books include *The Achievement of Wallace Stevens* and *Poetry Reviews of Allen Tate 1924–1944*.

Donald Davie is the author of *The Shires*, *Collected Poems*, and *Thomas Hardy and British Poetry*, which are perhaps the best known of his many books of verse and criticism.

Everett Emerson, who was editor of *Early American Literature* for twenty years before his recent retirement, is author of *The*

Authentic Mark Twain: A Literary Biography of Samuel L. Clemens.

JOHN FINLAY, who until his recent death lived in Enterprise, Alabama, published three books of poetry: *Between the Gulfs, The Wide Porch and Other Poems,* and *The Salt of Exposure.*

ROY FULLER, Oxford Professor of Poetry 1968–1973, has recently published *Available for Dreams* (poems) and *The World through the Window: Collected Poems for Children.* He lives in Blackheath, London.

CHARLES GULLANS, owner of the Symposium Press, has published *Bright Universe and Other Poems, A Diatribe to Dr. Steele,* and *Many Houses.*

GEORGE S. LENSING is author (with Ronald Moran) of *Four Poets and the Emotive Imagination: Robert Bly, James Wright, Louis Simpson and William Stafford* and *Wallace Stevens: A Poet's Growth.*

DAVID LEVIN has contributed poems to the *Southern Review.* He is the author of *Cotton Mather: The Young Life of the Lord's Remembrancer 1663–1703.*

JANET LEWIS (Mrs. Yvor Winters) has been writing a series of libretti for operas, the best-known being an adaptation of her novel *The Wife of Martin Guerre.* Among her many books of verse are *Poems Old and New 1918–1978* and *The Ancient Ones.*

DAVID MIDDLETON, author of two books of poems—*Reliquiae* and *Under the Linden Tree*—has a third forthcoming from Louisiana State University Press. He is writing a book on T. Sturge Moore.

RAYMOND OLIVER, a contributor to the *Southern Review,* is author of several books of poems including *Entries* and *Beowulf: A Likeness.*

CATHERINE PHILLIPS of Downing College, Cambridge, is the editor of Hopkins' *Poems* and Hopkins' *Selected Letters,* both with Oxford University Press.

HELEN PINKERTON (Mrs. Wesley Trimpi) is the author of *Melville's Confidence Men and American Politics in the 1950s* and *Poems 1946–1976.*

GROSVENOR POWELL's books include *Language as Being in the Poetry of Yvor Winters* and *Yvor Winters: An Annotated Bibliography 1919–1982.*

WYATT PRUNTY's most recent of several books in the Johns Hopkins poetry series is *Balance as Belief.* His book of criticism *Fallen from the Symboled World,* was published by Oxford Press in 1990.

KATHLEEN RAINE is editor of *Temenos: A Review Devoted to the Arts of the Imagination.* Among her many well-known books are *Defending Ancient Springs, Blake and Tradition, Collected Poems 1935–1980,* and three volumes of autobiography.

LINDON STALL, a contributor to the *Southern Review,* is author of *Responsoria,* a book of poems.

TIMOTHY STEELE's most recent book of poems is *Sapphics Against Anger.* His volume of criticism, *Missing Measures* was published by the University of Arkansas Press in 1990.

WESLEY TRIMPI is the author of *Ben Jonson's Poems: A Study of the Plain Style* and more recently *Muses of One Mind: The Literary Analysis of Experience and Its Continuity.*

CLIVE WILMER, who lives in Cambridge, England, is an editor of *Numbers* and author of *Devotions* and *The Dwelling Place.*